Geronimo Springs Museum Edition

Sierra County Historical Society

211 Main Street, Truth or Consequences, NM 87901

APACHE LAND

FROM THOSE WHO LIVED IT

EL PASO

R E P U B L I C   O F   M E X I C O

Ft. Qultman

Eagle Springs
Station

Van Horn, TX

BASS CANYON
May 13, 1880

VAN HORN
WELLS
STATION

El Muerto
Station

Barrel Springs
Station

FT. DAVIS

Wild Rose
Pass

Barilla Station

Leon Holes

FT. STOCKTON

Escondid

1   FRIO TOWN, TX

2   END IN SIGHT

3   JO-BOB'S RUN DOWN WILD ROSE PASS

4   MURPHY'S RANCH (ON TWO WHEELS AND A WHIP)

5   GAVINO'S GOATS

6   "BURRO" MENDOZA

7   MILLER THE KILLER

8   BARNEY TAKES TWO

9   SIX-SHOOTER'S SERENADE

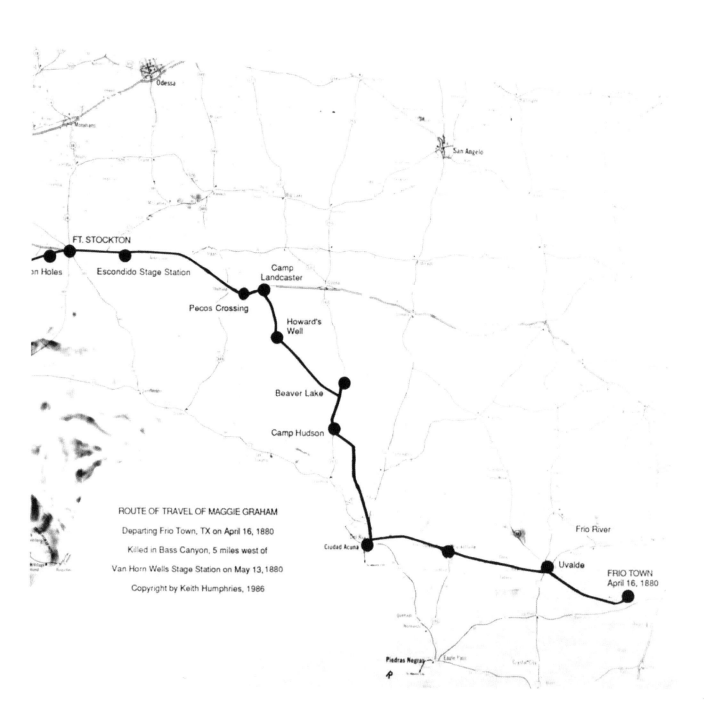

ROUTE OF TRAVEL OF MAGGIE GRAHAM

Departing Frio Town, TX on April 16, 1880

Killed in Bass Canyon, 5 miles west of

Van Horn Wells Stage Station on May 13, 1880

Copyright by Keith Humphries, 1986

ISBN-13: 978-1540588982
ISBN-10: 154058898X

Original Edition:

Copyright © 1988 by Keith J. Humphries
All rights reserved

Printed by The Printing Corner
1800 E. Yandell, El Paso, TX 79902

Printed in the United States of America
Copyright Registration Number: TX0002507367

Keith Humphries As I Knew Him

A Foreward by
Karl W. Laumbach

In 1997 I received a telephone call from Jim Eckles at the Public Affairs Office, White Sands Missile Range. For the previous six years I had been involved in the collection and interpretation of archaeological materials from the Hembrillo Battlefield, the scene of the largest conflict of the Victorio War, an epic battle between Victorio's Apache and the 9th Cavalry Buffalo Soldiers. Our work at the battlefield had been well publicized and what Jim had to say was interesting to say the least. An elderly gentleman from Las Cruces had just called him to say that he owned a .45-70 Springfield carbine that he had found "under a rock" in the Hembrillo Basin in 1929. As a college student at New Mexico A&M (now New Mexico State University), he had been interested in local history, became aware of the battle and had taken the time to visit the location. This was, of course, years before the development of White Sands Missile Range. In the course of our field work we found hundreds of cartridges from the fight but no weapons and the prospect of an actual weapon used in the battle was extremely exciting. And then Jim told me the bad news, the man had clearly and firmly told Jim that he "didn't want to talk to any stinking archaeologist!" And Jim clearly didn't have permission to give me his name.

My immediate response was that the man must be Keith Humphries. Jim was surprised and asked how I knew that. My response was that although I had never met the man, I had heard of his abrupt manner. Indeed I had long heard stories of Keith Humphries and his vast knowledge of local history and folklore. And of his paintings depicting scenes from early day New Mexico. Occasionally some of the paintings would be on exhibit. I remember rushing down

to a bank to see his Lincoln County War/Billy the Kid series only to find that they had been taken down the previous day. I had never tried to meet Keith largely because I had been told that he wasn't particularly welcoming and was cautious about sharing his knowledge lest some historian steal his material.

But the possibility of seeing and handling a carbine used in the Battle of Hembrillo was enough to quell any apprehension about meeting him and I had a long time friendship with Keith's nephew, Neil Loomis as my ace in the hole. Neil and I had played pool together since the 1970s and when asked, Neil agreed to introduce me to Keith. The meeting went well. Keith was courteous and very interested in the Battle of Hembrillo. He brought out the .45-70 carbine. The stock had that weathered look that comes from years outside but the action still worked, allowing us to dry fire an empty primed cartridge in the hope that the firing pin impression could be matched to cartridges recovered from the battlefield. When I drew him a sketch map of how I thought the battle unfolded and told him of the evidence that we had found, he became very excited, declaring "that's the way to do it".

Greatest Aggie

Keith Humphries in 1931.

Courtesy New Mexico State University Library

At the time of our meeting Keith was 90 years old. His hearing was pretty much gone even with hearing aids but his mind was sharp as a tack. On that first visit he showed me a copy of his book "Apache Land from Those Who Lived It" and then took me into his garage and showed me the 80 or so oil paintings of scenes gone by, each stacked upright in a long neat row. I purchased a book, took it home and was immediately and forever fascinated by the unique combination of paintings, historic photos and oral historical accounts lovingly cobbled together by Keith Humphries.

Born in 1907 and raised in West Texas from the time he was three, Keith, like many of his peers, had the pleasure of hearing tales of the Old West from those who had lived it. The difference was that with Keith, it became an all-consuming passion. Not only did he listen and enjoy but he remembered. And, as he grew older and went to college in Las Cruces, he spent his extra hours searching out Sadie Orchard, the madam from Hillsboro or George Coe of Lincoln County War fame or Billy Bates who had served as a packer for the 9th Cavalry during the Victorio War. When he found them he asked for their stories, he took them to the scenes of their youth and he took photos of those individuals and those places. In the process he compiled an amazingly diverse portfolio of information that covers West Texas, Southern New Mexico, and northern Mexico. His search continued into the 1940s when the last of the old timers began to fade away.

During his college days, he was a tremendous athlete, starring in baseball and basketball. A popular, outgoing guy, he was voted "The Greatest Aggie" in 1931. A leader in ROTC, he was the Captain of Company A.

After graduation and marriage to Gertrude Loomis, he worked for the New Mexico and Texas Highway Departments which allowed him to visit a variety of places and people that were important to his stories. He also began to write and publish his stories which he continued to do into the 1970s.

Keith worked as an engineer until World War II interrupted his search and changed his life in profound ways. He enlisted with the onset of America's involvement with World War II in 1942. He wanted to be a pilot but was denied the opportunity. Instead he enlisted in the army where as a member of the Army Corps of Engineers in the Pacific, he was involved in the island to island fighting required to defeat the Japanese. He didn't talk much about the war experience but it significantly changed the man. Various stories include waking up in his foxhole with all his comrades dead and having been one of the men who risked their lives to recover the body of famed war correspondent Ernie Pyle. Upon his return he was hospitalized for what we now know as PTSD. Not a man to stay down, he petitioned New Mexico Senator Clinton Anderson to have him released. He soon found employment with the Federal Aviation Agency and then, in 1949, White Sands Proving Ground, later to be White Sands Missile Range. During the 1950s he was awarded a patent and given official recognition for developing a tri-axial missile tracking camera mount, allowing missiles to be tracked in 3 dimensions.

Retiring from White Sands Missile Range in 1972, he took up painting. Taking lessons from local Las Cruces artist Cliff Donaldson, Keith soon developed a unique but consistent style. He quickly began putting the stories that he had heard from the old timers on canvas. Revisiting the scenes of historic events he took additional photos. A pilot for many years, he was the terror of the Las Cruces airport, crashing his plane more than once. He used the plane to take aerial shots of locations and travel ancient pathways in the air. Detail was important. If a man was left-handed and wore his pistol butt first, then that was the way Keith painted it.

In this manner Keith produced over 80 oil paintings depicting the stories heard in his youth. As he did so he conceived the idea of putting the paintings, the photos and his stories into one wonderful book. With the help of his wife, Gertrude, a long-time librarian at the Branigan

Public Library in Las Cruces, the manuscript began to take shape. It came to fruition in 1988 when the Printing Corner of El Paso published 270 hard bound copies with all the paintings in full color.

Unfortunately while a few books were sold and distributed at its release, most were still boxed in Keith's garage when I first visited him in 1997. He told me that his cost for each book was $100 and that he had expected the printer to help him with sales. Instead they delivered the books and an invoice for $27,000. He sold some cotton land in El Paso to pay the bill.

Intrigued by the book and the manner in which it brought first-hand accounts to life, I began to tell my friends and colleagues about the book. Many of them were interested in obtaining a copy. I would collect several hundred dollars and visit Keith. He would autograph the books and send me on my way. When I visited I would often ask questions about the stories. As Keith was deaf, I would write my question and hand it to him. One day, after answering several questions, Keith looked at me intently with teeth clenched and asked "are you crazy too?" I could only nod in agreement.

Given his age I became concerned over what might happen to his paintings after his death. He was very possessive of the paintings, having poured his life's passions into them. Neil suggested that I write Keith a letter and let him know how much I valued his book and the paintings. And so I did. A week or so later I saw Neil and asked him if Keith had received the letter. Neil, nodding grimly, said that Keith had waved the letter at him somewhat angrily exclaiming "someone's trying to butter me up!"

However my next few meetings were quite cordial and as a Geronimo Springs Museum board member, I began to negotiate a loan of selected examples of Keith's paintings to the museum. By January 2000, the loan was complete and an exhibit of Keith's paintings was soon in place at the museum. At the same time I nominated Keith for a New Mexico

Historic Preservation Award through the New Mexico State Historic Preservation Office. Awarded in May, 2000, the award lauded Keith for "Outstanding Accomplishment for Lifetime Achievement in Documenting Southern New Mexico Oral traditions and the History of the Nineteenth Century." In August, 2000, he agreed to a long term loan that sent all of his paintings to the Geronimo Springs Museum with the exception of a few of his favorites that hung in his house.

Early in 2001 with the assistance of Curator Sally Meeks, an exhibit of Keith's art at the Branigan Cultural Center in Las Cruces was arranged. The exhibit was heralded by a wonderful article on Keith and his work by Derrickson Moore of the Las Cruces Sun News. I presented a slide show lecture to the Dona Ana Historical Society that was followed by a reception in the Branigan Gallery. Keith very

Keith J. Humphries

At the Branigan Cultural Center in Las Cruces in 2001.

much enjoyed the day and the long awaited recognition. He passed away a year later on July 21, 2002.

After his death, his daughter Lois Carol (Bunkie) Griffith, donated the paintings and Keith's files to Geronimo Springs Museum. The museum is very proud of the collection and was extremely interested in republishing Keith's book as a fundraiser to support the museum. That goal was brought to fruition by a generous donation from David Soules and the volunteer but very professional effort by Pete and Morrie Drexler to produce a faithful copy of the original.

Remarkably, Keith Humphries' passion for the stories and the people depicted in his paintings began as a youth and continued throughout his life. Oral history was not an accepted discipline in those years and early oral historians are often criticized because they focused on the more dramatic incidents. While Humphries was certainly interested in the dramatic, he also recorded the more mundane scenes of daily life in southern New Mexico. Many of his paintings depict street scenes in Mesilla, Las Cruces and Kingston, others present settlers on the move or salteros returning with carretas loaded with salt. Although an engineer and not a trained historian, Humphries worked diligently to find the connections between the stories and recorded history. As a result, his story tellers have provided both historians and archaeologists with insights into the events portrayed.

Some of the stories have not been documented by historians and thus fall into the category of folklore. A case in point is the painting "Dead Man's Mine" which portrays the Spaniards mule train hauling gold ore from the fabled lost Spanish mine in the Caballo Mountains. And yet, Humphries informant tells a plausible tale of why and when the mine was there, thereby adding to a New Mexican legend that continues to draw treasure seekers into the mountains of southern New Mexico.

Humphries' art has been described as "Grandma Moses". Regardless, he was consistent in his approach and perspective, being more concerned with accuracy of detail than with proportion or style. Thus the paintings depict specific events, correct in detail based on site visits by the artist, first hand interviews and historical readings. And while they are accurate depictions, they do maintain a personal view point that was a product of the life and times of the informants that shared their stories. While the personalities and backgrounds of Humphries and his informants are present in the paintings they shine through most clearly in his prose. Often "politically incorrect" by today's standards, the language reflects the rough edged world that was southern New Mexico and West Texas in the late 1800s. Matter-of-fact, sometimes humorous, sometimes callous, Humphries' stories are the next best thing to going back in time and talking to someone who lived in that era.

And that is his gift to us. Enjoy!

Karl Laumbach
Mesilla Park, New Mexico

Photograph Credits

for the Geronimo Springs Museum Edition of *Apache Land*

Compiling a list of credits for the photographs used in Humphries book has proven to be quite difficult. Humphries states in his acknowledgements that all photographs not attributed to a source were in his collection. Much of the original material was apparently destroyed by the printer after Humphries death in the belief that there would not be a demand for the volume. The text of the book gives credit to the sources of some of the photographs. The stories make it clear that many of the photographs were taken by Humphries as he interviewed sources and visited locations beginning in the late 1920s.

Due to the loss of many of Humphries photo archives, Karl Laumbach has made a diligent evaluation of the photographs that might be held in one or more archives and has contacted those archives to obtain permission to publish them. Arrangements to use the various photographs have been finalized with:

• Teddie Moreno, Library Specialist at Special Collections and Archives, New Mexico State University (NMSU) Library, Las Cruces, New Mexico.

• Hannah Abelbeck, Digital Imaging Specialist, Photo Archives, New Mexico History Museum/ Palace of the Governors, Santa Fe, New Mexico.

• Rebecca Tabah Percival, Photo Archivist and Curator, Arizona Heritage Center, Arizona Historical Society, Tucson, Arizona.

• Linda Lopez, Director of the Gila County Historical Museum (formerly the Clara Woody Historical Museum), Globe, Arizona.

• Dorinda Millan, Director of The West of the Pecos Museum, Pecos, Texas.

Known Credits for Photographs:

Gila County Historical Museum formerly The Clara Thompson Woody Museum, Globe, Arizona:

Felix B. Knox, page 165

Sara B. and George Riley York, page 165

Special Collections and Archives, New Mexico State University (NMSU) Library, Las Cruces:

Eugene Van Patten, page 74, RG 88-102-002

W. L. Rynerson, page 77, Hobson-Huntsinger Collection

Lee Meyers, page 125, NMSU 00240622 Ms.0024

Charles Bowdre and wife, page 118, NMSU 0110081

Frank Gomez, page 122, NMSU 01100081

Robert Beckwith, page 122, NMSU 01360010

John M. Beckwith, page 130, Lee Myers Collection NMSU 00240627

Keith Humphries "Greatest Aggie", page v (Foreward), and page 201 (Biography) taken from the 1931 Swastika, page 50

Arizona Historical Society, Tucson, Arizona:

Cochise' Second Wife, page 185, Gatewood Collection

Natchez, page186, Gatewood Collection

Nachez (sic) and Geronimo, page 178, Gatewood Collection

New Mexico History Museum, Palace of the Governors, Santa Fe, New Mexico:

Joel Fowler, page 113, credited to Socorro photographer Edward Bass, NMHM catalog number 164508

10th Cavalry in Black Range, page 138, Humphries mistakenly identifies the men as 9th Cavalry, photograph by Henry A. Schmidt. NMHM catalog number 058556

Ethan W. Eaton, page 114, NMHM catalog number 122150

Robert Olinger, page 128, credited to Lincoln County Heritage Museum now owned by the Museum of New Mexico

The West of the Pecos Museum, Pecos, Texas:

Tom Duncan, page 35

Table of Contents

Preface
Geronimo Springs Museum Edition

When asked to undertake this edition of the out-of-print "Apache Land" by Keith J. Humphries, I immediately volunteered. I had looked long and hard to find a copy of this book and considered it an invaluable source of history of this part of the country. Futhermore, I liked the idea presented by David Soules and Karl Laumbach. Soules is a scientist who has recently been highly active in the history of the southwest and Laumbach is a renowned archaeologist who is also a Director of the Geronimo Springs Museum.

They wanted an edition that would be less expensive than the original but one that would keep true to Humphries' original. Fortunately, the paintings and photographs used in the book were of sufficient quality that my brother, Morris Drexler, was able to scan and descreen them so that they could be used in the present edition. The content of the original book was commercially scanned and I was able to use those results for OCR (Optical Character Recognition) to obtain an editable version of the words.

In keeping with the intent of this edition, I decided to keep Humphries' spelling (and multiple spellings and mis-spellings) in all cases. I did, however, make a reasonable effort to correct spelling errors due to the OCR process, although some may well have survived. The pages numbered with arabic numerals are the same as in Humphries' original edition with only minor changes due to word processing differences.

I have taken the liberty of adding a Table of Contents with the "story numbers" indicated although Humphries referred to only a few of the stories by number. (Some of his story numbers are in error by my accounting, but the context will make it apparent to which story he refers.)

An "Index" generated from the OCR'd text by Dawn Santiago was also added to Humphries' original. Since the page numbers in the present Geronimo Springs Museum edition are the same as Humphries' original edition, the Index may be used with either edition.

A "Foreward" written by Karl Laumbach has been added to the beginning of the book to give the reader a better understanding of the significance of this work.

A biography of Humphries written by Daniel Aranda has been added as an appendix to provide the reader with an appreciation of the man and his accomplishments.

Humphries' first hard-backed edition contained large maps on both the front and back covers for the area covered by events of his stories. The present soft-covered edition required a different method of handling those large maps. I have included both of his maps, but found it necessary to break them into two parts, each on a separate page. The maps are displayed on facing pages at the front and back of the book.

It is my hope that this present edition will afford the reader an experience very similar to that of Humphries original edition. At the same time, it is anticipated that the added features will enhance the book's usefulness and enjoyment.

James J. (Pete) Drexler
Las Cruces, New Mexico

Dedication

APACHE LAND, FROM THOSE WHO LIVED IT lay dormant for ten years for want of a master printer who cared more for the story than for the job of printing it. Bob Beck made all the participants "live" together in Book I. I thought he should do them all for the Southwest in Book II; that they might be together again in their *PASO POR AQUI* (they passed by here) in Apache Land.

I am sure Bob would like the way (and proudly so) his daughter Vicky finished "his" book.

PASO POR AQUI Credit -- Eugene Manlove Rhodes

Credit for typing, correcting and evaluating the stories in this book, APACHE LAND FROM THOSE WHO LIVED IT, goes to Gertrude L. Humphries, wife of the author. For many years, she worked them over when they first appeared as feature stories in newspapers and some first printed in monthly periodical magazines.

KJH

PREFACE

Most southwestern history is re-worked versions of writings and compilations of the past. This record book is different.

It is the stories of the Old Timers <u>who lived it</u>. It began in 1910, in a far-west Texas ranching community when it became evident the Old Forgotten people would soon be gone and, with them, their stories.

The writing began in earnest in 1972 on my retirement as a data-gathering engineer for 24 years at the White Sands Missile Range. The illustrations followed as sketches with a paintbrush in oil — loose and simple-like, as imagined—from going over the sites with the Story tellers (some several times). And in later years when the Ranchers padlocked their gates, I photographed the sites from the air. The newspaper files and libraries supplemented the dates and aided the weed-out of the chaff.

As to the quality of the illustrations, I can offer only what Will Rogers once said: "When you are a failure at everything else you can always say, 'YOU ARE AN ARTIST. NO ONE will know the difference.'"

I became addicted on history at age 3 while at our 9-Mile Spring Ranch on the road between Ft. Davis and Toyah "Cowtown," Texas, here where the stage drivers, freighters, cowboys, Cavalrymen came back for a last look-see, and stopped to rest their horses. Our neighbor's wife — 4 miles east— said, "Mrs. Humphries always sat a good table." In that day, what else was there to set?

My mother — a western Oklahoma territorial school teacher — "launched" me with the aid of neighbor Dr. Murphy. The weekly beggar, a Kiowa, came by and looked and grunted: "Heep big ears, make good scout!"

I have lived and worked in these southwest places: Toyah, Balmorhea, (Toyah Creek) Alpine, Van Horn, Pecos and El Paso, Texas; Socorro, Silver City and Las Cruces, New Mexico; Safford, Douglas Air Force Base, Douglas, Davis-Monthan Air Force Base, Tucson, Arizona.

This cover's all Apache Land from on and above the ground. By the end of WWII, most were gone (Old Timers).

As Gene Rhodes would have said, "*Paso por aqui.*" (They did pass by here).

KJH, The Recorder
12/13/89

RE-CREATION OF MAGGIE GRAHAM

Maggie about 19

Left to right*: John Little, b. Aug 1860; Mrs. Brice Little; Maggie Little, b. Oct 1858 (Penn) holding Edmond N. Little, b. Jan 1879; Brice Little; Girl unknown; David B. Little, b. June 1862; woman unknown; Sam Graham, b. 1858 (NJ); Harry Graham, b. NJ; gentleman unkown; Mary Little, b. 1864; Samuel L. Little, b 1867. Baby Edmond's name appears in most of Maggie's letters.*

From southwest Frio Town to far west Bass Canyon, Texas, stretches the rockiest, gulliest and hilliest 468 miles of all El Paso-San Antonio stage road.

The half east of the Pecos River was once Comanche now remanded to their reservation. The west one-half remained the most feared of the dreaded Apache Land, made up of driest of the sun-blistered desert, with mesas and escarpments. To bless that forgotten land of mesquite, catclaw and greasewood, the "Great Rainmaker" threw in a generous mixture of steely blue, serrated sierras as seen shimmering in the heat haze on far off horizons — something for the thirsty traveler to hope or reach for as man and animal

tracked deeper into the alkali dust and burning sands. An opportunity that beckoned from distant horizons was daily groomed in red-and-golden sunsets, luring the wayward traveler westward. And so it was with the Graham's 5-wagon train. They reached out, but saw only the sunsets, until one day in May in 1880.

This story, then a young story, came to light in the ankle-deep dust of a drought-stricken land at our Nine-Mile Spring Ranch on the road to Ft. Davis, south of Toyah "Cowtown," Texas, a hot July in 1912.

Freighter "Burro" Mendoza, one-time water hauler at the Van Horne Wells Stage Station, was maneuvering his 24 burros, two freight and one light trail wagons, filled with camp gear, a bitch dog with pups, a burro foal, followed by two feisty jacks, vital to the operation and "fathers" of the herd, that threw up their heads in the dust cloud at the first smell of water and stampeded to the fore front and into the spring.

Calanche and Evaristo came out of the spring, dropping their shovels, let out a loud chorus "Ah-yah, amigo mi!" completely ignoring their boy boss, on a little grullo pony nearby. They called me, "Mi Muchacho" (my boy). All three were ex-stage line hands. The camp fire burned late that night in Burro's menagerie.

The story research ended at Austin, Texas, with a Comanche solo flight over to Frio Town. Once cleared over San Antonio, it was clear sailing to Pearsall where I broke out under the overcast over the Frio River and followed it up to the old brown two-story Courthouse — the last of old Frio Town and the beginning of the story that began a Saturday, September 20, 1879. I circled low over old Frio Town an evening, September 20, 1979, in the fantasy of the twilight glow, the lamps, the lanterns and the candle light came winking out at you, for they had come from all around. Wagons, buggies, surreys, and patches of saddle horses stood drooped-hipped and at ease, like a bunch of cattle bedded down for the night, chewing their cud.

Years later, the N. O. Pierson family said they heard from an old lady who said her father had just arrived from Mississippi to work for Mr. Little in one of his sheep camps; said she was just a little girl when "her father carried her to the dance . . . the crowd was waiting from the courthouse front steps clean up to the top floor for Harry and Maggie to arrive and begin the dance."

It was back to the old axiom — look hard enough and long enough and you see only what you want to see.

Long white tables were stacked with food on the top floor and women fussing over them as only women can, like bees over honey. An orchestra was tuning up, for orchestras are never in tune. It is their way of getting on center stage.

The late Douglas Little at the Pierson Airstrip, after showing me in depth all of Frio Town, said, "It would be kinda nice if you let your imagination go." His father, Dave, who was Maggie's younger brother once said, "There never was anything like it, not in all Frio Town. It was a real dinger!" In all my west Texas courthouse dancing, do I recall doing a "dinger." You have to use your imagination.

I passed over the old Little Home at 200 feet on my flight, April 16, 1980, 100 years after it happened. A grandson of one who lived at the Robert home, near the Little Home, said that as Maggie and Harry's wagon pulled away, Maggie's mother tearfully stood trembling and half-heartedly waving a white hanky. Her Father, the big Scotsman, was staring at Maggie, who was standing up in the wagon, looking back and waving her favorite red bonnet. It was as if he knew he was seeing his little girl for the last time. I homed in on the Uvalde Omni and with the same radio got a recording of Ken Griffen on the organ playing "So Long".

As I skimmed over the old wagon road westward out of Frio Town, I could see my research coming to an end. My journalism instructor once said, "A story is a bunch of words. It's how you put them together and when you start living it, it's time to write."

For the next 160 minutes at a little less than 3 miles-per-minute, I covered the 468 miles of the Graham wagon tracks that had taken them 27 days, ending in Bass Canyon. I started living the story as I passed over Uvalde about 10 minutes after leaving Frio Town. Here the Daniel (Pat, age 48) Murphy wagon with wife Martha Jane (age 28), son Joe (age 8), daughter Sally (age 4), and baby James (age 2), joined up. The Murphy family was going to Silver City, NM, to open a brick yard. Also joining the Grahams were two wagons from Castroville (west of San Antonio, TX). A man and son in one and two young (reported as gamblers) men in the other.

Maggie in her wedding dress, reportedly taken in her home 16 September 1879.

4

SAN FELIPE (DEL RIO)   April 19, 20 (Mon., Tues.)

A beautiful camping spot with spring, cottonwood, orchard and a green meadow. It marked the beginning of a vast land of brown mesquite, greasewood and black brush, with springs fewer and farther apart and massacre sites that marked the road since its beginning in 1849 from Gulf ports to California gold. It was a vast and troubled land of the Comanche and Apache, since before Coronado and Onate. Maggie's letter best tells of San Felipe.

Excerpts from Maggie's Letters

San Felip Del Rio, Tex
Apr 20-21

Dear Parents Sisters & Bro's
    We arrived here about ten o'clock today, took dinner with Mr. & Mrs. Tardy. This is a beautiful place. I never saw anything prettier. There are beautiful springs, here they are boiling springs. The lady who Mrs. Tardy boards with has a splendid place. She has a nice orchard and a ditch running through the yard. Oh! I just think this is a lovely country. I am enjoying the trip splendidly. We live fine, have canned fruit, pickles, potatoes, onions, butter, eggs and fresh meat and sometimes we get milk and Harry made splendid oyster soup. He is such a good cook I don't do much cooking. Harry and Sam do it all. I have made bread twice. Your light bread lasted well. You can send some more. I sleep sometimes until breakfast is ready. The first two or three nights I was very much afraid but am used to it now. Our team does splendid. The little black came very near running away with us in Uvalde. Now call our team lazy. Old Pat Murphy (Daniel, See: Marriage Certificate) is with us. We wrote that to you in the postal card. He is so funny he keeps me laughing half the time.

OLD CAMP HUDSON
April 22 [Thurs.]

From San Felipe, it was crossing and re-crossing the lower Devil's River, so properly named.

From Hudson Crossing, the wagons had road trouble all the way up the river to Beaver Lake.

This road is traveled a great deal. We met Green Gullet this side of Uvalde. He is driving the stage, he talks as much as ever. I hope you are all well. I have been very homesick since we left but am getting along finely now. I miss Edmund so much, the sweet little fellow. I could see him laughing and throwing kisses at us all day yesterday. Don't whip the little pet no matter how bad he is. Well, I will let Harry finish this. He is out looking at this place with Mrs. Tardy. Much love and kisses to all and kiss little Edmund for Harry and I. I send some flowers I picked to the children in this letter. Sam is well and in fine spirits.

Mr. Little:
We are getting along fine. The horses have not lost any flesh- but are really better than when we started. Maggie stands the trip agreat deal better than I expected and all in all we are very lucky thus far. My love to all, especially to Edmund. Regards to Chris and husband. (This is probably the odd couple with little girl on left in Maggie's family portrait.)
Harry
Mrs. H. B. Graham
Kinney Co. Del Rio, Tex

Care of Tardy
Mrs. H. G. Tardy

BEAVER LAKE April 25 [Sun.]

Maggie posted a letter here, which best tells it.

Harry Graham and Mary Little from group photo taken 1879.

agreeable and remember me to all inquiring friends and accept a great portion of love from Harry and I. Be a good boy and take care of the sheep. I hope you will get fifty cents for your wool. Address your letters to Fort Davis and good-by. I wish I could see you all.

Maggie Graham.
Beaver Lake, Apr 25, 1880

My Dearest Brother

We came here yesterday and will stop until today noon and then we will start. Mr. Ramsy has a cow ranch here and we have had plenty of milk We will have to travel forty-five miles without water. We will carry as much as we can. We went five miles past this place and had to come back again to get water. It is about two miles off the road and we had a terrible time with the old mare. She would not pull across water or up a hill. I tell you I felt like killing her. Sam and Harry took her out and gave her a good whipping and then she pulled fine. Our horses look better than when we left home. Harry went fishing yesterday and caught six nice fish. One trout weighed about 4 lbs. They were very nice indeed. We had milk and clabber. I should have said prunes, fish, butter, Worchestershire sauce and bread for supper and fish for breakfast. Harry fryed the fish and of course they were splendid. I don't do much cooking. I lay in bed sometimes until breakfast is ready but we have very early breakfast. We have traveled over some of the most terrible roads I ever saw in my life and I don't want to see anymore, the largest rocks it was just up and down

8

hill and jumping off of rocks but the worst hills I've have come up was at Devil's River. I wrote to May from there. I assure you we had a time getting up there. We put in both teams to one wagon and then had to take some things out. You would have almost killed yourself with laughter had you been there at old Pat Murphy. (Daniel Murphy, age 48). He calls his wife Martha Jane (age 28) and me Margarete and he would say now Martha Jane, you and Margarete push on the wheels and we will drive out. I did not do much pushing. Mrs. Murphy and I drove and Harry, Sam and Murphy pushed the wheels and I tell you we got up alright. Well, I don't want to see anymore hills like that. D.R. is a beautiful stream we crossed it seven times and it is running at every place. Oh! there are some beautiful flowers growing along the road. I will send you one that I have pressed. I think when Miss Vale said this was a d—f— country she missed it when she has not traveled over the hilly part of Texas. Have you taken your girls out riding yet? Have you heard from Johnnie? Well, I don't think you can say we don't write often enough for we write every chance we have. Give my love to Johnnie when you write to him. Love to everyone at home and kiss little Darling Edmund for me and you can kiss Cora for me, that is if she is

HOWARD'S WELL   April 27 (Tues.)

It wasn't hard to visualize where the four wagons circled above the spring at Howard's Well, just where Anastacio Gonzalez's ten wagons had circled and camped just eight years before, this same month, known throughout the southwest as the place of the "burnt wagon train," and after supper where Harry had walked Maggie up on the side of the mountain to look at the graves, a landmark of ominous foreboding in this land of the Comanche and Kiowa.

The fear shown in Maggie's letter is evidence that she could have known something of the tragedy, and that the mind of Marcella Serna's baby did not really die as it was dashed against the wagon wheel, nor did Marcella's mother's, who was lanced and scalped, as is evidenced by the years that Marcella came back to pray there.

The circuit priest told Mrs. Huelster, the stage keeper's wife at Leon Holes, that the Mexican freighters confessed to him that they saw on stormy nights, the Grandmother, a saintly ghost, carrying the baby around the site of the 9 victims of the Burnt Wagons, both wailing and crying for the Mother. When the lightning became bad she ran — just as she did when the Comanches scalped her — back to their graves.

Maggie sensed "an Indian behind every bush, but there was safety in the wagon train," so she wrote. Only four wagons now, when before ten were not enough and with two companies of the 9th Cavalry, not three miles away. But that was 8 years in the past.

Howard's Well campsite for the Graham wagons. Also, site of the Gonzales wagon train burned by Indians April 1872 with gravesite on nearby hillside of the burned teamster mentioned in Maggie's letter.

The mail hack from San Antonio came through the next morning, changed mules and went on its way west to Ft. Stockton. It left no letter for homesick Maggie.

Note: Howard's Well is a ghostly site even today. I camped the night there amid weird-looking oil well pumps in a death-like stillness slowly raising and lowering their "heads" among the graves on the mountain side, or was I too deep in the story?

Long before you get to Howard's Well, no matter how you do it — ride, drive or over-fly— there is always an eerie feeling in the air.

SE to Beaver Lake and NW to the Pecos River, a sense of death always abounds. Some believers say it is only part of Howard's Well and the burnt wagon train.

To describe it is wasting time. You cannot relate the on-coming feelings of a young pregnant woman, first time away from home, in this raw and roughest of desert wasteland — not from one who knows of frontier Texas tales of Comanche raids and now only three days away from the Pecos — the eastern flank of the most dreaded of all Apache land.

Before the development of oil, I had driven the 40-odd miles to Howard's Well (between Beaver Lake and the Pecos) where nothing but coyotes and owls stirred the quiet of the night along the old gullied stage road and never saw a light.

I studied Maggie's pictures on a stormy night at Howard's Well. The remainder of the night, I saw two Mexican women, alternating carrying a baby, running, screaming from gleefully shouting Comanche horsemen with lances playing with their victims.

I awoke hungry and stiff with the decision to write this part of the story right out of my mind.

[On Oak Creek and at Old Camp Lancaster, Texas]
Tardy Ranche
April 28, 1880

My Dear Mary & Cora

Thinking that you would like to hear from this old traveler I'll "drop" you a line. I have just finished baking bread & of course it was splendid. Sam did most of the baking. I am sitting in the wagon writing this. It is sprinkling a little & I am afraid I might melt if I were to sit outside so concluded to move in. This is a rather dreary looking place. Mrs. Tardy is coming out here to live soon. She will have a sweet time . . .

[handwritten letter image — facsimile]

. . . of it. They have a rock house and two rooms and no doors and very small windows and grass roof. We washed yesterday, Harry, Sam and I. Harry washed nearly all my clothes as I am too lazy to do much of anything lately except talk and you may be sure that I can do plenty of that. John Hanning took supper with us last night. We had jelly, batter cakes, sardines, pickles, milk and water cress. There is any quantity of it growing here. I enjoyed it immensely. John looks very much like Bro. John. I'm also sure I know what you think. He is not half as goodlooking as Brother Johnnie as you have never ever met anyone that who in your estimation. There is a nice milk house here. I am

. . . *going up to look at it with Harry when I* finish this. Mrs. Murphy's baby[*] is crying, it is very entertaining. Harry says he wishes it would change the tune for awhile and cry Yankee Doodle. He cries nearly all the time. You can imagine how we enjoy it. Sam says he would choke it if it were his. The mail passed this morning and we were so disappointed in not receiving a letter from you. We have traveled over some of the roughest roads I ever saw. We came down two hills that we had to tie ropes to the wagon and pull back on them and tie the wheels and I tell you I have had enough of such roads. Last Sunday we camped at Howard's Well.

[*] *This baby was a two-year-old boy, says Glenn Harper, a nephew of the boy.*

and Harry and I went up on a mountain and of course I was almost frightened to death. I imagined there was an Indian behind every bush or rock That is the place where the Indians burnt that train. A long time since I saw the place where it was burnt. I tell you it was no fun to be camped there but we were with a train. There is any quantity of cedar here and beautiful flowers and the prettiest cactus I ever saw anywhere. I would like to send some to the Dr. I know he would like to have them. Well Cora how are you and Tompkins progressing.

I suppose you and Mary will give him a nice game soon, a little lump of imperfection I feel for him but don't break the little man's heart for you know that would be terrible and good Christian little girls like you and Mary would not do anything like that I know. Oh no, but your sister would. Harry has just shed his pants and taken off all the buttons. We will have soup for dinner but not just soup but oyster soup. He is just an old hand at cooking. He can rattle the pots and pans and get a meal ready while I am thinking about it. Sam is no slow hand himself. He is the best

coffee parcher I ever saw anywhere. Send your coffee to him if you want it to look nice. I have fallen two or three times getting into the wagon. I almost dislocated a limb or two but nothing serious. However we have killed three snakes on our trip and they were fine large ones, too, and of course one is enough.

We stopped at a camp to buy some milk one day and the children looked like last years pigs and their mother had half her dress torn off. Oh! she was very charming. She could charm a man with both eyes out. When we asked how the road was farther on she said its worser than what we had passed over but we managed to wash the milk down some way or other. Cora, I am just about the color of the colored girl Mrs. Price had working for her. You and Mary can take a good look at her and then think of me, but I am growing fat and sassy and feel splendid, only homesick sometimes but I am looking forward to the time when we will return to the beautiful lands of your little home. Send a copy of Tompkin's letter, if you please as I know you would not part with his precious letter. I must end for fear you will faint trying to read this letter. Of course I don't want you to do that. Sam says to kiss each other for him but he would rather kiss you himself. Harry and I too. Mr. Andrew. Our love to everybody in Frio Town and accept a kiss for yourselves and love and a kiss to home folks and to sweet little Edmund boy from me. Write soon. Maggie. Sam will finish this. Our regards.

John Henny looks much like your John, not so pretty you think. Well, I will have to close as my space is limited. Tell Dave I will write to him in a few days from Stockton. I should like to know what poor fellow you two are giving a game. Kiss each other for me. I would rather do it myself but you see how it is. Present my regards to inquiring friends, keeping a good share for yourselves as I remain yours truly,

Sam Graham

Please write us at El Paso

THE PECOS CROSSING
April 28, 29 (Wed., Thurs.)

Tardy's Ranch
April 28th

Dear Friends
Mary and Cora

Maggie has left this space for me to fill. She has told about all herself. Murphy's child is keeping up a delightful racket not an unusual thought it needs choking. My lips have been sore ever since I left Frio and I did not kiss Dave. It must have been someone else that caused it. Maggie is lively and full of fun. Keeps us all bouncing around and she is much braver than Murphy. He is the biggest coward I ever saw. I hear you are writing to Tompkins. I should like to see letters. Enclosed find cactus flower.

Once over the rim, I cut back on the throttle, gliding quietly into wide Pecos River Valley, where even the wind whistling around the cabin had an ominous tone to it.

Here the wagons rough-locked their wheels and slid off the treacherous east escarpment 400 feet into an 8-mile wide valley holding old Camp Lancaster and the old stage station at the junction of the sweet water of Live Oak Creek and the briny alkali of the unpredictable Pecos, known since 1854 as the Military Crossing. Lancaster, the Angel-of-the-Southern-Road, known by the troopers as the Indian burial ground. From here at H. C. Tardy's Ranch, Maggie posted her last letter of record with John Henning, the mail hack driver.

Tardy listed 1800 head of cattle on his 1880 census — showing how the cattle business was already growing. The Slaughter brothers had moved their cattle out of Frio County in 1879 to New Mexico and Arizona.

It is believed that Harry Graham was heading for the unsettled upper San Simon Valley adjacent to John Slaughter's large San Benardino Ranch straddling the Mexico-Arizona border. Here Mexican cattle could be bought cheap for cash and by just driving them across the line.

At the Pecos Crossing (some few hundred yards above the present bridge), the four wagons crossed to be joined up-river by another — James Grant, a post trader from Ft. Concho (San Angelo).

The next day the five wagons crawled out of the wide limestone-rimmed valley into the land of bolsons, sierras and escarpments. A land where the wise traveled with guns at the ready and at night through the worst of Apache land (a no-fight superstition).

They had no emergency plans, camping at will, traveling within sight of each other and depending entirely on the horse-backed Sam Graham (age 22 with 2 years' Texas Ranger service) to lead them safely into the promised land, where the evening golden sunset beckoned them on.

ESCONDIDO SPRINGS
April 30 [Fri.]

A wide long valley nestled between friendly hills with good grazing and plenty of good spring water. Here Bill Hobbs, station keeper, years later said he warned the Graham wagons of reported Apache renegades operating along the stage road west of Ft. Davis.

The good watering here was where the freighters most always "cut" their whisky barrels, called the mule-skinner's sample. A half-gallon from each barrel was replaced with water. One barkeeper in Ft. Davis said "it kept the soldiers on their feet longer — giving the "girls" time to ready them for soldiering again.

Replica of Escondido stage station at time Graham wagons stopped there in 1880. Bill Hobbs was station keeper.

Believed to be Peter Gallagher Farm Center, northeast and on Comanche Creek near where the San Antonio Road entered Ft. Stockton. Maggie could have acquired the fresh eggs and milk here in 1880.

Maggie passed this house in Ft. Stockton in 1880.

FORT STOCKTON   May 1 [Sat.]

A post of military design gable roofs, adobe walls, warehouses and corrals. Nearby Comanche Springs with its abundance of good water once was a stopover for the annual raidings of Comanche into Chihuahua since the beginning of the mission/settlements. They looted, plundered and dared their victims to follow — leaving only enough livestock for "seed". On the West side of the spring was a warehouse, two stores and two saloons. Here the Herman Kohler store later stood as an institution of honesty, good-will and credit—open days and nights to everyone. Cowboys were known to charge their tobacco and staples with signature or marker and if broke, could sleep on their saddle blanket on the floor.

Maggie probably posted a letter at the Young store. Here a military poster warned of renegade Apaches and water shortages west of Ft. Davis.

Due to a family fire, no record of other Maggie letters were found.

17

LEON HOLES
May 2, 3 [Sun., Mon.]

Years later, Mrs. Herman Huelster said that she was the station keeper's bride at the "Holes" when the five wagons came in to camp, graze their stock and wash their clothes at the deep springs that overflowed into a meadow of grass. Here the road split left to Chihuahua and was heavily traveled by freight wagons from the Gulf ports. She said the young bride never let a west bound mail hack driver leave without a second look through his mail sacks.

Mrs. Herman Huelster, age 80 (in 1939). Station-keeper's wife at Leon Holes and Barilla Station in 1880. Talked with Maggie.

Louise Humphries Adams standing in old corral of Barilla stage station dressed as of 1880.

18

BARILLA STATION
May 4, 5 [Tues., Wed.]

The spring at Barilla was running dry and the Huelsters warned the Graham wagons on leaving Leon Holes. If it came to water rationing, the twice weekly Concord carrying passengers got first choice over the daily mail hacks. Freight wagons and emigrants would have to take their chances.

Barilla Station was the end of 34 miles of droughty desert — a mile longer than the waterless plain between El Muerto and Van Horne Wells, the heart of the forbidden land. After the Graham wagons had left Leon holes, the Huelsters took over the Barilla Station where the Apache rumors came daily with the mail hack.

Years later as a 10th grader on a Saturday deer hunt, night overtook me in the mountains some miles west of old Barilla Station. I walked tired and sore-footed toward the only light. The mountains loomed up dark and ghost-like with the receding twilight. I was a stranger and they took me in. It was the Herman Huelster's ranch. That night I heard my first stage line story. German men don't talk much; they just sit thinking and smoking. Their wives do it as part of the house work. This is Mrs. Huelster's story as I recall.

A few days after the Grahams had gone up Limpia Canyon, Jerky, the mail-hack driver, came into Barilla Station one midnight, overdue — slewing on two wheels, seesawing the reins to four wild Mexican mules, their bellies pumping, nostrils dilated — eager to be out of Wild Rose Pass.

Jerky, a bearded six-foot-four, all legs and arms, jumped from the buckboard throwing the reins to Huelster, the Station Keeper, saying, "Hermie, I've got to be past Cayonosa before daylight!" — his boots stomping up little dust cones all the way into Mrs. Huelster's kitchen.

Ten minutes and five cups of black coffee later, Jerky grabbed a handful of baking powder biscuits, throwing them into his open buckskin shirt front, said, "Don't worry, Mrs. Huelster, a patrol is comin' down Limpia Canyon." Out the door he vaulted into the hack. Braced, spraddle-legged, he shouted, "Let `er go, Hermie!" Huelster and a Mexican released the ears of the leader mules — flinging themselves to one side as the team shot out the gate in a cloud of dust into a moonlit sea of greasewood and mesquite as far as the eye could see.

I asked Mrs. Huelster about the travelers of that day: She said, "They were the Concords, mail-hacks, and mostly military freighters from the Gulf. Long mule team wagons and yoked Mexican oxen wagons. They always camped here. To see a blonde woman cooking was a saintly sight. Just a blonde was enough for the Mexicans. The gamblers were the most considerate . . . the cowmen the most respectful . . . the preachers and priests the hungriest. The Mexican freighters always came into the station hat-in-hand, bowing as they left, blessing themselves as if they'd seen the Virgin Mary. Me and my blonde hair!" she laughed.

I thought — out there in this vast and troubled land with that set of souls to save there should be enough sinners for a priest and preacher, both to have a field day.

Anton Aggerman, horseshoer who shod Harry Graham's horse at Ft. Davis in May 1880. He was later a soldier at Ft. Davis.

Trees at front edge of wing are where the Grahams camped while at Ft. Davis. Had the corrals been rebuilt, this would probably be as it was in 1880.

FT. DAVIS
May 6, 7, 8 (Thurs., Fri., Sat.)

The Graham wagons camped on the east side of the fort's corrals at the big cottonwoods and spring, where all travelers stopped. Nearby was the S&S (Sender and Siebenboin) store and warehouse with a blacksmith shop next door. Here Anton Aggerman (then age 23) worked as a civilian farrier (horseshoer).

It was the same day as his birthday, Friday, May 14, 1880, he said, when "the eastbound coach came in at sun-up, just as I was coming to work. It came in a run, paused to let a well-dressed woman out at the first Chihuahua Hill Saloon, then on to the stage office where the guard threw down the mail sacks, and then ran across the parade ground straight to the hospital. It was so unusual I borrowed a customer's horse and galloped over to the hospital just as four men were carrying a badly wounded man inside, followed by a priest in black, clasping a cross and doing his wig-wag signals of a final prayer. I knew the man must be dying."

"Not until the next week, when the injured man's brother came to the shop with a horse to be shod, did I learn that he was the new deputy to Sheriff W. T. Wilson and was the younger brother, Sam, of Harry Graham now in the hospital, and, for whom I had shod a horse the week before." Sam then recounted the Bass Canyon fight in detail.

The five wagons had rested their stock, washed clothes and checked their team's feet. Harry and Maggie stocked up on staples at S&S Store, enough to last to Franklin (today's El Paso), 200 miles distant.

Evaristo, stage hand at Barrell Springs stage station with relative.

BARREL SPRINGS STATION
May 10 (Mon.)

The westbound stage pulled by 6 nail-hard Mexican mules passed the Graham wagons short of Barrel Springs. A bad sign — six mules, said old Evaristo, years later (he was horse tender and hay cutter there).

The driver said he wanted six of the best desert mules, the fastest, for he aimed "to pass through Bass (Canyon) in the dead of the night." Said he liked the "smell of early morning Eagle Springs rancid bacon and old El Paso eggs."

The stage guard spoke up, "You can always hold your nose and eat them eggs. It's good to be alive." The station keeper, also the cook at Eagle Springs, said to the passenger "If you can't smell 'em they ain't dead, go ahead an' eet them eggs. If they's any fresher, I'd eet them myself." A sharp looking passenger added his word of wisdom, "What difference does it make if the Apaches make you dead, so are the eggs."

These are stories of Evaristo, Calanche, and "Burro" Mendoza. Neither could read or write. Didn't know or wanted to know with two jugs of wine, plenty of Bull Durham and a cool twilight, they preferred to live it all over again.

Would that we had Maggie's letters from the Pecos to Van Horne Wells. Evaristo said, "Cuando Los Apaches estan danado (when the Apaches were bad)" they always counted the passengers and the travelers. Didn't know when the military would be coming looking.

He remembered the Graham wagon train — two women and 7 men, all well armed. They looked safe, but seemed concerned only about water.

The last eastbound coach brought in a whiskey drummer, who also sold caskets. The Station Boss said he had it good "coming and going". The drummer cursed the road back to the Wells, "The rocking fore-and-aft on the thorough braces was fine, but where you bottomed out in a gully, it made for holding a bottle ... rough on the teeth." The dust in the coach was good for business.

EL MUERTO

May 11 (Tues.)

Glassner, Johnston's companion, bartered with the train master of the 7 wagons (following the Graham's 5 wagons) . . . "added protection of 2 guns for water from their water kegs." It was 34 long, dry miles to the Wells (Van Horne). The offer was declined.

Johnston, a Texan with frontier knowledge, said years later, "Stupidity in the Apache country was like flies in the station corrals and in the kitchens — everywhere."

Calanche, who was a horse herder at El Muerto, said the last week's stage came in a cloud of dust, a passenger with his head hanging half out — coughing dust and throwing up his whiskey, made a run for the spring saying, "This dust is killing me!" The station keeper growled, "A snoot full of mule dust is better than being staked-out in an ant hill. Puke up that gut-rot an' come on in, there's coffee."

The Grahams could have heard the station keeper as they filled their water kegs at this spring.

A saloon keeper on Chihuahua Hill (Ft. Davis) said their worst whiskey made them men passengers braver than the best water. For man's fears are many. Sleeping it off on the dusty coach floor is the best panacea, but leaves the face ghost-like until the coach guard shouts, "Station water — all out!", then the dash for the spring — wash the face and he is brave again, until on to the next station.

VAN HORNE WELLS

Midnight, May 13 (Thur.)

Johnston and Glassner left the "Wells" the night before for Eagle Springs Station, said the Indian situation looked as bad as the water shortage.

The five and the seven wagon trains left El Muerto jockeying for first water, ignoring all the danger signals. There wasn't a station keeper on the line who wouldn't admonish, "Wait for the military escort, at least until you build up a larger caravan and travel in the dark. Most of all, when you don't see Apaches, that's when to be most alert."

The Graham wagons arrived first at the Wells in the quiet of night, just before midnight. Their horses commenced whinnying and leaning into their collars long before a lantern came on within the station walls.

The El Muerto stage station in the 1930's.

Calanche, the stage line hand at El Muerto Station about 1917-1919.

21

Maggie's grave midnight 13 May 1880. Left to right: Priest, Driver, Madam, Guard, Sam Graham, Harry Graham, La Ponte — station keeper, Mrs. Pat Murphy, Pat Murphy with two of their children, and "Burro" Mendoza.

Note: Harry, at his request, is standing for a last look-see at his beloved Maggie. He had been sitting propped up on the Murphy's wagon tailgate during the burial.

Harry Graham was walking beside the wagon talking to Maggie. Shown here as being shot, he is falling reaching up for his Winchester. Maggie grabbed it from the scabbard and is loading when shot in the head dying instantly. Husband Harry, badly shot, crawled under the wagon to play dead.

Brother Sam is shown in far mid-picture riding back; his horse was shot from under him. He went off over the falling horse's head hit the ground running and scrambled up into the rocky bluff making like a rock squirrel.

BASS CANYON

May 13 (Thur.) Past Noon

Robert Johnson, a Texan with Indian fighting experience, left Van Horne Wells the night before with companion Glassner. He could get no cooperation between the two wagon trains as to how they would go through Bass Canyon. Disgusted with their haggling, he rode in the night to Eagle Springs Station. Here, the next afternoon, the Seven Wagons stormed into the station—their horses frothing at the mouth, sweat-wet and hardly able to stand. They came in shouting at the top of their voices: "Musta been a hunnert of 'em! **Apaches!** The rest are all dead . . . killed!" Nothing about helping the train . . . saving only their sleazy hides. On sound of Murphy's bugle, the Apaches broke out of the canyon allowing the "cowardly" Seven to stampede out of the canyon and on in to Eagle Springs.

Johnson, with two helpers from Eagle Springs, rode back to bury Grant and help the Grahams and the Murphys into Van Horn Wells.

Grant was shot off his wagon seat not knowing what hit him. Maggie tumbled off the seat, falling down by the wagon wheel. Harry, badly groin-shot, crawled under the wagon to play "dead".

Sam Graham, scouting a quarter mile ahead of the Castroville wagons, broke back on first shots for the canyon. His horse shot from under him, he went flying over his horse's stumbling fall, only to scramble up into the bluffs making like a rock squirrel — leaving his $300 in his saddle bags for the Apaches to buy much-needed Mexican ammunition across the river two days away. (Mexican traders have been known to send word to the Apaches — the Victorio campaign of 1879-80 — of cartridges for sale in accordance with the Apaches' needs . . . payment in gold, of course. It matters not who gets killed with it.)

Footnote: *Dan (Pat) Murphy settled in Silver City, NM (about two weeks after the fight) and ran a brick yard. The Murphys had three more children — some living when I lived there—unknown to me as I had yet*

Looking eastward down Bass Canyon from the air. The lower far right "X" is where the Castroville wagons were when the firing started. The large "X" is where the Graham wagon stopped. Others think Harry crawled into the brush alongside the road. It was probably Murphy's bugle that saved his life — more credence to the bugle story. Murphy's rifle was in the wagon bed under the bed clothes and with <u>only</u> three cartridges, said his oldest daughter in Silver City years later.

You are looking eastward down Bass Canyon. The first and far left "X" is where James Grant was killed. The two Castroville wagons are out of this picture. The center "X" is where the Graham wagon stopped. The far right and distant "X" is where the Murphys fought the attackers. Beyond and lower in the canyon by one-quarter mile, is where the cowardly Seven Wagons bunched and made no effort to come to the aid of Murphy.

(Footnote continued)
to find Frio town — the starting point of the Maggie Little story.

Murphy died there at age 54 in 1886 — a boozer. Martha Jane, worn out and tired, died at the early age of 42 in 1894. Sam Graham passed in Texas in 1951 at 93. Harry, when last heard of, was a bridge foreman on railroad construction in Mexico.

Most of the Littles are in Pearsall and Frio Town cemeteries. Maggie, is still at the Van Horn Wells Stage Station site, alone and almost forgotten, in not too many years some idiot on a horse with a rope will lasso the railroad ties protecting her grave,

to drag them away to fuel a branding iron fire. The gully that is forming there will wash the mound and the protective rocks away, back into natureland. And her passing — with her unborn baby — will only be a word or two on some forgotten page.

You need not "pass the hat around" to move her body into Van Horn town, for cowmen move only cattle — to good grass. When they smell fresh manure coming on with the spring rains, a smell they enjoy most, all the way into town and up to the Bank. (It is believed Harry Graham never appeared in the Frio Town after the fight. He was considered a good and fine man.)

Prologue

Ellen Garrett, an English woman, was a gifted clairvoyant who it was said could communicate with her son, a pilot killed in WWI. Years later a similar spirit appeared in a B-17 pilot killed in the same area of France during WWII.

Thirty-two years after Maggie's passing, a beautiful girl grew up in Van Horn, who also danced in the old brown sandstone courthouse there as Maggie did in old Frio Town. Both married at 22. Maggie died eight months later just 13 miles southwest of where the other life began.

Some students of the Ellen Garrett school believe that Maggie's spirit was dormant for 32 years and would appear again in some related host. The old paisanos of Apache Land believe the spirit never dies — just jumps around from one dead to the next one dying and comes out most often on stormy nights when the lightning strikes twice near the same spot. One strike to kill the "old" (spirit) and the other to activate the new "one," so say the old stage hands along the stage line. Even the Apaches feared to be about on stormy nights.

I think it only fitting and proper that Maggie be moved to the west side of the Van Horn cemetery and a monument placed at the old grave site with these words:

"MAGGIE LITTLE GRAHAM,
age 22, so young,
so long ago died west of here in Bass Canyon,
May 13, 1880. Killed by the Apaches."

They buried her at Harry's request 300 feet from the NE corner of the stage station, "for to keep her company," he said. This move should keep her in good company. I know, for I have danced in their old courthouse.

It was a sad day after the war when on my first trip back over Van Horn, I noticed the old courthouse had been torn down. It was then I decided to finish the Maggie story. That the generations to come might know of this brave young woman who has been "sleeping" there, forlorn and forgotten by all but a few.

The Humphres (so spelled then) and the Littles — English and Scot bookprinters, competitors — feuding 20 years before King Charles II and Cromwell (one of whom then in power) decreed the Humphres brothers' heads for the guillotine.

Wisely, the brothers took the first night scow for Holland and from there a 4-rigger to Boston Colony, in 1640.

When asked why all this bother chasing Maggie. She could be your Grandmother, so? He answered his own question: "The genes are after you!"

"You just have to do it so," I said. It's her PASO POR AQUI (she passed by here).

Above, the late Douglas Little at cistern of the old Little home some several hundred feet NW of Courthouse, Frio Town.

At left, Douglas Little at entrance of Frio County Courthouse. Through this door, Harry and Maggie passed to lead the dance, September 16, 1879.

Story teller at Maggie's grave.

A portion of Apaches taken prisoners by Mexican Colonel Terrazas at the Tres Castillos fight October 15 and 16, 1880. Shown here working their way back to the Mescalero Reservation, they came upon the railroad construction crew 4 miles west of Van Horn, TX, November 1880.

The End In Sight

Between 1911 and 1916, while working on our West Texas ranch, Calanche told me he quit the stageline for a job as cook's helper on the Texas & Pacific track-laying work-train about 4 miles west of Van Horn, Texas in October 1881. There, a few Apache stragglers appeared south of the work-train, where unarmed Chinamen were laying and the Irishmen were spiking rails, westward up the canyon road-bed.

They looked starved. He waved them in — he said, speaking Spanish which they understood—to the cook's car. They came, reluctantly, every eye cautiously on the work crews. They looked longingly at a dressed beef hanging nearby, the first fresh meat they'd seen since the massacre at Tres Costillos, the October 15th and 16th before, between their Chief Victorio's band (less than 100 men, women, and children and out of ammunition) and the Mexican Colonel Terrazas' 260 combined troopers — some 110 miles southwest.

They'd traveled only by night from Chihuahua City in a desert still alive with vengeful patrols, both Mexican and American cavalry. Nights were so dark, not even a bird's nest could be found. No food. Rabbits caught were few.

Calanche set out pans full of hot soda biscuits that the women gobbled down like marshmallows — not a wince of pain, for Apaches don't cry.

The woman on the right with the papoose, as a captive in Chihuahua City, was given to a wealthy family. Months later, the "Dona" (mother of the household) — after the captive woman gave birth to a full-blooded Apache, and after she told of the rape and being repeatedly passed from one soldier-group to another while enroute to the city — gave her a black shawl to cover her face, a knife, and a mule and escorted her beyond the city. There is "that" feeling among "all" women, when a baby is born, that transcends all plateaus of hatred and is strong among Spanish/Mexican women.

The woman with the small daughter admitted to many atrocities and had been traded between goat and sheep men who gave her access to the herbs needed for early miscarriages. She preferred being a cook in a goat camp to that of a domestic in the village with the ever-jealous wrath of hateful wives.

The single squaw with the gun — a Victorio's sister type (Lozen) — was smart, aggressive, and with the knife a boundless demon of vindictiveness. As all women were, and resigned to it, she was ravaged repeatedly as the price of captivity — on both sides since the Governor's edict of a bounty on Apache scalps — priced downward from men to children since the 1830's.

This squaw, beautiful, aggressive, and high spirited, was remanded to the city jail, where she was passed from guard to guard as the opportunity and her endurance allowed, until discovered by the fat, egotist warden, who claimed her for his solamente (his only).

Not many nights later, as he lay fat, pig-like, exhausted, and in a drunken stupor, she slit him up the middle like a dressed hog — cut the jailer's heart out, took his gun, and in the dead of the night disappeared northward in the desert.

Long ago, in an Ojinaga Saloon, an old Mexican officer of the Apache period retold the Tres Costillos' fight to a room full of drinkers. The sober sat listening intently as he described the grit and guts of the Apache women. How many fought to death with only a knife.

He admitted the Apaches were out of ammo after the first short volley — then it was a massacre. It is a wonder what a few drinks will bring out . . .

The drunks slept on through the story, as drunks always do, all except one, who raised his groggy head from under a cloud of flies and to the surprise of all, and in good English, said, "That ish just the kind of woman I'm lookin' for," and passed out, his head falling back in the beer-soup on the bar.

Other "Lozen" type stories have it that an Apache woman made it back from Mexico City to the Mescalero reservation with only a knife.

Note:

It has been reported that Apache Chief Nana, with no less than 20 warriors, was off scouting for much needed ammunition. This bunch joined up with a band at Rattlesnake Springs (20 miles north of Van Horn) and was responsible for the killing of Maggie Graham the past May 1880. Most of both parties got themselves nicely killed at the north end of the Diablo Mountains by Ranger Captain George W. Baylor on January 17, 1881. They still had several items of the Graham wagon train in their possession. Sam Graham, the leader of the Graham train, also in this party, wanted to kill the women and children prisoners for his having lost his horse (killed), saddle, and bags with $300.

Had he been Apache-wise, Maggie and his money would have been with him in Arizona — smelling the cow dung of freshly purchased Mexican Cattle.

Credit to Ranger George W. Baylor's report.

Jo-Bob in north side of Wild Rose Pass doing his story. Moses split the Red Sea. I moved the mountain on the left forward to catch the rising sun.

Looking north up Wild Rose Pass and old stage road crossing Limpia Creek 13 times between Ft. Davis and the Pass.

JO-BOB'S RUN
DOWN
WILD ROSE PASS

Jo-Bob, the mail hack driver, had topped Wild Rose Pass — 13 miles north of Ft. Davis (Texas) — the beginning of a June dawn in 1879, with the ending hanging in uncertain doubt as Jo-Bob's four wild Mexican mules raised their ears, snorted, and bolted from the stage road.

Mules can smell an Apache a quarter-mile away, avow the old paisanos of that day, and will climb a mountain rather than run an ambush.

And Jo-Bob had smart mules. The S A & E P stage line would have no other. Mexican-bred mules are smart, or soon get that way traveling the canyons of Apache land.

Jo-Bob said, one July day in 1912 at our Nine -Mile-Spring Ranch, he'd just topped the Pass and had pulled up to "blow" his team, looked back, and saw three Apaches climbing out fast, two with lances, pushing their horses to the limit. He hung his Winchester scabbard behind the seat, out of reach but in full view, tucked his .44 six-shooter under his buckskin in his waist band, threw his jacket over his new double Wells Fargo (sawed-off shotgun) and laid it handily behind and across the seat, to sit on like a turkey on a nest. "This Turkey," he said, "was getting ready for a turkey shoot," and laughed with the sureness of one of Jeb Stuart's cavalrymen before First Manassas.

Jo-Bob, of 66 years, was enjoying his first time back along the old stage road after 33 years of waiting.

"The Apaches were coming within yipping distance when I yelled," said Jo-Bob, "and snapped the black snake over those mules backs. They needed no urging — just exploded from their nervous crouch and off the mountain we went. The Apaches had taken the bait."

"Those mules laid their ears back. All you could see in front of the buckboard was wringing tails and flying mule feet. It was a sight to see," grinned Jo-Bob.

"I wrapped the reins around my leg, began fumbling in my pockets for cat-r-ridges for a Winchester they could see was beyond my reach. I was beginning to feel like Cousin Bill Williams when he took that Yankee dispatch rider "out" as he came fogging down Granny White's Pike after Chickmauga. The big Apache on the near side was closing fast, a big grin on his face like a wave on a slop bucket. He raised his lance to gut stick the left leader — to slow us down — while the right side Apache was positioning for a heart thrust into the right leader, for the pile-up to come down by the jack

30

pine at the foot of the hill."

"That's when I raised up, reached behind, came up with the double Fargo. At five paces, I bet those barrels looked as big as water buckets. Then I 'sawed' him off that hoss, real clean an' nice — sent him on a fast trip into Apache heaven. That's better than they had planned for me."

Had Grandma Williams been there, I thought, she'd a' swore that Jo-Bob had served with Hood's Brigade. He had their way of telling things.

While Burro Mendoza was hooking his team up that day at the Spring, Jo-Bob reasoned it all out for us: the Apaches had planned the pile-up at the foot of the hill — before I could reach the flats for better running in the road and freedom to swing the Winchester — having never seen a double Fargo before. This Greenhorn they'd plan to hang, like a butchered hog — head down, over a slow fire — while they gorged on fresh mule meat, to his agonizing screams — dinner music to the Apache's delight.

Calanche and Evaristo nodded in gratitude to their stage line friend. Anyone who kills an Apache comes as a Mexican delight, as they had suffered from them for years. Until the Veterans of Hood's Brigade came home, smarting from defeat, to loosen their wrath on a cause they could win.

Mrs. Herman Huelster, the Station Keeper's bride at Barilla Station, asked Jo-Bob about the graves up in the Pass. All he would say was he set two stolen horses free because their riders, he knew, wouldn't do a thing about shoein' good horses.

Evaristo said his friend was delivering a load of corn from Dan Murphy's Toyah Creek Ranch to Ft. Davis when his team shied from the road up the Pass. He rolled a couple of skeletons — what the buzzards and coyotes had left — into a gulley and piled rocks over them — an Apache burial, not knowing until this July day in 1912 that he had buried a couple of Jo-Bob's "friends," who wanted to hang him high over a dinner fire.

In the Fall of '25, while returning from the Alpine College to Toyah Creek in our Hudson touring, I topped the Pass and was fast on the downgrade — my head out in the windstream — looking for the grave when I accidentally bumped the gear shift. Popping it out was easy, getting it back was something else on a 16-percent grade. Boulders, in a winding wagon road? I tried double clutching. Slewing the curves on two wheels. Gears chattering and the brakes beginning to smell.

Plenty of daylight was beginning to show

W. L. Kingston, early Davis Mountain cowman, standing on new highway near where Jo-Bob took the second Apache. Both were buried near the "X" mark.

Grandson, Keith Griffith, history addicted — looking at the place where Jo-Bob "sawed off" the first Apache.

between me and the seat. Rocks flying against fenders! I yanked on the handbrake, the cable snapped. I knew then it was Mary-Ann — from-then-on-in!

The grave passed in a mountain-side blur. For a fleeting moment I sensed the Apaches were laughing at me. What one can see when the Great Rainmaker above starts reaching out . . .

"Not yet," I said aloud, comforting, on a fast falling road. "No-o-oo, not yet, not yet!" For a man's fears are many and for the moment I knew how that Apache must have felt looking into the barrels of Jo-Bob's Fargo.

Hang tight and hope was all I had left.

How I got down to the old jack pine stump I'll never know. But one thing sure, I'd scattered a lot of rocks out of the old stage road.

I just sat there by the pine stump wondering what old Jo-Bob, Calanche, and Evaristo would say to this story. I'm sure Jo-Bob would have said: "Serves

you right, ridin' that contraption, an' awaistin' time going' off to College."

Calanche, a quick thinker, who progressed to head horse-herder at the El Muerto Station would say, "Why for you boys go around, always een a beeg hurry?"

Old slow Evaristo, who got no higher than horse herder at the Barrel Springs Station: "Why you don't stop and feex thos' b-brakes? Eet might keep you from keelin' yourself."

A good question, Evaristo, "Stop and fix those brakes" — wherever you are in a World-gone-by.

The mail hack driver from Ft Davis, going into Murphy's Ranch (July 1879) enroute to Seven Rivers, Lincoln Plaza and Ft. Stanton.

INTO MURPHY'S RANCH
ON TWO WHEELS AND A WHIP

Jo-Bob came into San Solomon Springs tails high and wheels bouncing — about dawn a July day in 1879.

Shown here with the stock herder holding open the gate for the driver's sweat-lathered mules as they came wheezing past the limestone walls of the 300-ft. square from a three-mile, down-hill run, all the way into Dan Murphy's ranch.

"Mi Muchachos!" the stock herder called the boys. One stepson of Murphy, the other his friend Riley, 19, two years older, went up on the roof as the sound of Jo-Bob's .44-40 Winchester came floating down in the stillness of the early mountain air.

The driver of the Miller-Murphy mail hack had left Ft. Davis for Ft. Stanton in the dead of night to clear Limpia Canyon and Seven Springs — both Apache havens for ambush — and be out on the flats with plenty of running room by good daylight.

It was a round-trip-a-week with water stops at Nine-Mile and Toyah Springs, a change at Seven Rivers, then Placitas (Lincoln) before hay and grain and a curry comb for the mules at Stanton.

All went well until four beady-eyed Apaches, on fresh stolen horses from the main line station at Barilla, jumped Jo-Bob on the shady side of Weinacht Hill (later so named). That's when the serenade started. Letting the mules run loose-reined and wild-eyed in the road, young Jo-Bob braced, spraddled-legged, yelling and levering his Winchester as the Apaches, running with the rising sun in their eyes, yipping gleefully, lusting for a lance thrust into the belly of a mule.

This story came to me 34 years later, when I was 5, from Jo-Bob who had walked into our Nine-Mile Spring Ranch. With his bandana kerchief he was wiping his brow and the other hand fanning the heat with a derby, asking if this was "the right road to Solomon Springs."

I felt sorry for this lost-looking pilgrim. "A fired fireman from the railroad strike", no doubt. "And, maybe, a one-time mule skinner looking for dirt work."

Not knowing that here standing before me was one of my boyhood idols. A real live stage driver . . . in derby and store shoes. And me, a skinny, bare-legged boy on a crow-bait pony; for the drought was upon the land.

I called to Burro Mendoza, who was hitching the last of his 24 burros (six, four-ups) to three freight wagons, one loaded with salt, the other with barbed wire, and a light trail wagon for bed and board — chuck box and burro feed.

This man in the derby said, "Just call me Jo-Bob." I said, "This is 'Burro.' He's goin' to McCutcheon's Seven Springs Ranch. He'll drop you off."

Then there was a wide grin on Burro's face. And I sensed the smell of "rain" in the air.

Jo-Bob was a young main "liner" (stage driver) on the main line between Ft. Davis and El Paso when Burro was young Mendoza hauling water at the Wells Station (Van Horne) in 1879 and '80. And Calanche and Evaristo were cutting hay and herding mules at El Muerto and Barrel Springs. Both here now at Nine-Mile Springs digging for more water when Jo-Bob came in that July day in 1913.

A little later when I looked southward toward Star Mountain all I could see was a ball of stifling dust, Jo-Bob was riding high on the lead wagon,

Burro's long legs barely clearing the dust from the big left wheel burro he always rode. And his arms were see-sawing in the dust pall as he talked up to him.

They'd be camping at San Solomon Springs and a disappointment it would be for Jo-Bob, for the old limestone corral walls had long gone into foundations for the adobes at La Mota, Calera, and La Mata — the Mexican settlements along Toyah Creek. The old Dan Murphy adobe had long melted down or been hauled away.

But these two old stage line hands would have 25 miles of good talking and plenty of road dust to remind them they were now in this sun-blistered, drought-stricken land — where once the ridges waved in gramma grass and tobosa lined the swales and it was rightly known as Apache Land.

And so like all old drivers, they most always hopefully came back for a last look-see. But it is never the same.

Note: This possibly could have been Ed-W, a relief driver. Both drivers knew of this, a short-lived mail route.

Hez Kountz's father's farm was 2 miles down Toyah Creek from Murphy at La Loma, a Mexican settlement. Their ranch was 9 miles Southeast into the mountains. A treat was to go to Murphy's store where keeper Ike Dempsey, long on the sauce (whiskey), always presented Hez with a peleoncillo, a rock-hard candy, and a hammer to crack it.

Hez Kountz of Balmorhea, Texas, between 1937-39.

33

Toyah "Cowtown," Texas' Youngblood Hotel and Citizens Bank. Today standing tall, but that's all — just standing vacant. Toyah's first and last store was in the lower portion of this hotel. This store's warehouse and the one for the Toyah Supply Co. (my father's in 1913-14) was the supply source for "Burro's" freighting.

GAVINO'S GOATS AT TOYAH, TEXAS

The goats and old Gavino are long gone, but there still remain a few of the Old Timers there — still hanging around in this land of creosote bush and mesquite — where onto this same land one day, long ago (1914), a lady stepped off the train in Toyah — when it was really "Cowtown," Texas. There in the summer heat, she rolled her eyes far off and far out on the simmering, heat-hazed horizon — all the way south to the Davis and north to the Guadalupe mountains, and from under a flowery hat, snorted, "What a God-forsaken Land." Gathering up a chalky handful of rustling, taffeta skirts, she elevated her powdery nose skyway, and shook her "tailfeathers" right into the faces of the curious, but friendly, onlookers before disappearing into her Pullman.

But this I remember best — it was a fast freight that got the goats and the drought got the cattle. The man in the main was ole Gavino, a fat, likeable Mexican, in faded blue overalls and a floppy black hat with a wizened little wife and many mouths to feed — all happy people in the forsaken land.

Gavino was too fat for cowboying and too lazy for windmilling, so Dad made him head herder to a bunch of feisty goats. I was five and past, the younger of two boy viceroys to this same passel of smelly goats.

On "election" Gavino took over immediately, appointing my older brother to head-herder and promoting me to prestigious waterboy. He went on back into the shade to sleep his way on up to "chairman-of-the-board" — a coveted title for any man in overalls, much less owner of a big railroad watch, which he consulted often after four in the afternoon, while stroking his luxuriant moustache.

Much could be learned from Gavino. Every time a nanny sampled a loco blossom (and died), there was fresh goat meat on his table. And so it seemed the poisonous weed started blooming summer and winter.

Dad, a newcomer in 1910 to this sun-blistered, drought-stricken land, had much to learn from ole Gavino.

But it was the fast freight — running wild, rocking and rolling as it came rattling down the San Martine grade, the Engineer's red cap way out the window — like a turkey in a Thanksgiving coop — that bothered old Billy, the big ram, most. He led his fool herd right out onto the tracks to see what he could see and who dared his sovereign rights to this part of greasewood and mesquite Texas.

As the whistle came screaming old Billy braced, snorted. His head went down, his horns laid back, and up came his tail as he shot up the tracks, followed by the six hundred.

In less than six seconds — less time than it takes to say "ba-ba" — we were out of the goat business.

The two boy viceroys cried and ran to the "chairman-of-the-board" — snoring gallantly in the shade of his "office" — under a cloud of flies, playing tag for flicks of food over his moustache. But Gavino didn't seem to mind. He was considered a good sleeper.

He rolled over on his fat belly and out into the sun to report post haste, as a good chairman would, of his concern to Dad — a bedridden tubercular, where Mother was on guard, and valiantly busy snatching cigars out of his mouth as fast as he sneaked them in.

Gavino lost his chairmanship and his family went back to straight beans and tortillas — not that they seemed to mind.

It was a sad day in this drought-stricken land when the word came out that the banks over the Southwest were beginning to close their doors and the Cattle Buyers were coming out of their "holes" like the rats of Hamlin — offering prices commensurate with your last rains.

So began the big drought of 1915 and the beginning of the end to our cattle.

Somehow it gets to you — this forsaken Land of the goats and Gavino — as it gets to the others, who must know, for they are still there and will probably stay on to the end — like a rattlesnake charming a cottontail. That hidden charm unseen by the Lady who didn't look long enough before shaking her "tailfeathers."

Note: For years, every time I'd fly over old "Cowtown", I'd see those old red brick buildings still standing down there, empty and forlorn, ghosts of Yesterday — the Bank, Hotel, and my first School — monuments to a once good life in a happy land. And there still remain names I best remember, like Tom Cargill (Mr. Toyah), Georgia Daniels, Janey Joe Duncan, McAlpine, and Mrs. Keasey Duncan — a few of the "Boys and Girls of Yesterday."

Tom Duncan, early Toyah cowman in the Davis Mountains. (Courtesy of Pecos, Texas Museum)

35

"Burro" Mendoza, lifelong freighter at age 94 in 1941 and water hauler at Van Horne Wells stage station in 1880. He worked all of West Texas.

"BURRO" MENDOZA, THE FREIGHTER

Old Timers in Toyah "Cowtown," Texas say he's old, old, and freighted with burro-teams a long, long time. How long is long, and how old is old?

Gillermo Mesa (Burro) Mendoza is shown here in Pecos getting ready to die. He hauled telegraph poles, stock salt, and houses all over west Texas for 50 long years. That's how long is long. His hands are ham-size, gnarled, and horny. His sphinx-like face is furrowed deep with a myriad of wrinkles — sand-etched and sun-tanned. He's 94 (in 1940). That's how old is old.

At sunrise, two heavy wagons stood in line on the east edge of the salt lakes southwest of Guadalupe Peak in what is now Hudspeth County. Eight thousand pounds of salt — four tons at $25.00 a ton — to be delivered at the ranches and El Depot, as the Mexicans called Toyah. Behind six spans of four-up, long-eared, drooped-hipped burros, hooked in tandem

to a common chain and half asleep in their traces, stood each loaded wagon. The first pair of burros (all others were four abreast) was at the wheel — the left-hand wheeler saddled. The seconds — the swing team; the thirds; fourths; fifths; and the sixths — and all up to the leaders, all stood resigned to a long day ahead before water at a charco (hole) or a spring — if it didn't turn out to be a dry camp. Then to be hobbled and belled for the night where there was feed on a tobosa flat.

In from the greasewood and mesquite came the dogs and the boy — the viceroys of the extra herd — driving an old belled jenny, the maternal leader of the "change-off" stock, kicking her heels in the face of a mischievous jack. Around her crowded the extras that could be thrown into the spans, making four working abreast on the long grades; or the flats, should they have turned into mud; or the arroyo crossings, if they had gullied too deep.

The drivers' bedrolls were on top of the tarp-covered salt. The chuck-box lid was fastened, and the water kegs' new toe-sacking lids were deftly wired down.

A mesquite fire had burned into gray ashes and was now smoldering under a dumping of Arbuckle grounds.

The 'skinner' mounted the wheeler. The wheeler sagged under the extra saddled load. Long stirruped legs barely cleared the ground. Across the burros' backs cracked a 30-foot bull-whip accompanied by a loud "Hep!" The whip left its dusty mark across the leaders' rumps. They leaned into their traces, barely raising their doubletrees and the forepart of the heavy chain. The fifth pair took their crack in like manner, adding their shoulder-weight to the mass of double and singletrees pinned to the chain. On down the line the driver's whip played the scale. By the time he'd brought the whipstock across the wheelers, the big wagon hubs had begun to slowly groan, and the broad-tired wagon wheels to track painfully along the edge of the salty lake. The #2 wagon in slow-motion followed out leaving a feathering of dust that had gradually risen.

Toyah-bound, the whole push moved out at its two-mile-an-hour gait, due back at El Depot in 5 to 10 days.

And so came the stock salt to the ranches of that early day. Some of the first went to Joe Seay, west of Toyah, in '89. Other trips followed. Some to Ab Tinnin's at Rustler's Springs in 1883; to Bill Casey on Cherry Creek; to Cowan's "VH Springs; to

Reynolds' "X" Ranch at Kent; to the McCutcheon's Limpia and Seven Springs Ranches; and to Popham's "U" Ranch out on the Barilla.

Later the cattlemen's wives began moving the children into town to school, so the menfolk said. And the men began to run their ranches in the wintertime from the south side of the store fronts — each with a pocketful of pecans and a sharp knife. And a T-Model Ford stood nearby, hood-saddled with a hundred-dollar saddle. That is when "Burro" Mendoza began moving houses into town.

His biggest feat was moving a 4-room frame house across Salt Draw. Salt Draw can be a half-mile wide and swimming-to-a-horse, when — and if — it rains. Those that saw it said there was a wagon under each corner, burros working two four-up teams to each wagon. "Looked more like 32 rats moving a case of whiskey — if the whiskey had had a gabled top on it," one fellow said. Another quickly added, "Whoever saw a case of whiskey with any kind of a top on it?" So goes the levity in the Bible Belt of Apache land.

Ella Frazer's home about 400 feet southwest of saloon where younger brother Bud was ambushed.

Whatever she may have said to Miller after the sneaky killing, I'm sure he deserved. I object to sleazy remarks just to glorify stories.

I remember when she came to our isolated farm in a snow storm. Cars stalled in the flu epidemic of 1918 and all our family was bedridden.

Ella will be there when the Great Rainmaker passes out the stars.

Ella Frazer, age 25

37

Left to rigth: Jim Miller with shotgun; Pat Flowers, barkeep (questionable by some as Tom Pate); Andy Cole; J. D. Shelton; Bill Earhart (Miller's accomplice); Johnson Tate (still sitting); and J.E. Jerrell (one of my informants) heading for the back door.

MILLER, THE KILLER

I was three when the train first pulled into Toyah "Cowtown," Texas where we ate at the old adobe saloon, then a Chinaman's restaurant. The bar was now the lunch counter and had the tables served anything but food — not cards and whiskey as they once did in this wild and troubled land—Mother, the good Baptist she was — would have huffed and puffed her way right out of there blowing more steam than the engine that pulled us in.

Almost three years later I was passing Ella Frazer's house and this same saloon-restaurant enroute to my first school. Each evening at dark I delivered two one-gallon pails of milk for a Chinaman's reward of cake and stories of early Toyah. John-the-Chinaman pointed out to me, as a boy with big ears in Buster Brown shoes, the spot where Bud Frazer sat and the door where Miller came through.

The Old Timers say for a fee some lawyers will defend any criminal. That's how Miller got acquitted according to Tray Humphries, after Miller put his "letter" in the Pecos City church, then moved it and the trial to Eastland for the acquittal. Jim Scanlin added "They just planted a paid-off patsy on the jury — just one was enough."

Bud Frazer as a young man. (Courtesy of Barney Hubbs, Pecos, TX)

Above, J. E. Jerrell. (Courtesy of Mrs. Howard Chandler, Granddaughter)

Right, Tom Cargill standing on grave of Bud Frazer,. Born about the time Frazer was massacred in 1896.

On September 14, 1896, the morning sun glistened along the railroad rails running 18 miles eastward from Toyah, to where the night before two of the meanest men that ever plagued this troubled land left Pecos for a night ride westward to do as dastardly a crime as was ever committed in the droughty land.

Bill Earhart, set-up man for executioner "Deacon" Jim Miller, and Miller both stabled their mounts in the dark at Fast's wagon yard and sneaked into the hotel where they took up their watch from an upper front room facing southward across the railroad to the saloon and Ella Frazer's house, some 300 feet farther out, where her brother Bud was visiting.

The next morning Earhart came early to the saloon to bait the trap and around 0900, as usual, Bud came in. Earhart got up and gave him his chair at the card table facing the north front door, his back to the mid-saloon partition, Frazer's usual position of watch.

Earhart sauntered out the front door, spit out a sizeable cud of tobacco, dropping his hat — Miller's clue — while watching from the hotel window, that the pigeon was on the nest. Earhart went back in, took a chair to hawk the game and listen for Miller's footsteps on the front boardwalk. Shown here in the illustration is Earhart getting up, removing his chair to give Miller a clear shot at Frazer.

Note: Bud Frazer came in from the restaurant side entrance into the saloon through a door (not shown) at the bottom of the illustration and between the beer barrels.

Earhart had signalled to Miller, in the hotel window on the north side of the railroad some 500 feet northeast of the saloon, that Frazer had taken his usual chair facing the north door. J. E. Jerrell is shown vacating his chair for the back door.

The old hotel, a wooden two-story, was sometimes known as the Luckett or Alvarado Hotel.

Bud Frazer's only daughter was a good friend of my mother. His sister Ella was a nurse to anyone sick or in need throughout the ranch country and saved my life during the flu epidemic in the winter of 1918.

Other informants were Ella Frazer (life-time family neighbor and friend), sister to Bud Frazer; Tom Riggs, brother of Barney; Monroe Riggs, brother of Barney; Stump Robbins, friend; Lon Robbins, friend; Tray Humphries, friend; J. E. Jerrell, and Mrs. Robert (Eula) Frazer Baker.

Bill Earhart's first shot missed. Barney Riggs ducked and fired second. The ball is shown nicely exiting behind his left eye. John Denston saw and "chickened" out. Barney took him from behind and in the head as he ran streetwise.

BARNEY TAKES TWO

Here in early October, 1896, at Pecos, TX, is the Orient Saloon, better known by the old timers as "the place where Barney Riggs took care of a couple of 'Deacon' Jim Miller's murdering friends."

Named "Deacon" because he always put his "letter" in the church where he planned his murders, or acquittals, from services done for hire. "Deacon" Jim wore a steel breastplate under his dark coat for protection of the blackest heart God ever gave a man. His water-drinking habits in gambling saloons stood him high in church circles.

Bill Earhart and John Denston came down from Eddy (Carlsbad) to kill Barney Riggs, brother-in-law of Bud Frazer, whom Earhart and Miller had murdered a short time before in Toyah.[1]

Where old timers — who whiled away their time from store fronts and boardwalks as their horses stood loose reined, droop-hipped, switching tails and stamping heel flies into the dust — were saying: "it was this-a-way, boy, and don't let anybody tell you any different . . ."

Barney, Toyah-bound from Fort Stockton, had heard the murder story, so he saddled a fresh horse and set out for Pecos saying, "he had a little business to take care of."[2]

Miller was in jail for the Frazer killing. His friends were on the prod and prowl looking for a backside shot at Barney. When Earhart and Denston came into the Orient to inquire of Barney, guess who walked in from the back room in a bartender's apron? Earhart bristled, leveled his gun at Barney's face, saying "you should have left the country," and fired. Barney ducked, sending a .45 slug right smack back in his snarling face, taking out his left eye. Denston "chickened" and dove for the front door. Barney fired and missed— shaking his apron — and followed him, blowing his cowardly brains out as he started up the street.

Some of the more colorful writers of today say Denston ran up the street getting the back of his head blown off, not that Barney couldn't have done it. Only modest Barney and those whom he told really know.

So there you have it from those who lived there then, and to a man agreed: that Barney was a good man with a gun—better than two to one.

Notes:

1. This story was re-told to me in our Toyah Creek Store (Saragosa, TX) in 1922 by Barney's brothers, Tom and Monroe, in the presence of such old timers as Stump and Lon Robbins, Bill and Roy Chandler, Ed Steckler, and Pink Harbor, all of whom were familiar with the affair and the original saloon (not at its present site.) The apron Barney wore is questionable.
Barney later said he expected them to be wearing steel-lined vests hence plucked their heads.

2. Some say Barney's wife went from Toyah to Pecos with him — shotgun on her lap — in a buggy.

Tom Riggs, younger brother of Barney

Stump Robbins, good friend of the Riggs and Frazers.

Late photo of Barney Riggs shortly before he was killed by his son-in-law in 1902.

Barney Hubbs, "Mr. Pecos," 1976. Namesake of Barney Riggs, long time owner of the newspaper.

THE LATE APACHE LAND

Apache Land stretches from the Pecos River (TX) to the Santa Cruz (AZ) — a vast desert troubled and plagued by raiding Apaches, fearless and determined to destroy everything Mexican except the "seed" for survivor.

All the villages were held in bondage and servitude, some with as little protection as a priest praying and blessing every living soul — in a land where guts and guns were the law. The village fortunate enough to be near a presidio (whose few men were poorly trained, underpaid and afraid) somehow survived.

How to see and record these isolated villages, where once they lived in mortal fear separated by remote mountain ranges — here where an aeroplane beat the horse all to hell.

After years of walking, horseback and pickup riding with the old story tellers "who lived it" — now comes the fun and photography. The above Dragonfly was a low-wing, two-place, slow-flying Fornaire, good in the low mountains of Texas with airstrips and High-O gas.

Then came the hard part. The high Sierras of Mexico without weather reports, gas or airstrips for low-wings. The inevitable had to happen. An emergency out-of-gas landing on a packmule trail in the pass between Bachoachi and Esqueda (here

where Mangas Colorado's Mexican wife took his first captive to raise; a boy of four in 1834).

I slept under the wing and was awakened by the tramping of feet. A pair of billy goats were flexing their muscles before a young nanny in first-heat, when up drove their owner, raggedy and dirty as his goats, in a T-Ford. "I was a stranger and he took me in." He drained in a quart can four gallons of his gas in four trips to my 'plane (my count), took my two twenties ($40) as he eyed the distance to Douglas (AZ) at 40 miles. Figured on taking my last twenty somewhere short of Douglas. You never show money in Mexico.

How I got that Fornaire out of the pass on Mexican gas, I'll never know. I made the Douglas airport on a dead-stick glide. The engine popping and banging to the high heavens. The hanger emptied on the railroad side thinking the train had jumped the track.

Bill Mueller of Southwest Air Rangers (El Paso) put me in a Piper Comanche with a 1200-mile range and 18,000-foot ceiling. It turned the highest Sierras of Chihuahua and Sonora into chicken-and-dumplings. No more leaving my car keys under the seat. No more flying with empty pockets. That dime I threw out while climbing the Fomaire through Bavispe Pass, I now can keep.

SIX-SHOOTER'S SERENADE
[On South El Paso Street]

As the years pass, I think of the times I have stood reflecting in the middle of the street where Louis Abrams said Dallas Stoudenmire once stood ending this "symphony of the six-shooters" with his last shot into the helplessly wounded Campbell who took a third shot to put him down, having never fired his gun, the handsomest pearl-handle of them all.

This story is a natural for the "bang-bang" writer who never misses the drama of gunplay and is a good place to start backing up the story of the "Symphony of the Six-Shooters", staged in the horse manure and dust of South El Paso Street between the present Del Norte Hotel and yesterday's State National on the corner of El Paso and San Antonio Streets. A frontier town's musical at high noon— high noted by the "six-shooter section" — all sharps

and no flats — with the newly elected City Marshall "conducting" and sending the ever-alert city populace scrambling into nearby alleyways and doorways.

A day to remember, this April 14, 1881, a month before the railroad came and the addition to the ground floor of the old Central Hotel at the north end of El Paso Street.

Louis Abrams (at age 19) said he had just outfitted himself in a new store suit and derby at Sol Schutz on West San Antonio Street and had turned the corner at the Pony Saloon, looked south on El Paso Street where a street full of Mexican horsemen (vaqueros) were around a wagon that was pulling away from Keating's Saloon near the present corner of El Paso and West San Antonio Streets.

Louis was going south, passed Poney Saloon

David Abrams, standing second from left, in front of his store on "Tree Plaza" and at the head of South El Paso Street in 1869. Son Louis is one of the small boys at age seven.

Louis Abrams in 1940.

and a Mexican peddler's burro cart in front of Monday's Market on his way to meet his father, David, at the famous Globe Cafe. The elder Abrams had preceded him to Zach White's Grocery to interview a clerk for a prospective bartender's job in his Clifton, Arizona, saloon.

To avoid the flies and the stench of fresh manure-laden dust of standing horses, he crossed the street easterly to the new red brick State National Bank at the northeast corner of El Paso and San Antonio Streets. Louis said he never walked past a bank that he didn't feel good. The Abrams' interests were principally in merchandising — stores, saloons and hostelries — certainly not in horsemen and guns.

At the new bank stood two to four Rangers lolling and nursing their Winchesters cradled in their arms. Some held the gun as if it were a warm milk bottle; others like a woman holding a wet-bottomed baby. Possibly among them was a young Ranger, Sergeant James B. Gillett, who at the time Louis did not know, and he sensed trouble in the air.

He then crossed southward to the Lone Star Saloon where another Ranger and more curious bystanders were watching like coyotes around a

The Abrams Hotel, one of the Abram's properties in Silver City, NM. Louis lived here in his later years.

newborn calf — just waiting for the cow to make a wrong move. These bystanders were looking west across the street at three men talking by their mule mounts in front of Judge Buckler's office and adjacent to Keating's Saloon.

Then Louis turned the corner and went into the Globe Cafe on the east side of South El Paso Street between the Lone Star Saloon and Ben Schuster's store. In the Globe he saw a large impressive looking badge-and-vest man who hurriedly ordered his lunch and disappeared quickly down the Street as if still interested in the large group of Mexican horsemen escorting the wagon southward and were then nearing the Overland Stage building.

Years later, Louis said the Marshall went there to meet the stage, reportedly bringing in new prostitutes and to apply his "business tax" and to check out the "merchandise." Louis' apartments in his Silver City Hotel were considered "good" for the wild growing mining community on nearby Chihuahua Hill.

Not long after Louis sat down to a white linen table in the cafe, a shot broke out across the street. If you had been standing then in the middle of the

street, that day, between Ben Schuster's (east) and Zach White's (west) and stretched out your left hand northward toward the Central Hotel— palm down— your thumb would be pointing at "Doc" Cummings (brother-in-law of Stoudenmire), shown (on page 46) coming out of the Globe in apron and with a shotgun to assist the new City Marshall. Your index finger would be pointing at Dallas Stoudenmire, the new Marshall who was firing on George Campbell (your middle finger). Campbell had run out into the street after Hale had shot down Krempkau, shouting that he wanted no part in the shooting, his gun still holstered.

To back up the sequence of the event, the reverberating echoes of the first shots had hardly died when Stoudenmire, on his way back from the Overland, charged up the street toward the Globe. He opened fire on Hale (your little finger), then standing behind the right pillar post. In keeping with his Civil War style, Stoudenmire was running and firing, missing Hale, but killing a hapless Mexican who had been buying candy at Zach White's storefront where David Abrams had been talking to the clerk.

Hale, busily finishing off the gutsy Krempkau (your fourth finger) who was down but still firing on

45

Nineteen year-old Louis Abrams (photo on p. 44) was inside the Globe Cafe at the time of the shooting. Shown left center, in apron and armed with shotgun is "Doc" Cummings, brother-in-law of Marshall Dallas Stoudenmire. The marshall has just shot George Campbell.

him. Hale was unaware of Stoudenmire then moving up the street and firing at Campbell, breaking his right arm. Campbell, attempting to cross-draw his gun with his left hand, took Stoudenmire's second shot (as shown) in the belly that put him down for good.

Campbell lived until the following morning and his deposition is the basis for this change. I believe it was ex-Ranger Gillett who told of it in Alpine, in 1925, how Stoudenmire who "popped" off a shot at Hale for a "credit killing." Hale was then down, mortally wounded, from Krempkau's last shot.

Of these three who fired the approximately fifteen shots in this "symphony," Hale probably fired four or five, Krempkau five or six, and Stoudenmire four — no more. Had they stood in the middle of the street howling to the moon at midday firing all shots at the moon, they couldn't have gotten them off in four or five seconds, as some have reported. Louis estimated more like 30 seconds.

Although I talked with half a dozen or more people on South El Paso Street in 1925 who "knew where to dig under the plaster," I missed finding "that peck of lead balls" they said were there all those years.

If all the uncles and grandfathers who say they "saw it all" were there, the town had to be empty, for all were at the "symphony." This would include the one who said he saw by the gun flashes at midnight on a New Year's Eve from down in the Modern Cafe in the basement of the Mills Building (built more than 25 years later). He too had too much to drink.

It is reported the Mayor and the City Council, who had lost their claim by Campbell for backpay after his discharge as Marshall, were not saddened by his death at the hands of their new Marshall. The Mayor left town for a few weeks on being told by Stoudenmire that "he was running the town."

And he did for about a year on "whiskey and gun smoke" until he "badgered" himself into his own killing.

Shows a Saturday night dance on the west side of Van Horn, Texas and the north side of the railroad. This congregation of Mexican laborer's are here for the replacing of railroad road-bed ties. First (1900) since the railroad was built in 1881.

Note the Mexicans on the roof-top. One is firing his pistol off into the air. The other two are drinking from tequila bottles. The first one to finish always helps the other. When both got drunk one falls off the roof into the crowd. His amigo (friend) tried to save him and also fell. These two are dragged out of the doorway and allowed to groan and sleep it off. The pistoleer shot himself in the foot trying to get off the roof. He lay groaning behind the dance hall. The dance went on as if he were a dog whining out in back.

The dance got started late as you can see. The freight train engineer got his chance (as all engineers did in that day, just watching and waiting). If he could catch a horseman near the tracks, from Toyah to El Paso, between Van Horn and Sierra Blanca, he had a perfect trip.

The man on right (ground) had just ridden in from the Rock Pile Ranch on a borrowed horse to play. His horse went home (south of Van Horn 25 miles) without him. He told this story in 1917 while warming up for a Mexican Dance on Bragado Hill, a dance hall one mile east of Balmorhea, Texas. He was still a violinist, but didn't ride with his violin anymore.

SAVE THAT GEE-TAR [GUITAR]

JOHN HOLYLAND TAKES A BRIDE

Husbands spoke of it in hushed tones when within earshot of Protestant wives, and referred to it as that "Domino Parlor down on the River."

Concha's Cantina Colorada straddled the old cattle trail crossing since cattle became a commodity on both sides of the River (Rio Grande). Known as Cucaracha (cockroach) and on the north as Rustler's Crossing — both names fit. Before 1900, the trade was at its highest when the Rurales on the south and the Rangers on the north were at their lowest. The Ladrones (mountains) were the holding trap when the river (Rio Grande) was at flood stage, and suspicious fires were seen along the river.

The law of the land was with the Rustlers, those smart enough to elude both Rurales and Rangers, and bright enough to "sell" on the opposite side of the river. So the Cantina prospered with the movement of the cattle. Which way didn't matter to the "girls" for gold was good from any pocket.

The "girls" put out the red drawers on the clothes line - it was the all-clear signal that Concha (the owner) had departed down river for Presidio-Ojinaga to pay her "taxes" to El Grande. (The Big One, although small, fat and bald). But Concha came back (as shown here) a night early, without paying the "fringe" benefits, for El Grande's wife who had come along with him from Chihuahua City.

Shown here is Concha firing her second barrel over John's head, for he was a good customer. The big Gray had gone airborne on the first shot, sending John's hat and head into the line of fire. Birdshot at ten paces could be cooling to John's thoughts of domesticity with his Chili Pod — shown here riding tailgate.

To Concha no $30-a-month cowboy was going to make three-day wives out of her prime stock.

Holyland was getting too far along in years for bronc stomping and longed for the domestic life of greasing windmills and riding fences, and had been eyeing our three-room frame house at the Jones Place. But Concha's double Fargo "cooled" that idea into just another cowboy's dream.

But it was the drought that got the cattle, and the bank got the ranch that sent John back to bronc stomping (until thrown up against a saddle horn; alone, mangled, and in severe pain, operated on himself, and was found bleeding to death at a remote ranch north of Toyah "Cowtown," Texas.

So passed on in the 1920's my first real cowboy hero, as did "Red" Jennings (from the V-H's, shown here on the center Black), also handy with the rope and the "girls." He died when his horse stepped into a prairie dog hole. Both were one horse, one rope saddle cowhands — none better. Both "cashed in" doing their trade.

Texas folklore has it John's mother was a nurse, a laundress, a camp follower in Georgia, there presenting her husband with a son. He never made it out of the fight at Kennesaw Mountain in '64. She found the trench they buried him in. Came back to Texas — a cook with a baby — on a bull train (oxen).

Many doubt that Holyland was John's real name. His secret — with respect for a father who never saw his son.

The stage running into a Nana ambush near Lucero Station as told by Marcos who was at Lucero, that 28 June, 1881.

CHIHUAHUA STAGE AMBUSH

This stage ran between Chihuahua City and Paso del Norte from the 1860's to the Railroad in 1883. Marcos said the cab was burned off in the ambush and was replaced. Note the similarity to the one refinished.

Stage restored by a Las Cruces Doctor on display in the Holiday Inn. Note the paneling.

Believed to be of Luis Marcos, blacksmith on Toyah Creek, ex-ferrier (horse-shoer) at Lucero Station. Here gathering feed for his pet burro and wood (not shown) in a two-wheel cart for his adobe fireplace and cooking.

Goat Camp Well . . . good year-round water between Franklin (El Paso) and Fort Fillmore on east side of the river valley.

THE WATER STOP AT THE GOAT CAMP

One dark night during Mexico's darkest hour (1865) this old coach —then a young coach — deposited in Paso del Norte one Don Benito Juarez at the back entrance to wealthy Inocente Ochoa's place. Don Ochoa was also dedicated to the cause of this liberator Don Benito, president to be, and whose cause was vitally predicated on receiving a secret arms agreement from a sympathetic benefactor to the north (U.S.).

Later that night an empty, unescorted coach unsuspectingly crossed the River and the next day by noon past, under a hot sun, made a water stop at the Goat Camp for six of the fastest and best mules on the whole Chihuahua run. The road ran along the east mesa, above the mosquito belt and bosques, recrossing the river west of Fillmore and into Mesilla in the dark of the night and therein began the real reason for this picture-story.

If you are a Dreamer, and can fly and dream, take off early, go southwest from Mesilla, over the old Janos-Mesilla freighting road, past the "mal pais" and on into the Potrillo Pass. And there, if you'll look hard enough and long enough — just at sun-up — you can still see them — driver, guard, a coach, and the six gallant mules bathed in a mirage — far off and far below on the desert floor—tiny and seemingly unafraid.

Then a dust trail enters the Potrillos under a sudden burst of speed, as Apache horsemen storm into the road behind the coach and into the dust cloud boiling up into the Pass.

Then it's just corn-fed mules outrunning grassfed ponies on to the safety of Ascencion.

Rumors have the dispatches going from Janos to Casa Grande to Chihuahua City and back up to Paso del Norte, its starting point barely 45 miles south of its destination, all this to avoid betraying eyes of the "Judas for the French Cause." How many "thirty-pieces-of-silver" the coach passed in that long circuitous route no one will ever know.

As one in the State Department, stirred deeply in this delicate situation (France was our once benefactor), said: "Give the dispatches to Kit Carson. Only he knows the way to She-hua-a-hua-a," (thinking Benito was still in Chihuahua City). That's a pretty good pronunciation from a "stand-up collar and forked-tailed" official in Washington.

The coach or its sister could now repose in the Holiday Inn de Las Cruces in dignity and splendor, graced in new red and yellow paint to cover the scars plagued in "mordidas" by the Apaches and Highwaymen throughout its long desert life and carrying under bodement more unsolved secrets than all Watergate.

Much historical dust dripped from its iron rimmed wheels before and after Terrazas disposed of Victorio's Apaches at Tres Castillas.

Thereafter the area blossomed like cockleburrs in the spring as the old coach carried more of the "garden" type variety of thieves, robbers, and gunmen; hauling preachers, priests, and padres; miningmen and cattlemen to say nothing of the promoters and politicians whose greed for silver and gold lay buried under that age-old guise - for God and Country.

The coming railroad put the old coach into secondary use until retired and forgotten in a military armory in Chihuahua.

If you'll read widely enough you may put some of the story pieces together, but most helpful will be an old picture showing the Chihuahua stage resplendent with driver, guard on the box, sacks of mail and baggage in the boot and attendants busying with the harness. Four mules abreast, in front of the wheelers, awaiting the crack of the whip, the coach will tear away from Lucero's Station, northbound into Apacheland with the dust boiling from its wheels as it fades away into the distant past save for this old picture and the deeds of those who care.

Then came the Texans down Lohman St. in Las Cruces, NM, 1877 across the Water Street ditch to the Molina (flour) Mill. The Davis wagon train enroute to Arizona and California follows behind.

THEN CAME THE TEXANS

The Rio was drying up between Fronteria and the Goat Camp Well, the antithesis of what it was when Onate crossed in 1598.

There was a stench of dying polliwogs and decaying fish. The wolves stalked the bosque bottoms for beaver with no place to hide. The drought was upon the land, even the water in sand traps at the old Fillmore Crossing to Mesilla was unfit for man or beast. So it was on to Las Cruces for the California-bound Davis wagon train, shown here coming north on the old Camino Real — now Campo Street through sandy boondocks, soft on oxen feet but hard on the muscles.

A thirsty but proud people, they'd stopped at the slag dump of the Stephenson-Bennett smelter on Tortugas arroyo and village to change into their Saturday night's best. The latest Yellow-Rose-of-Texas dresses, last washed and ironed in Franklin (Texas), were now on dirty, grimy bodies.

At the smell of water, they all broke for the Acequia Madre — their heads up — said the Davis diary, for they were Texans, proud but seemingly in a foreign land.

Shown here are the local women offering them water from gourd dippers, for Spanish custom was still practiced - women didn't belly down, however thirsty — in front of men.

Inside the left compound and placita begins the barbecue preparation for the next day's wedding fiesta for the young lady (far left) being watched by her abuela (grandmother) lest some wild Texan forgets his manners, or the daughter - not yet quite sure — blows the wedding.

On top of El Molino, the old priest, long in years of devoted service, is here shown relegated to official "Bell Ringer" — signaling the coming of a wagon train—possible sales of grain feed, flour or beef. He's a lifetime guest of the Old Mill and now guest of German Miller and his young native wife who is admiring the latest fashion from San "Antone" (Texas).

In the distant center right is the B. Dailey's home, prior to sale to Nestor Armijo, early wealthy New Mexican merchant, rancher, and banker, and before the advent of the School and Convent located between El Molino and the Armijo's. Today, the remodeled home is also home of the Pioneer Savings and Trust.

Here marks the spot where a motley few of thirst-crazed cattle and a passel of thirsty goats tore past for the wastewater ditch below the mill, lest it too disappeared into the river sands.

When Grandma Davis, in her late 80's, and her niece Lollabell, in her late 70's, came through Las Cruces in 1937, I showed them where the owner of the Mesilla carreta, pointed them to the way up the acequia (now Water Street) to the local camp site — then below the Lucero Mill (same acequia) and at the old high school football field at North Main and East Picacho.

They walked slowly around the old football field as if looking for something lost, living it over again, I thought, so I quietly drove away. The next day, they would be going back, the last of the Texans, back home to die. They most always do, back to the old nesting ground. But it is never the same.

You are looking over the site of present Las Cruces Building and Loan at Cordoba's Mill, also known as El Molino. To the right is the end of old main street. Behind the mill are the Dona Ana Mountains.

EL MOLINO - CORDOBA'S MILL

Wild may be the storms over the Dona Ana's (mountains) — sweet may be the water in the Acequia Madre (mother ditch). First came Onate in 1598 — "paso por aqui" (they passed by here) - with his herds, carretas, soldiers and settlers up the watery thread of the Rio Bravo. Summer dried the water to below the river sands — a river dividing a land of bolsons, mesas, desert — its banks sun-dried and sun-blistered stretching from the Gulf of Mexico to the Three Spanish Peaks of southern Colorado, a land of the Pueblos, wisely built on the upper reaches for want of surer water. It was a droughty river in June and July — only the local rains sparing the new life in the land of the new living.

Mill builder Salvador Cordoba ventured southward from the upper Rio Bravo del Norte from the village of Cordoba, near Taos, 250 years after Onate went north — to build a new mill on a new acequia — wooden plowed with oxen from the river near the ten-year-old village of Dona Ana — for a new breed of settlers from the villages of San Elizario and Paso del Norte and a new generation of babies baptized before clawing their way up from the cribs infested with flies and mosquitoes to be men and women of the fields. And so life went on in 1849 and a new village of The

Los Cordobas, Taos, County, New Mexico, (1934). This village 'tis reported that Don Salvador Cordoba departed to build the first flour mill on the acequia madre (mother ditch) in Las Cruces sometime between 1846 and '49.

Crosses was born (Las Cruces).

Shown here in 1853 (p. 56), the distant rider is going up Main Street to give his confession to the priest at the church.

The carreta has brought wheat from the field near Mesilla for grinding.

Visiting are the carreta owner and the man irrigating the field of chile, beans, and corn west of present-day Loretta Mall and east of First National Bank and Mutual Building & Loan.

The history of this mill is well documented by the late Katherine D. Stoes, early valley pioneer since the early 1870's. She told it best, long before I came along. I will be one of those who owes this fine historian much. Credit is so easy to give.

Mesilla Ferry in high snow run-off showing ferry bringing an ox-cart and oxen to Mesilla side. The mail rider from Pinos Altos is swimming his horse to save fare. No charge for riders.

THE MESILLA FERRY

The ferry site at present is in the river bed and planted in cotton. To reach this point, go east from the southeast corner of the plaza, out Parian street onto Barker road for about half a mile toward Las Cruces.

If you were to leave the southeast corner of the Mesilla Plaza by La Calle de Parian (the Market Street) and take the Las Cruces road past the old Mesilla Times adobe for one-half mile to a large, old and green cottonwood, you would be near or at the river crossing.

The upper crossing was southwest of Dona Ana known as the "Indian Crossing" for as far back as Man himself. The lower crossing is at Ft. Fillmore — both fords — until you got up to the narrows above Ft. Selden (in the 1870's) and on above to San Diego (at the Tunico Cone in the 1850's) — both operated by men with block and tackle. If the River was high, wild, and rough, it's best to wait at some nearby saloon, if it is not military payday, for things might get equally as rough.

Shown here one late August evening in 1861 is a boy rider for George M. Frazer's and Antonio Torres', short-lived line, known as the Pinos Altos

Annie Frazer, wife of Barney Riggs who is featured in Story 7.

George M. Frazer (1828-1908). Entered Mexican War in 1849 at 18, served with Joseph E. Johnson. Was wagon master for the Army in Santa Fe. Opened T&P Hotel in Mesilla with George Ackenback, another Mexican War Vet. Frazer, with a partner, started the first mail and passenger route to Pinos Altos in 1858.

T&P Hotel as it appears today. Here (1858) first daughter Annie was born in Mesilla.

and Mesilla Express. This was until Apache Mangas Coloradas put them out of business; and the South and North began killing each other.

The boy rider rode at night to avoid the Apaches and delivered the next day such dispatches as went to Dona Ana, Las Cruces, and Ft. Fillmore. Shown here on the ferry with his saddle. Pay only for oxen and horses. No charge for swimming in the river.

The River jumped over to the west side of Mesilla, taking with it the largest Lesinsky warehouse out of southwest Las Cruces. Then, for no better reason than lack of water, the ferry and ford existed alternatingly depending on the snows in the upper Rio Grande watershed.

Mary Edgar Frazer, traveled in first wagon train from Arkansas to El Paso (Franklin) in 1849 — escorted by Johnson and Frazer. Married Frazer in Dona Ana in 1858. Raised 8 children and died in El Paso in 1893. Son, George A. (Bud) was a Sheriff in Pecos, Texas, was killed by Miller in Toyah. See Story 7.

You are looking east through the main entrance from Las Cruces via the river ferry into the southeastern corner of the Mesilla plaza. The building to the left is where Billy-the-Kid was tried in 1881. The building to the far right is the site of present day La Posta Restaurant.

The street to the right once serviced the early Butterfield Stage line in 1858. The Little Merchants usually hung around the street leading south from the southwest corner of the plaza or this is the area the stock were corralled. Butterfield and later N M & T stage line had offices in that area. Also this road leads south to Santo Tomas and the river crossing at Fort Fillmore.

The illustration typifies the 1860's and '70's.

THE LITTLE MERCHANTS

The Little Merchants of Mesilla of the early 1870's were boy-merchants who roamed out from the dusty streets of the village (shown here at the southeast corner of the plaza) to the bosques and river bottoms for wood — burro-packed back to the homes and fireplaces for copper pennies, while herding a passel of feisty goats — fresh nannies with full milkbags — guarded by a cantankerous old billy who ruled his herd by his horns, and anyone who questioned his sovereign rights thereto was in for some of the same, be it on the river bottoms, the grassy ditch banks, or out on the mesa tops.

So began the careers of the boy merchants and more particularly one Lorenzo Lujan, who grew up to clerk in Lynch Brothers' Colorado store (a mile east of Hatch, New Mexico), then on to farmer-renter and bridegroom in 1879, then 19, to a beautiful Mexican "flower" of sixteen — the belle of Santa Barbara (3 miles northwest of Hatch) — until she was captured in October 1879 by Victorio's Apaches in the cornfield outside

Loma Parda (4 miles northeast of Santa Barbara).

Lorenzo followed her captors from Lloyd's Ranch southwest to the "bleeding" site of the Mexican wagon train massacre and on to the Floridas, southward to Janos and Corralitos, where he lost the trail in the Candelarios north of Carrizal. Nowhere was there a trace of the captors trading her for guns or ammunition.

Mexican beauties just don't disappear from Apaches, but become pregnant and are lost forever — more to their families, and on into the nothingness of Time, with the hopelessness of Evangeline.

Lorenzo next appeared at El Presidio — at the Texas river crossing — again to become a merchant with two good horses and a canvas-topped wagon selling apples from the Ft. Davis orchards to the railroad and roundhouse at cowtown Toyah, Texas.

One day in 1911 Lorenzo camped at our Nine-Mile Spring with a wagonload of apples enroute to Toyah — in Homberg, black coat and square-toed merchant's shoes, and a businessman's smile under a short-cropped moustache. He pulled the tarpaulin back from over a bed full of windfalls for Mother to see. She smiled and shook her head. Then he pulled out a gunny sack of hand-picked Winesaps to which she nodded, and he smiled back as if he knew he was dealing with a Missouri-bred farmgirl who knew her apples.

On one of his many stops in 1916, I noted that Lorenzo was graying at the temples, and white streaks were threading his moustache on the classic Grecian face worth the turning of any eye to see, still dressed in a style beyond that of an apple peddler, and with a Santo and crucifix hanging under the bows of his wagon.

Some say that he prayed at each overnight camp — always toward that steelblue knife-blade of a mountain — the distant Guadalupe Peak, northwest — El Capitan of the range and guardian of all Apache land.

Others vowed that the priest at the little chapel back of the railroad roundhouse said Lorenzo knew his bride from Santa Barbara somehow made it out of the Tres Castillas massacre of October 1880 and was seen watering her mules one early dawn at Van Horn Wells by Guillermo Mendoza, the stage stock attendant.

Shortly after that, an ex-Turkey-Track cowboy at Rattlesnakes Springs' cow camp caught a buck and two squaws, with a papoose and a boy-child butchering out a calf. They looked like scarecrows on scrawny Mexican mules — so poor that he didn't pull his Winchester but let them go on up the canyon toward Crow Springs, gnawing raw meat and fighting their mules into a struggling trot. (Crow Springs is the first water south of the Mescalero Reservation on the raiding route into Mexico that is as old as the Mexicans and Apaches).

The last time I saw Lorenzo was in 1921 at the Saragosa Farm on Greasy Row. He looked more "religion" than "apples" and carried his crucifix dangling from the front bow of his wagon. His smile was slower, and not so wide, his eyes misty with that far-off, glassy look as if he now somehow knew . . .

What he never knew was if his bride's son was his son, or if he was only a Godfather, in name, to an Apache named Lorenzo — who made it "home" — and was now living on the Reservation.

'Tis rumored that he finally married, and that his widow followed him in death some years later in a dusty, windswept West Texas — a sun-blistered, forlorn, drought-stricken land where if two lonely roads cross and two windmills spike the distant horizon — with a ballot box and a post office - they make a town.

Out there Lorenzo is buried, a good man, religious, honest, and a merchant to the last.

Cocono, the wine merchant, came out in the evenings when it was cool. This illustration is typical of near the southeast corner of Mesilla plaza in the 1870's.

COCONO, THE WINE MERCHANT

Cocono always came out on the dusty Mesilla streets in the late afternoon dressed in his red sash to sell his barreled wine for nine cents a quart from his wooden-wheeled carreta behind a yoke of dedicated steers.

Cocono was just that homely as shown, known by a name for little girls to giggle at and little boys to tease and be chased after— for he waddled like a duck.

He was anything but shaped like his Mexican nickname. Only his face resembled that of a turkey neck.

Mine trail on north side of La Cueva rock trailing up and left to the mines beginning with Spanish era. Wealthy mine owner Don Antonio Garcia from El Paso del Norte operated in this area until Apaches shut him down about 1810.

HI-GRADE FROM THE HIGH COUNTRY

Mule trains from the high country came down from the west side of the Organs in the early 1850's by night when the Apaches, for superstitious reasons, did not attack.

Folklore and history has it, and only in part, that these same mines were Spanish before 1822 — patrolled by Cavaliers in plumed headgear and blacksmith's metal clothes, rattling their sabers at the backs of Apache slaves, and keeping their long pointed mustaches waxed in anticipation of that day again of bosomy ladies in the King's court.

They came down from the Santo Domingo de La Calsada, the Santa Susana and the Refiego mines where deep in hardrock and quartz ran streaks of silver, threads of gold and nodules of lead for the furnaces (smelters) of Hugh Stephenson at Tortugas Arroyo.

From nearby rock corrals to the mines, the arrieros (muleteers) would keep the pack mules on down the trail with their two cowhide mochas filled with hi-grade ore.

Resting at the river smelter, the mules would roll their salty backs on the silt-laden banks. There the arrieros would divide the train. The larger mules with the gold ore would go on via Janos to the Corralitos and Chihuahua smelters and after 1850, they did their fandangoing in Mesilla.

They would dance and drink the night through, to violin and guitar, with their spider-like legs flaying the air — bells jingling on pantaloon bottoms — going every which way, up and down, and out. Sometimes out the door by request and force — or because of a rising sun. One aghast Paisano said they danced more like jumping crickets when touched by a branding iron.

The arrastra and the furnace men at the Corralitos smelter would, when the ore trains failed to arrive, retire to the shade of the Cantina and obligingly discuss at length *los razons* (the reasons) for the delay or for as long as the tequila lasted.

If it had not been for the Senoritas at Mesilla, Janos, and Corralitos, the mule trains would never have gotten through, prophesied one fireman. Los Arrieros, the Comandante and his Rurales, the Federales and the Apaches . . . ? Who can you trust with gold — even in the rock?

One furnace man in the cantina vowed, before emptying the first bottle of tequila, that it would be better if the Apaches took it. For they were always hungry for mule meat. Likely, before you'd reached their second camp site, you'd have found it dumped. The aparajos and mochas (cowhide pack sacks) would be on their feet "*en nueva botas*" (in new boots). The campfire bones would tell where the mules went. "*Los 'paches no es tontos.*" (The Apache is no fool). "Becos' no 'pache lak' to carry a rocks een hees han's." Where would he find an arrastra and a furnace?

By the third bottle, the Revelers would wisely and in guarded whispers assure you that under no circumstances would you go for help to the Rurales or the Federales!

"Becos' theen you weel have to cru-sh eet and coo-k (smelt) eet an' *todo para nada.*" (all for nothing). Besides, none of the gold would get past Chihuahua City.

One of the older furnace prophets began in a faltering manner, "Who ees at fault? *Ees eet los arrieros* for losin' thos' mules? *O los 'paches'* for findin' theem? *O el Comandante* with hees Rurales? *O los Federales* - thos' solgers?" (soldiers). He then lowered his glass, looked up into latillas and belched — a heavenly relief from tequila over sour beans — and continued, "O ees eet beco' no Ma-n can e trust heemself?" He wavered as if in deep thought, belched again, and fell over onto the table in a sea of warm beer to snore it off. The soberest of the lot summed it up best, "*Por Dios, y mil gracias para las muchachas y los arrieros.*" (For God, and a thousand thanks for the girls and the arrieros). The painting shows the mules loaded with ore sacks, camp supplies, and a cook tent. A yearly sight most common in Mesilla Plaza, when as many as 100 mules and 40 arrieros passed through in one train with trade goods from Paso del Norte to Janos, Bavispi, and other Sonoran Villages. This road ran southwest from Mesilla straight to Janos. You fly over it to see it — only faint ruts and mesquite lined (from the bean seed droppings).

NATIVIDAD PADILLA'S father was known as
El Senor, and was captain of an ore-packing
mule train from the Organ and Caballero
Mountains via Santa Rita Mine and Janos, to
the smelters at Corralitos for a period before
and after 1822.

The salt hauler's left the saltbed 25 miles north of San Augustine Springs two or three days before. They are shown here 3 miles from the springs which they left before dawn and now after sun-up approaching the Pass with 12 miles to go before reaching Don Ana sometime after dark. A hard 4 days if Apaches are quiet.

LOS SALINEROS – SAL PARA CAMBALACHE

Coming up the San Augustine Pass (Organ) are the Dona Ana Salt Haulers returning from their annual trek (beginning in 1840 and until the coming of the railroad in 1881) to the Salt Beds above Lake Lucero and northwest of the White Sands Monument.

When the Apaches were known to be camped at the Hembrillo Canyon Springs, they returned along the east side of the San Andres Mountains, stopping at El Ojo del San Nicolas (the old Barbaro Lucero Ranch) and the San Martin Springs (the late W. W. Cox ranch) long after the Spanish Dons (sheepmen) were starved out by Apaches, and before J. Bull of T. Shedd operated Road Houses on the road between Blazer's Mill, Lincoln Plaza, and Las Cruces, early county seat for Dona Ana County.

Dona Ana was also a trade center of note — a "paraje" for the weary on the Chihuahua-Santa Fe Trail. All wagon trains camped there — bought or traded in salt.

James W. Cox, son of owner, at site believed to be an early San Augustine Spring Spanish sheep ranch established in early 1790's. An array of rock pens and remains of two adobe's believed built by Franciscan Friars. The foundation of which lasted through T.J. Bull (1848) and W.T. Shedd. W.W. Cox bought from Wilde and Davis in 1893.

In distant left, in the sunshine-shadow line is San Augustine Springs. The salt laden carretas came up the gully to cross thru San Augustine Pass — a hundred feet higher than the present highway.

San Augustine Springs is out of the field-of view, to the left. The trail came up into the Pass from the left lower right corner.

WILDY WELL SHOOT-OUT

A political shoot-out took place at 12 paces at dawn on July 13, 1898 in the McGregor Firing Range about seven to eight miles east of the Oro Grande.

From left to right shown here are Ben Williams on the dirt tank bank by the windmill, Clint Llewellyn showing his head from behind the metal pump house shed (problematical), and next is Pat Garrett -- seeking another term of sheriff and who was the root of the whole fracas with his deputies, said such Old Timers as Gene and Walt Baird, Jose and Felipe Lucero, and W. W. Cox, adjacent ranchers to the west of this site. Center and falling is Kent Kearney, sometime school teacher around Tularosa, earning his spurs the hard way — as a law man.

To the far right is Jose Espalin, a sometime friend of Oliver Lee and who warned him as he was leaving the Cox Ranch, "Quidado, estan extranjeros" (Look-out, there's strangers about). He is shown here jumping off the west end of the frame shack adjacent to the adobe that dates from Apache times with its remaining parapets and port slots for roof firings.

From trips back with knowledgeable ranchers such as Walt and Jim Baird, McNew and Gilliland, I still don't know if they stood on the roof or behind it on a ladder or on a wagon behind the shed.

Pat Garrett did learn that shooting at Oliver Lee was not the same as shooting Billy-the-Kid, with a steak knife in his hand, and not knowing if the man in the dark bedroom was a friend of Maxwell or another Bounty Hunter. Had he not hesitated in saying, "Quien es?" (Who is it?) that shooting might have turned out like this one.

One day in 1932, Oliver Lee, while at lunch at our ADT Fraternity House to see his son Vince, told about the same story as he told William Kelleher in 1937, who unlike most folklorists documented it, which makes him the Historian of this story.

Footnote: This illustration is as I saw it on two occasions while flying from west to east over the site at the same time of day as it occurred.

The long (oxen) freight wagon loaded with military freight for Tucson, are climbing sandy West Mesa, Spring 1877, owned by Tully and Ochoa of Franklin (present El Paso, Texas). The train master told the Mexican farmer family (ox cart) if he'd be at Mesa top by sun-up, he would put his family aboard the last wagon. She miscarried at Mesa top. The family buried the stillborn at Slocum's station and went on to the Mimbres or Gila River. See Story 24. The stage coach is from Silver City now 3 miles from Mesilla.

WEST MESA, WESTWARD, HO!!

The German Huelster family settled in Ohio and New Braunfels, Texas, in the 1840's from which came two Frank Huelsters — one to Barilla Station (West Texas) and the one shown here as train master for the Tully & Ochoa, one of the largest military cargo freighters between Franklin (El Paso) and Tucson in 1877.

Huelster is the man on the left center horse, here shown as wagon master for 8 wagons — 10 yoked oxen — each doing 10 miles or more a day, depending on the availability of water. He is shown here "cooning" up the west mesa road just south of Picacho Peak — the sandiest, longest, highest, and most difficult grade between Port La Vaca, Texas, and the west coast — the first of many freight and stage roads with difficult grades, known as "Heartbreak Ridge."

While camping at Picacho Village (near the last two big distant wagons shown leaving on p. 69), Huelster told the Mexican farmer from lower El Paso valley — bound for the new farming valleys of the Mimbres and Gila Rivers — that if he would be at the top of the mesa by sun-up, he would put his family aboard the last wagon — the bed and chuck wagon. This farmer was dubbed by Huelster thereafter as the "carreta family" for their mode of travel, a common expression in that day when it was not polite to ask a man's name.

At midnight, as Huelster walked around his wagons at Picacho, he noted the "carretas family" astir. They were not to be left at the top of Heartbreak Ridge — not in these times of Apache raiding. In the illustration you see a determined farmer, a family man of five married years. Such was life in that day.

The woman miscarried at the mesa top but went on to Slocum's Station where Mrs. John Slocum, a Mexican wife from Carrazal, advised her to go on with the wagon train and she would bury the stillborn infant — a faint grave with a replaced cross was still there in 1929.

Priesser — a stage-riding guard — is shown waving to Huelster "that all is clear — no Apaches on the road" and who later confirmed Mrs. Slocum's story, and the story of the Mexican wagon train of 12 wagons and two carretas massacred 5 miles west of

Slocum's in October 1879. Here the Mexican farmer was returning to El Paso Valley. He was buried with the other victims by the W. L. Rynerson posse. His wife and two little girls went into Mexico as Apache slaves for "use" and trade. Blind at 90, Huelster was living with a Mexican woman in Agua Prieto, across the line from Douglas Air Force Base in Arizona, where I was stationed in 1943. He filled me in on the "carreta family."

Heartbreak Ridge today is just a sandy grade of greasewood and mesquite — the final approach to the southwest runway of the Las Cruces West Mesa Airport, where you hardly see the traces of the wagons and carretas. To those who wish to know, may this picture tell you where to look.

Jacobo Chavez was born in Picacho, 1863. He grew up and lived with the stage and freight lines. He sold wheat, corn, vegetables and fruit to all the travelers before they started their climb up the sandiest, longest grade between San Antonio (TX) and San Francisco.

TURKEY SHOOT ON THREE JUGS OF WINE

For years after the running fight with the Apaches, one wet October 13, 1879, along the old wagon road between forts Fillmore and Thorne in the rough of the west side of the Las Uvas — Mesilla's Kokono, Trujillo, and Madrid would go back with the relatives of the victims to rebuild their cairns, replace the crosses and say respectful prayers for those hapless five of the seventeen artisans and farmers, who were more adept at following the plow than the Apache into ambush.

And for the years to come in the Dona Ana, Las Cruces, and Mesilla saloons, gossip had it that had the unfortunate seventeen "good men and true" known there were 70-odd of Vic's best out there (mounted on Hooker's stolen cavalry, armed with Government carbines and ammo) waiting eagerly, they all would have "opted" for a late bed with their wives on the old worn excuse "too wet to plow."

It had also been said of this same story, the Raconteurs would, after looking around the room (saloon), refer to it in guarded, whispered tones, as "the Apache Turkey Shoot."

This story came to me first, by way of three jugs of Mesilla wine, told within the same corral walls where the posse came in, to stable their run-down mounts and deaden their sorrow in Bean's saloon, for already the young married had hastily bathed while riding through the Picacho slough and had cut out for home — too eager for the welfare of their half-dead mounts.

In the Fall of 1927, I met with Kokomo, Trujillo, and Madrid in this corral where the posse came in looking more like Lee's ragged "remnants" retreating from Petersburg in 1865, than the jubilant seventeen of four days before who had sallied forth to teach the Apache a lesson.

Shown in this aerial photo looking west is the type of terrain where the fight took place. Van Patten, the leader and Armijo wrote in the local paper of a hard 2 hour hand-to-hand fight. (Apaches don't fight such, it's all or nothing.) The Parks family, who were forced back to Slocum's when told of the newspaper account, "poo-whoed" the story. After Trujillo, who lived on the Mimbres and ran sheep in the area showed the author in 1933, the grave sites of the luckless five who rode (as 17) gallantly to the sieged at Lloyd's ranch, ran into an ambush about as shown at the far right "X" in the photo.) The remaining four men ran back-tracking along the old Fort Fillmore-Fort Thorn road as shown. Young Jones the left "X" is near where he fell. His fellow men, Hickey and Van Patten, on the fastest horses reach Slocum Ranch first-reporting a 2 hour hand-to-hand combat. If running like hell, quirting your horses tail is a form of combat. There is nothing shameful about being prudent when in a hornets nest of 70 well-armed Apaches. The Old Timer's I talked to said, "It's doubtful if the prudent runners got off a killing shot."

Lloyd's Ranch, looking south up-canyon. The Rock house and corrals stood between the rectangular marker and the windmills. The rocks were salvage for the house, shown. This was the original ambush — off to the right from the car—that created the episode. George Ackenback with six, went to see how the people at Lloyds were surviving the Apache horde coming from the Black Range, along the Rio Grande farms, enroute to Mexico, two days ahead of Major Morrow's cavalry.

Colorado, Southeast of Hatch, now known as Rodey, was the departure point of the original Seven — Ackerback, Garcia, Melendres, Torres, Cosme & Victor de la O. Since 5 were buried (at Lloyds) a son of one de la O, age 15, had to have been along. Ackerback and Torres, riding behind came out to fight the next day for the bodies with the 35 that were driven back to Lynch Brothers (at Colorado). Walled-in wagon and livestock yard, store, saloon, and you name it, for it was long ago that day — Oct. 10, 1879.

I learned long ago — beginning at age four on a west Texas ranch — to get a good story from the paisanos, it takes WINE. Three jugs for three Tellers. One to loosen 'em up; two to start an argument; three to get the story, and put them to sleep. Repeat it the following Saturday night. If it comes out the same — you've got the story.

When I asked them, "Why the three miles between the first and last grave," Kokono, the sharpest, came right back at me, "Eet ees not becos thees me-en (men) wan to mak a fight with theese A'paches. Oh! . . . NO !!! Eet ees becos theese hor-ses don all ron (run) the same." There's a bit of philosophizing in every jug — the more wine, the more philosophy.

We were closing in on the second jug when Trujillo raised it — cradled it in a bent elbow, miner's style — closed one eye for better alignment on the opening — when out gushed the last cupful — over chin, whiskers, and through his mustache. Quick, and rapier-like, out shot a long and practiced tongue — catching the droplets before they hit the corral dust. And I thought, "Won't the flies have a feast here — come sun-up — changing from horse manure to sweet wine."

Then Madrid said he'd heard in the Las Cruces saloon that it was Jaciento Armijo's race mare that cut Van Patten's black stallion out in the narrows of the old road (see illustration), both men whipping

each other over their heads in their search for the business end of their mounts — sensing the warm breath of closing Apaches.

From the signs in the road, the race mare didn't help Sanchez from getting "boxed-in" — Apache style, for want of a faster horse and more running room. They cut his throat, just enough to bleed him out for the squaws to come up and watch, smiling as he slowly fell from a staggering, blood-soaked horse. Then they went to work on him with their knives.

Some think Pancho Beltran (or was it Lam) fell from his gut-shot horse (see illustration), breaking his leg. The squaws worked him over, gleefully bleeding him out in the private sector for as long as possible. When he showed signs of fading, they beat his brains out slowly with a rock. Such butcherings were the squaws' pleasure — believing that in dismantling a man meant he (his spirit) could never father a son to fight.

The Bucks, leaving the squaws to do their work, saw and took to a 12-wagon train (Mexican freighters from the lower El Paso Valley) two miles westward on the Silver City road.

Three miles west of Magdalena Gap they lanced the oxen, leaving them struggling in their yokes, in the road. Shot the men under their wagons (poorly armed, mostly muzzle loaders) — taking two women for ravaging and three children for barter or slaves.

When Van Patton, on the black stallion, came smoking through Magdalena Gap shouting at the John Parks' wagon train, "INDIANS! INDIANS! GO BACK!!!" as he flashed by, they saw only wheezing nostrils, ears laid back on a head pointing eastward, pounding the 3-mile road to Slocum's (also known as Mason's).

Years later, when I met the Parks, I showed them notes from the newspaper account of Van Patton's and Armijo's stories of the "Two hours of hand-to-hand fighting." Then they said, "As we were leaving Slocum's, 'the 17' rode out that morning and they (the Parks) had gotten only as far as Magdalena Gap when `this man on the black' came smokin' through the Gap shouting 'INDIANS!.' There wasn't enough time for a fight — the distance to the ambush. A running fight, maybe — if running is fighting — but not two hours . . ."

About a week after the fight, friendly Apache scouts (attached to Morrow's command) reported finding three bodies rolled inside Army blankets —which he doubtless didn't need in hand-to-hand fighting.

The Parks passed the Freighters' burned-out wagons and burial site, very shortly after, they viewed at length the battleground. (As did Agnes Meader Snyder and family, some time later). All vowed if anyone drew blood it was this man in the small yucca barricade, a short distance eastward, on the side toward the "Running Fight." It is believed this fight had hardly ended before the Freighters' fight began, although two miles apart.

From the tracks of the horses turned loose at the yuccas, marks of a large knife used in frantic digging "in," and many empty .44 cartridges — this site was the answer as to who filled the blankets — before the Apaches "cut" him down, with the yuccas around him. An unknown, unnamed fighter, a "Viking of many stormy seas" — since the blankets were found southwest from the Floridas. The squaws salvaged Armijo's blankets.

Agnes M. Snyder, who made the wagon run from Victorio at Alma (see Roberts' Cabin story) the following April, when shown this same newspaper account, huffed, "You don't kill Indians running — at your back."

Rancher L. F. Burris (in the 1930's) showed me the grave of the Freighters and some of the muzzle loading guns found nearby. But most of all, I wanted to stand on the spot. So I aligned and stepped off the distance (as given by the Parks) to where my nameless hero had made his stand. I wanted the truth, for there'll never be a picture or name for this hero to leave in this Apache land. His "Paso por Aqui" (He passed by here) unrecorded save for the Parks, and this book.

Van Patten (who came to Mesilla in 1858 with the Butterfield Stage) led the Seventeen "good men and true" from Mesilla and Las Cruces to relieve the Colorado/Lloyds group and lost Jones, Barragan, Sanches, Lara and Beltran, in the hour hand-to-hand running fight. Van Patten Photo: Courtesy of Dona Ana Historical Collection, New Mexico State University.

The MEXICAN MASSACRE, a train of 10/11 wagons and three carretas (carts) about 30 miles west of Las Cruces on the main stage and freight road to Silver City and the west coast, (13 October, 1879) a group of poor lower Paso del Norte valley farmers returning from peddling their fruit to Silver City miners were caught in the path of Victorio's horde of fleeing Apaches (75/100 Bucks and 140 squaws and children) driving their commissary of stolen cattle, Mexico bound.
Lower right: Mexican farmer's wife in Story 22, making a run with her children. All were taken captive/slaves.

THE MEXICAN MASSACRE

A Mexican train of 12 ox-drawn wagons, sellers of lower El Paso valley fruits and produce, left Silver City when the early October rains (1879) made oxen travel easier (more water and grass) and were returning (shown here) three days short of Mesilla when Victorio's Apaches, about a hundred Bucks and a hundred and forty squaws and children — Mexico bound — struck them 30 miles west of Las Cruces and west of Magdalena Gap, leaving consternation through Apache land.

(The above illustration is based on what was seen during the burial by parties of the Parks' wagon train.)

Van Patton had lost five of seventeen of his "Home Guard" in an ambush 2 miles northeast of this site. Van Patton came tearing through the Parks' Wagon Train, then in Magdalena Gap, "on a black horse throwing mud and scattering rocks," shouting, "Indians! Go Back!" They saw only a shirt-tail of him tearing down the road eastward to Slocums, said Jim Parks of Duncan, Arizona one day in 1937.

Site of Mexican massacre and grave of 10/11 men — marked in 1929 by an old juniper stump post.

Van Patton and Armijo did write from Slocums glowing dispatches to the local paper of "bravery and hand-to-hand fighting for two hours." The Parks saw, as they were leaving Slocums for Silver City early that morning, the seventeen riding westward through the Gap — all strung-out, like children going to a picnic — enroute to Lloyds' Ranch to bury the five killed there two days before, and were supposing the Indians were now being followed by Morrow's Cavalry into Mexico.

Then in about two hours this black stallion came tearing through their train "smoking up" the road to Slocums.

Since ambushed bodies were found scattered over a three-mile run, it had to be a running "hand-to-hand fight" — the Apaches doing the killing and the Guard doing the running.

Later, after the military had reported the number of Apaches, it did seem prudent to "run and tell" — if you're riding the best horse. Van Patton did decline the next day at Slocums to go back with the Rynerson's burial party of 70 to 80 "good men and true," which didn't make for a good "Major" in the Home Guard. He said his horse "was tired" — with only 24 hours rest and grain in Slocum's corral. Maybe, he was waiting for the newspaper to hit the Las Cruces streets.

The large wooden cross at the common grave had long fallen into decay by 1929. The railroad reached Deming in March, 1881 and the old road travel had stopped. The years had rutted and washed out the road, and the relatives from the lower El Paso Valley no longer came annually to lay flowers at the

grave. The large rectangular plot — with time — began to settle and by 1937 it was 8 inches lower than the surrounding "berm".

In the picture, on page 75, runs the horseback traveler (riding with the train for protection) "who, if he had ridden on through in the night would have left grandchildren instead of a half-dug, half-size foxhole among the shot-down yuccas," said Jim Parks, who picked up many .44-40 cartridges, evidence he was the one who left three wounded Apaches —their blooded blankets found at the Portrillo Spring.

The common grave is just beyond the carreta fleeing to the right—as shown in far right center. One carretta was found the following day with the oxen grazing in the grassy swale off to the left, its occupant sitting upright, like a judge, very dead, a lance hole through his belly for a slow bleed-out — an Apache's delight.

"The women—what happened to them?" I asked. "*Ellas partirse para cielo en el primero noche ante.*" (They went to heaven the first night after.)

Guns found by the Burris' where the wagon train was burned.

L.F. Burris, Rancher in 1938, who had established a ranch here some years after the fight. The site is behind the adobe and to the right of distant hill. The adobe is on the old road.

W. L. Rynerson, (attorney and ex-California column volunteer, 1862) was in charge of the burial detail at the three fight scenes, if you can call a massacre a fight. Two Apache corpses were found 15 miles southeast, believed killed by a horsebacker, well armed Anglo riding with the Mexican train (oxen, and slow) because he as a Texan, believes a man is no man that won't stand and fight, (this birthed at the Alamo 43 years before). The Parks (also Texans) said, on studying the site, the man had to be carrying a Winchester or a Henry and two .44-40 six-shooters to empty that many cartridges. The Mexicans had only a few ancient muzzle-loading cap-and-ball guns. (A Texas family in 1915 came to Duncan, AZ, to see Jim Parks' about a lost relative returning from Silver City in 1879.)

CREDIT: Photo W.L.R. Hobson, Huntsinger Collection, New Mexico State University Archives

James Parks, a boy with his father's wagon train, that was looted in Magdalena Gap 3 miles west of Slocum's; only by turning the oxen train loose, grabbing a horse surrey, they dashed madly back saving his family. A man named Hickey (one of the fleeing fighters of the Van Patton's Seventeen) "high-tailing" it out of the ambush — saved the Parks'.

William Bates, arriving at Slocum's near midnight, tells Simeon Eby, driver, to hold up until word comes that Major Morrow's command (coming down from the Black Range) has cornered Victorio.

BATES' RIDE INTO SLOCUM'S STATION

It was a rainy October in 1879, when the mud delayed the Santa Fe-Silver City Stage at Mesilla, thereby delaying the midnight change at Slocum's Station — 28 miles west, and in the center of Apache "Fairway" — their raiding route from Ojo Caliente (NW of Monticello) to the Sierra Madres of Mexico.

Long ago the Church put out Mexican settlements along the northern frontier to bring the Apache heathens, supposedly, closer to God; but actually brought them in closer to the green fields of "eaten" mules, riding horses, and beef cattle; and it soon became a way of life — raiding these hapless settlements, and a form of recreation from fighting Navajos and Papagos where no quarters were ever given.

Victorio's Apaches had "cut-up" Major Morrow's Troopers on the Animas (Creek) and were "sliding" out of the Black Range onto the fairway south, but on which side? Billy Bates' pack train was held at the Placers (NE of Hillsboro) when the word came to "hold the stage at Mesilla!"

From years of staging and scouting, Bates had a "nose" for the Apache and an eye like an owl in the nighttime, so turned his mule train over to Presser — heading his horse south for Slocum's — holding to the foothills, above the valley (Rio Grande) where the cornfields would be crawling with Apaches.

The first horse change was at Trujillo's south of Hillsboro, 12 miles more, under a peek-a-boo moon, (in-and-out of the rain clouds), and on to McEver's at Lake Valley.

Then another horse and 25 miles of open country, feared most even in the night time — crossing the fairway short of Mason's Ranch — his last hope for a fresh horse,

Each guest room at Slocum's was fitted with a fireplace with juniper or mesquite root wood. Photo —1938.

then through the Uvas, 17 miles into Slocum's.

Bates came cautiously into Mason's — from behind on the mountain side — determined to make a run for the rocks. But everyone had gone to "fort-up" at Lynch Brother's store and wagon yard in Colorado (Rodey, SE of Hatch).

Bates watched the road and slowed to a walk, before rubbing his mare down, fearing pneumonia from fatigue, the heat and the damp.

Soon, from up in the rocks came a long whinny, high up on the bluffs. Then, in trotted a big speckled Gray, coming in on the damp scent — an Apache-wise stud — pawed the mud, and nickered like he'd found a lost troop of cavalry mares. Bates, years later said as we sat in the old kitchen doorway at Slocum's, "Horses are so human. I hate to see the roads all cluttered up with cars."

"I switched saddles to the gray," he said, "and led the mare some miles up into the Uvas. She tried to follow but soon gave out." Today there is a "horse canyon" named in the area.

He continued the last leg of the ride, "I let the big Gray out that last hundred yards. I wanted him to come into the station in style."

Then his misty, old eyes looked out through the gap in the low, east adobe wall, out through where once stood a heavy timbered gate, and on beyond toward Las Cruces — out there into 55 years, years of nothingness but time.

Bates had come back to sit for a day and dream

in the middle of the fairway, but like the Apaches, all had passed him by.

Bates' last words were, "Go find Madam Malissa, in Silver City — she's the last living woman on that stage."

Louis Abrams, owner of the old Southern Hotel, said: "I'll show you where Malissa lives. Her room isn't far."

Madam Malissa was known by all the cowboys who come to town to horse around in her stable of young fillies; mining men said she had the most marketable by-product of high grade in all the mining lands. From out of the dark, business men came and went — by her back door.

When I asked her if she remembered the stage ride, she smiled faintly, her low voice had the intonation of a plantation parlor, and I almost felt I could hear the rustle of crinoline.

"Yes," she smiled, "I remember it well. It rained all the way down from Soccoro (she had a "House" there). A man from the "34" (newspaper), in Las Cruces said, 'Don't go to Silver, stay here! The telegraph is down! Lynch Brothers (Rodey) said the corn fields below Palomas and around Santa Barbara were "loused" up with Apaches. Morrow's Troopers were still following . . . still hanging on, two days behind."

She said, "No squaw was going to get my clothes. I had a Derringer strapped to my leg." Modestly and without reservation, she showingly

South walls of Slocum's Station in 1937-8.

clamped long slender fingers around what many a cowman from Vegas to Silver City had offered a kingdom for the exclusive rights to and I saw and understood how many a "past" could be forgotten in the long ago day here in Apache land.

"It was mud from Mesilla to Slocum's," she continued. "That man they called 'Sim' (Simeon Eby, the driver) was good with the mules in the mud."

"I watched the guard check the barrels of his double Fargo," she added, "before we got into the narrows of Rough-and-Ready and I checked my purse. Had a horse pistol there with six bullets and a box. A real old 'hog leg'."

Then I realized why so many cowmen wanted Malissa. She not only was beautiful but she had spice and spunk and a figure that would make any man stay at home.

When I said in 1934 to Uncle Billy, "Let's go see Slocum's," a glint came into his tired old eyes and his handle bar moustache spread with a glow that you only see when you break out flying from overcast skies into a full moon.

He would be going back for a day, back in time from Oct. 1934 to Oct. 1879 — 55 years since he rode four horses down the Apache fairway — all 65 miles of mud flats and rocky canyon walls. I flew it once — straight across - 50 miles in 15 minutes one dark rainy night just for the feel of it. What Billy did in a day and a half night — that my great-grandkids might read about it 200 years after it happened one October 1879 — long after the walls of Slocum's had melted down. After Billy will have been forgotten — save for those TODAY who might read of it.

Wm. M. (Billy) Bates, scout and packer through the 1879-80 Apache Victorio campaign. He drove the stage from Silver City to Georgetown and later settled on a ranch east of Mule Creek. He lived at 615 N. Florence St. in El Paso, January, 1940, at age 88.

Slocum's from the air in 1974 looking west. How time has taken its toll.

Shown here is Slocum's Station about 26 miles west of Mesilla on the Silver City road. You are looking west at an Apache attack that failed. Simeon Eby was driving, using the whip. The Silver City Madam, the only passenger, was doing her part.

THE SILVER CITY MADAM

Shown here is Simeon Eby bringing Madam Malissa into Slocum's Station in time for supper as told to me by Bill Bates and Priesser, who later scouted for Major Morrow's command.

The renegade Apaches had jumped the coach in Rough-and-Ready Gap, between Mesilla and Slocum's on the Silver City road. Priesser, riding shotgun, had kept them back the two miles or more until Slocum's and was almost within reach when the Apaches made their move — one going for the lead mule, the other two firing on Priesser and Eby.

John Slocum said later, to Bates, that Eby should of known he had no shootin' help here — just two Mexican hostlers, not good riflemen, wife's relatives. And he, Eby, brought them right up to the gate.

Priesser told it the next day in the Silver City Continental Saloon, that he was holding 'em back, good, until the Apaches came in close. He had just two loads in

Thomas, son of Simeon, Stage driver from Las Cruces to Santa Fe 1857-8 to late 1870's. And from Las Cruces — Mesilla to Silver City 1870-'81. Eby, Sr. is buried on his Mimbres Ranch, (1912) and was an early member of the Las Cruces Masonic Lodge.

Slocum's Station from the air, October 1976. The stillborn Mexican birth (story 22, West Mesa) was buried near the northeast corner of the Corral in the upper left corner of the picture. The arroyo took it sometime after 1929.

his Double Fargo — a real saddle emptier -- that Fargo. Then from behind and under his seat came this BOOM! BOOM! He looked down — saw this big "Hog-leg" (six-shooter) poking out the window, "talking back" to the Apaches. Malissa was working this six-gun. The leading Apache was too far out for me so I just "dusted" his hoss. It was Malissa's second Boom that "sawed" that renegade off his hoss — nice and clean like. The other two gathered their fallen comrade and disappeared toward the Potrillos.

Madam Malissa was the first of three prominent Madams in this mining and cattlemen's era. I had the pleasure of meeting her in her sundown years in Silver City, across the Big Ditch and in a part of the old Southern Hotel, then owned by Louis Abrams. Billy Bates, stage coach driver in Arkansas and California, and who later drove from Silver City to Georgetown said, "Go see Malissa, she can tell the story best."

I visited Slocum's low adobe walls, with Bates in 1937, where we sat in the dining room doorway, center and west end of the compound when he told Priesser's story; also where he ended his famous rainy night ride in October 1880 through this vast land swarming with Victorio's Apaches.

This ride is another story from this wonderful man, a rancher, who at age 87 in 1939 was living on North Kansas Street, El Paso. Folklore has it that Bates was more than fond of Malissa and I could see even in her late years she was a real "looker."

Priesser later became a mining assayer in Engle, New Mexico, shipping point on the AT&SF railroad. He couldn't have said it better when he said, "There she was, Malissa's two little white hands - gloves off - working this big six-gun like a man."

Malissa always carried two six-shooters in her handbag and a Derringer strapped to her leg while traveling between her Houses in Santa Fe, Socorro and Silver City. When asked why, she always replied, "Where's there's gold, there has to be guns." Malissa was a good woman for her time.

Las Palomas, N.M.T. Here operated the most notorious dealer in contraband — selling guns and ammo to the Apaches during the outbreak of Chief Victorio from the Mescalero Reservation in 1879-'80. Shown here is Juan Felano's store on the east side of the compound; the gate being near the southeast corner, showing the nearby river.

CONTRABANDISTOS

As I stood among the graves in front of the old church a half-mile northwest of old Palomas (9 miles south of T or C, in 1927); here where, Estanesloa continued his search; I thought of the children slaved, the women ravaged, and the men mutilated and scalped in that Apache holocaust of 1879-80.

Palomas was a tiny, walled-in village with outlying fields, cattle, a trade center, and a traveler's delight. Tiny, unafraid, centered here in this turbulent Apache land, where to survive meant "getting along" any possible way — even if by trading in that early (1860) day prudently, if possible, with profit—hence the title CONTRABANDISTOS, traders in contraband. One of such prospered in Palomas, another in nearby Canada Alamosa (Monticello) near the Warm Springs Apache Reservation, while others —Mexican villages with less military protection, were plagued with the scalping knife at their throats.

It is, and always has been, especially since the scalp-bounty years of the 1830's and 40's in northern Chihuahua — trading one's blood for another's silver. The church

84

The waters of Caballo Dam creeping upon Las Palomas in 1942.

was against it, yet helpless to do anything about it.

Then Estanesloa motioned me to an unmarked cairn, saying, "Thees ess eet! Thees ess heem — Juan Felano!" with a certain amount of middle-age pride for being one of the few who, as a boy, watched his father and others of Loma Parda bury the twenty men, three women, and two children of the massacred wagon train — just nine miles south of where we stood (see Story). This is the same Palomas where Juan Felano was the "John Doe" trader of contraband, over whose business door — in brazen Spanish (the Apaches' written language) — were these words: *Rifles y cartoches para vender en plata.* (Rifles and cartridges for sale in Mexican silver). Rifles selling for $17.00 in Silver City went for $100.00. Cartridges costing a nickel for $1.00. A $300.00 purchase of .45-70 cartridges netted $6000 profit. A bountiful supply of the Apaches' favorite rifle, the cavalry carbine, existed all over the Southwest, but "getting" them got "sticky."

One old Dona, the proverbial black shawl over her head, treading the Palomas road churchward after she accepted a ride one Sunday in 1929 surprisingly answered my question in the best of English, "Juan (Felano) always gave generously on Sundays to the passing priests (from Janos to Santa Fe) and of his best wines."

The American officers, not knowing the meaning of the words, passed through his portal without looking up. They bought eagerly and thirstingly of Juan's cool dollar-a-bottle beer.

How many of these dollar-cartridges went into the bodies of the 5 massacred at Loma Parda, the 8 at Lloyd's Ranch, the 10 on the Jarralosa, and the 14 Mexican farmers from lower El Paso Valley (west of Magdalena Gap) among the others, totalling around two hundred, is not known. Ambush of travelers, freighters, prospectors, or better still, any army pack mule or freight wagon with ammo was preferred to Juan Felano's blackmail prices. The military scouted the "Juan's" to ascertain strength, position and areas of likely ambush. When Chief Victorio came into Canada (just below Ojo Caliente) with a gold Mexican cigar holder dangling around his neck, the Trader then knew business would soon be picking up.

While querying a folklorist in Monticello in 1929, he put it this way, "Does one die more easier or queeker with a neekel cartocha than weeth '*un para un peso*' (one for a dollar)?"

I answered, "I have no way of knowing."

He shot back sharply, "Too bad you were not one of theem, you say, CON-TRA-BAN-DIS-TOS!"

I did not find out until later that he was a local trader's grandson, high in political circles.

An aerial shot looking Southeast and down river. Rectangular markings show the old walls and the adjacent stock corrals on the east side. The small square is where the Old John Cross (Las Palomas Land and Cattle Company) stood, branding some 10,000 calves in good seasons.

The Southwest corner as it appeared in 1927 thru 1940, before the Reclamation Service bulldozed the walls down.

The Southeast corner as it was after the entrance was made in the west wall, opening across the Silver City-Santa Fe road after 1870.

This old church stood across the road going northward to Santa Fe.

This color illustration is the old road some 9 miles south of Las Palomas. The women and children in the surrey trailing the train (far left) were buried beside the old road. The graves were still visibly marked in September, 1927. This road was moved west from near the river bed in the 1930's.

THE LOST WAGONS

Only the old Paisanos of Apache Land remembered or cared — I have skimmed off the brush and eliminated the Caballo Lake that you might see 103 years ago — about what happened between Hatch and T or C to a southbound wagon train of 12 or more wagons, 15-20 men, 3 women and several children who were burned as a pyre on their ambushed wagons by 40 Mescalero Apaches in March of 1880.

Many years of research, including a trip to the National Archives, have produced no names — nothing.

Mostly folklore by the Paisanos who were at the burial — Anastasio, Angel, Trujillo, Madrid, and Madre Maria Medica (the medicine mother and practicing mid-wife — comadre — and home doctor to all young wives with their first-born from Angostura to San Jose. She, who had lost her young husband to the Apache near Janos, was now traveling with a young French priest northward to her relatives at Santa Fe.

The Apaches killed the priest for his hat (see Apache wearing hat) and left her stranded in Las Palomas.

Some folklorists have it that it was the will of God. Others added that the Priest should have been traveling southward to Chihuahua for his sacraments, instead of northward with such a young attractive widow. With that many nights on the trail, he could easily lose his vows faster than he lost his hat. Many of the old male Paisanos — who would sit in the twilight, smoking and dreaming of younger days — would agree

The wagons were strung out from the water's edge (as shown) to the foreground oil drum. The woman firing on the Apache (center) (p. 88) was actually in the first wagon at the drum. Her baby (she birthed just after) was buried just to the right of the drum, said Madre Maria; old and grey, from Santa Barbara and Colorado (Rodey), on my first trip to Hot Springs (Truth or Consequences), as told me in the fall of 1927, as she was catching a ride from Hot Springs back to Colorado. When the car passed the spot, she said in Spanish, "WAIT!" All 5 of us got out and saw History at its best — first hand. (She died; a few years later, but not before giving me her story.)

to a man that under such conditions they wouldn't mind losing a hat or two.

On page 87 and shown in the upper left is a canvas-topped two-seated light rig with one of four horses shot down as it made a run-back from the ambush. Two women and the children were buried in a single grave off the road. On a replenished wooden headboard, on the anniversary date of 1927, appeared these words — "*Las Mujeres y Ninos*" (The Women and Children). It is believed that Madre Maria Medica in her passing through the area kept up this grave as she did the one of the pregnant woman — shown here firing her husband's rifle at one of the mounted Apaches. No one escaped a Nana ambush.

In which of the remains of the burned-out wagons was this woman's husband? Madre Maria said she was buried alone with her newborn baby that lived long enough — squalling loudly — for an Apache to pick it up by the heels and walk over to a wagon wheel.

By 1929, the area was a scattering of low, hardly-discernible, earthen mounds. Waxed paper flowers appeared annually at the graves until the early 1930s when the road was moved west from the river. By 1932, the travel had ceased on the old road and with it passed Madre Maria. Francisco Madrid passed away some ten years later at age 94 in a one-room adobe in Colorado (Rodey). With them went the last of the old paisanos — an era of who remembered and who cared? Without them, there would be no story.

By 1939, the rising Caballo waters were creeping northward, clutching at and relegating most of the area to a watery oblivion. Today, July, 1987, this entire road from Palomas to Caballo Dam is covered by water — the gravesites lost forever.

Footnote: I have the legal location of their graves but they will not be revealed. Let these souls rest in peace as they wanted to be left alone. (Believed to be a Pennsylvania religious sect.)

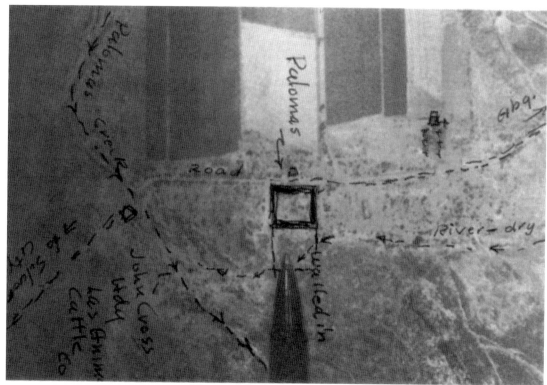

Upper right in the aerial photo: a later church and yard
where (probably) some of the early graves were moved. The
old church is shown across the road to the left of the walled-in
compound. The river portion, in this photo, is dry and under
the pencil pointing to the right center.

Credit for the aerial base: SCS-USDA District Office.

The tree (in the old road
coming out of the river
bottom) is where the surrey
turned back and made its
run for Palomas, according
to Madre Maria. The last
wagon was just climbing out.
(Apaches set good traps)

The color illustration: on the center horse are Private George F. Allen and Private John E. Simmons, from Company "L" of Captain Curwin B. McLellan, Sixth Cavalry, deserting at Canada Alamosa (near present Monticello, NM) in March, 1880. I kept the scatter stones (their only marker after 1927) placed on their graves until covered by the Caballo Dam waters in 1988-9. These two, and the baby in LOST WAGONS, are a few of the graves "watched" for more than 60 years until completely obliterated by "progress," (The Caballo Dam.)

THE DESERTERS

The Apache at center left is holding up a Cavalry Carbine. The Deserter, on the black horse, is bluffing with an empty .44 Colt as they leave the road for higher ground from the ambush site (distant center) where the other Deserter lost his horse and arm to Apache fire.

The deserters had been riding alertly along the road, (west of present day Caballo Lake), watching more to the rear for the Cavalry than for Apaches, waiting in the ravine ahead.

Sun-up and freedom from soldiering — the young romantics' thoughts of the up-coming brown-eyed senoritas lurking in the cantinas of the gold mines in the security of Chihuahua, deadened their awareness to the Mescaleros plaguing the road from Socorro to the mines of Silver City in 1880.

The price of passage through Apache land was high for these two.

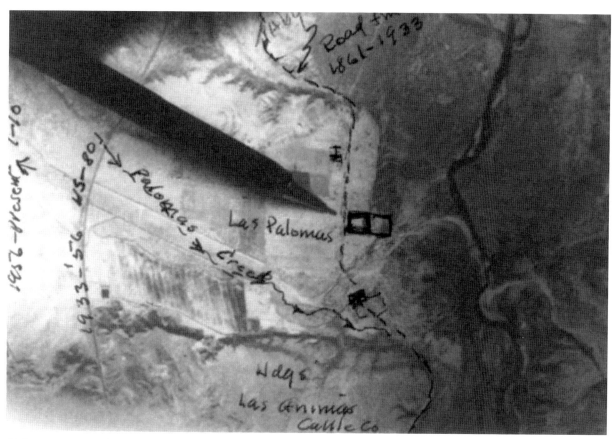

Palomas at pencil point is where the deserters traded their military carbines for cash and their service .45 pistols for civilian .44 cal. revolvers. They lived about three hours after the trade and 12 miles down the road to Mexico.

Beyond this point, 400 yards, the valiant horse went down — ran his heart out. Sixty yards farther on scrambled the Deserters from the pile-up — for their final and inevitable climb.

One deserter, crazed and badly wounded, did crawl 30 yards farther on as if in vain hope he might somehow reach his "Kingdom" in Chihuahua.

Valiant men in death almost always do. It's their way of saying "goodby." Old Indian fighters used to say it's the only way — the "gutty way to go!"

Anastacio from Loma Parda, passing shortly after, saw the stripped and mutilated bodies and spread the word northward to Cuchillo.

FOOTNOTE: The deserters' names could faintly be seen in the late 1920's on weathered headboards that soon went for campfire. My stored records from 1912 through 1937 were vandalized and destroyed during WWII.

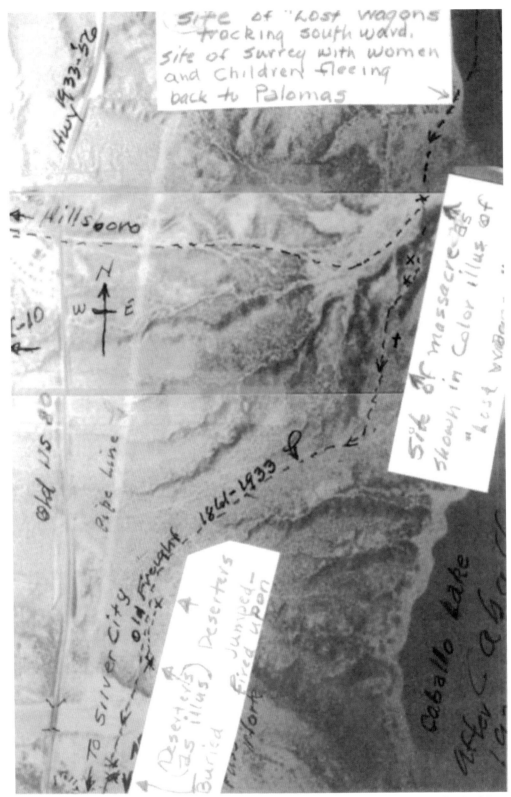

Text visible on the aerial photo (as note markings):

Hwy 1933-56

Site of "Lost Wagons tracking southward. Site of surrey with women and children fleeing back to Palomas

Hillsboro

N
W — E

I-10

Old US 80

Pipe Line

Silver City
Old Freight — 1861-1933

Site of massacre as shown in color illus. of "Lost wagon..

To Silver City

Deserters (as illus) Buried

Deserters fired upon jumped upon

Caballo Lake after Caballo

Why this aerial photo is so important: to the right is the Caballo waters. To the left, the (first) old road in dotted line. Second road left, was used from about 1933-56. The present I-10 farther to the left, and not shown. The present state road to Hillsboro crosses I-10 to the left of where it crosses U.S.-80.

The upper three "X's" bracket the wagon train massacre in story 28. The lower three: the upper "x" where the first horse was shot down. The second went down at second "X", and the graves are at the lower, third "X", as illustrated.

Aerial Photo: Courtesy of SCS-USDA, Department of Interior.

92

Ft. Craig, between mail box and Rio Grande River. Paraje, the river crossing, to the right, since Onate's time, 1598. North end of the Jornado del Muerto. (Journey of the Dead).

SNAKE IN THE BOX

The acting young commanding officer at Ft. Craig, a major, rode over to the reservation at Ojo Caliente (50 miles SW of Craig and 43 miles NW of T or C) in 1876 and told the Apaches that if they didn't stay on the reserve and quit raiding, "trading their loot from Mexico for contraband in the United States (guns and ammo), he would take their horses."

Tough! thought the Apache. "But the Mexicans have many horses and mules and the White Eyes (Americans) have many guns."

But when he added "impound their 'work horses' (squaws)," that called for a decision and a reply. The Apache had no written language. Trade was done in Spanish, which they spoke well. They needed no whiskey. They had their native Tezwin, made from the abundant sotol or agave. Tezwin would put an Apache on a killing "high" quicker than Mexican tequilla and gut-rot whiskey, combined. But their "work" horses? The squaws took care of all their needs while jumping back-and-forth — jumping across the Mexican border — depending on the soldier's and the side that was the angriest.

J.W. Crawford (scout), at his sutler store at Ft. Craig, after 1880

Courtesy of his sister. Socorro, NM, 1933

Nothing could be more stupid than international law when it came to chasing Apaches.

The impounding of their squaws demanded an answer. One with teeth in it. Teeth such as a rattlesnake's fangs.

The Craig mail orderly would go for the mail-box before dawn, after the Santa Fe midnight stage had passed. Most orderlies' minds, at that hour, would be on beer and nearby Socorro senoritas.

Once he opened the box lid, he would about have time to reach the Officer-of-the Day's quarters and on to the infirmary to the doctor, asleep, before this "dream" faded into death.

This story came to me from an old Apache on the San Carlos Reservation in 1934-35, during my travels crossing the reserve between Globe and Safford, Arizona.

I heard a similar story, at Socorro in 1933, from "Captain" Jack Crawford, who scouted out of Ft. Craig in the Victorio Campaign of 1879-80, who was also a sutler at the Post until it's closing.

Crawford dressed as he scouted into Mexico after Apache Chief Victorio in 1880.

Looking north and approaching the real "Stairway to the Gods (Apache gods)." Deadman's Mine has hung tenaciously on Eyebrow Ledge since Spanish times (1822) and on the west side of the Caballos Mountains, 70 miles north of Las Cruces, New Mexico.

The Spanish ships lost much of the gold to the hurricanes in the Gulf, where wooden-hulled sailboats were tossed helplessly about as if they were peanut shells in a modern clothes washer.

DEAD MAN'S MINE

This story was almost 100 years old when I first heard it from Natividad Padilla in front of his mud-chinked, juniper-post jacal on Whiskey Creek, south of Ft. Bayard, N.M. in 1938. He said he was born in Janos, Mexico 108 years ago and his father, he called him *"El Senor,"* was head arriero, or *El Capitan* to a pack train of 100 Mexican mules packing hi-grade ore from El Cobre (copper mines at Santa Rita) to Corralitos and Chihuahua City via Janos. Mules bred in the fields of Janos, raised on mesquite beans; corn fed only when packing two mochas (cow-hide bags) of hi-grade ore slung across an "A" frame or sawbuck pack saddle — 75 pounds to the side.

Shown here is El Senor's pack train "tip-toeing" down the west side of the Caballos — down the stairway to the Apache Gods. In some places, their forelegs stiffened like rods and their rear ends slid on their hocks. One false step and the

A close-up of the mine on Eyebrow ledge.

ore scatters to the chasm bottom and the mule went for coyote bait. But the train must keep going — lest some lurking Apache above had rock rollin' on his mind.

Natividad showed me a small, very old painting of his father on a grullo mule done by another amateur in Chihuahua City. A man of the 1830 period — firm in heavy beard, a large hat of beaver — turned down, and of snowshoe shape with the boot on top to accept the long black hair, tied in back with a red ribbon. A jacket of chewed deer skin, the fringes frayed and some missing — as sometimes used in haste to wad a muzzle loading rifle. The breeches tight at the buttocks, flared at the bottoms, where once bells might have jingled in corral dust or jangled over fandango floors. Spurs of copper and soft iron, wrought from the furnaces of Corralitos — partially hidden by one concha-stud tapadero. A Hawkins rifle of maple stock and a lock partially hidden by the hand.

During the high Spring winds, the beaver hat went into the bedroll and a red scarf bound the hair snugly to the head, knotted in the rear.

From Janos to El Cobre was almost three times the distance from El Cobre to El Rey (the King's mine — an "Eagle's Nest" on the west side of the Eyebrow Ledge far above the river and nine miles below T or C, N.

The Palomas river crossing was at the future Las Palomas (1860), the first crossing for El Senor's only trip - with a year's production of El Rey's hi-grade, yet to be challenged by the Apaches, although they watched from far off Ojo Caliente.

From El Rey to El Cobre, the worst mule trail then known. The river was crossed, with ore bags, only during the dry June season and under the best conditions.

Then the ore would lay in wait at El Cobre for the August-September rains. For only then the spring seeps (camp sites) between the Divide and Ojo del Perro (Dog Springs) would come "alive." The travel time from Cobre to Janos was half as long as to El Rey, all flat and Apache infested country.

Was it the second trip to El Rey? Natividad does not remember. His father, Apache wise, after one trip gave up on the mine and the "stairway" as a trap for ambush.

The Apaches "took" the next train of arrieros at daylight as they were loading their mules at the mine. They feasted on mule meat while watching their victims slowly starve — thirsting for the river water below.

LEE NATIONS, an early-day cowboy with the John Cross, Palomas Outfit (1880-90's). With his son Emmett and me, Lee showed us the mine on Eyebrow Ledge. "Smart cowboys never rode up there," he said "Only dumb arrieros on mules, driving mine workers (jail prisoners) with a bull whip at their backs."

The old men of Palomas used to tell how the priests traveling from Janos to Santa Fe would stop and say prayers for the arriero's relatives. From the Apaches trading at Janos, they learned how the arrieros would look down on the river screaming deliriously to be thrown off the mountain. As they weakened they were made to crawl back into the mine, the tunnel sealed by large boulders, an appeasement to their Gods.

The story tellers used to say on stormy nights the ghosts of the arrieros would come out on Eyebrow Ledge begging the Palomanians to come up and unseal the mine and let the arrieros go back to their wives in Janos.

Jim Moffett, a Kingston miner, said it was not until the late 1870's that two Irishmen prospectors from Lake Valley found the tunnel. They cleaned out the skulls and snakes and started a vertical shaft to

reach the ore vein below and near the river's edge. But that is another story.

Father Lorenzo was at Palomas when the miners' mules came in. He went immediately to "Ghost Mine on Deadman Mountain" to say their last rites (as folklore grew, new names came to old places).

Lorenzo was as bald as a cue ball. The Apaches tried to scalp him, gave up in disgust and threw him into the shaft with the miners.

Later, Colonel Hopewell, manager for the Animas Cattle Company — branding the "John Cross" — whose headquarters was on the acequia madre just below Palomas, heard of the mine in the 1890's and sent cowboys with giant powder charges to close the shaft "before some deer-hunting, homesteader fool finds it and breaks out with a rash of gold fever," said the late Lee Nations, a Texan, who worked for the "John Cross."

FOOTNOTES: This story was made of three parts, by three tellers. Their pictures taken over 44 years ago; and older were the pictures of Palomas, although it was not there during El Senor's time — only a river crossing. For aesthetic and other reasons, I have altered the north peak and mule trail. Palomas is too close, but since it was not there, it does not matter.

Shown here is the village of Leasburg, as it was in 1879, two miles southeast of Fort Seldon between the present railroad and the valley proper. (Railroad came in 1881).

A WARM NIGHT IN LEASBURG

In front of Adolph Lea's Saloon. Lea, an ex-Army man, dealt in saloon trade—catering to all with hard money—soldiers, travelers, freighters, cowboys—anyone with a lust for whiskey and women. In 1869 there were four saloons, gradually drying up and finished with the coming of the railroad. Shown here are three of John H. Slaughter's cowboys who were holding a herd of 2000 cattle while waiting for the river to run down, and naturally, gyrated to the saloon. Also, a favorite spot for the Troopers in Blue. The three Troopers had been out to Shedd's San Augustine Springs Ranch (now headquarters of Jim Cox Ranch), looking for some oxen reportedly run off by the Apaches. Before long the War between the States broke out all over again, Texas fashion. The madam in the background is shown sending her fleetiest "girl" down the street to another saloon where she had been sending free drinks all afternoon to a couple of Deputies from Las Cruces and Dona Ana. The help never came, for the two Deputies had been discussing violently, all afternoon, the affairs of state and were now snoring under a cloud of flies. Flies, they say, are fond of

warm beer and sweet wine. The cowboys left the saloon to the Troopers — and one to be buried in the little cemetery just north of Fort Seldon. This story was going around in the area after 1884, according to the late Bill McCall, who ranched in the canyon west of the Fort. The Trooper was accorded a full military burial, with honors, and died in action and in the service of his country.

The post complement in May 1879, consisted of one Lieutenant and twelve enlisted men.

John Slaughter, this May 3, 1879, was not with his herd at the time and probably was down at Las Cruces enjoying the comforts of the Armijo Rooms or Amador Hotel. He was recently married, in 1879, in Tularosa, to a young girl, Viola Howell, age 15-16. Now at the age of 38 years, he chose to spend more time in his spring buggy than on his horse, in the dust of the herd. He was on his way to establishing the famous San Bernardino Ranch south of Douglas, Arizona. Viola was the girlfriend of Bob Beckwith killed in the Lincoln County War of July, 1878 at Lincoln Plaza.

This coach, from Santa Fe, is departing the Headquarters Building about midnight.

THE COLONEL'S LADY

It's a long day that begins at 0200 A.M. in the morning; the moon is out and the horned owls are hooting far across the river, above the cottonwoods, high up in the stony crags of Mount Robledo, and there is that ever present "smell" of Apaches in the air.

The post is all astir. The candle lamps were lit in the enlisted men's barracks an hour before they started winking in the maid's room, adjacent to her lady's in the colonel's quarters. Soon she was a busy shadow passing from room to room like an ant plying from honey to hole, for it takes a lot of fussing to ready her ladyship for nearly 275 miles of New Mexico and Arizona road dust — all the way to Ft. Lowell (Tucson) — two days and a night of dusty jolting through Apache land, for a wedding of the colonel's niece, and for lady gossip, band music, lemonade on the veranda, and to touch again fresh linen, crystal, and Wedgwood. It had been many long months of frontier tedium since duty on the Potomac.

The moon hangs high behind the two-story adobe headquarters building, the flagstaff in the parade square with useless cord and pulley, for it is yet four hours before reveille and the sergeant-major has already gone through the barracks searching every trooper's duffel for the best equipment for show and duty — a blanket, canteen,

99

The same coach reported as departing at sunup, both stories described as departing to the west. The latter version is shown approaching the ferry. Some of the advance guard have already crossed the river (Rio Grande about 10 miles above Las Cruces, NM).

cartridge belt, side arms and carbines, straight-heeled boots, shined — the best campaign hats — if too large can be sized to fit by turning sidewise that will, in the dark, pass any lieutenant's inspection, and stay there with "crupper," even at the command, "Load carbines — at the gallop!"

By 0200 A.M., Sgt. O'Day was already rousting out, by shake and name, the best of his better troopers, for escort duty — a slight tinge of soldierly pride in his barking Irish brogue, followed by a demandingly firm reminder to his young saloon-brawling hot-heads — his best horsemen and finest marksmen - that their duty was first to the colonel's lady, then God and country.

You can bet O'Day's escort will go into Fort Cummings, a credit to any campaign colonel, and hopefully the succeeding relief escorts will be the same — in respect to her ladyship. Then on to Bowie and into Lowell — as tried troopers daring the lusty Apache into action - not as parade soldiers from the department of the Rio Grande.

The National Mail and Transportation coach rolls up the dusty street between the Headquarters and Q.M. corrals washed in moonglow — dignifiedly quiet — with veteran Simeon Elby on the box see-sawing the reins to six nail-hard mules with Bustin' Baker riding shotgun with a sawed-off double Fargo, loaded with 00 buckshot, who reportedly had covered himself with glory (Southern Cause) at Antietam and who casually walked off the field of conflict at Appomattox — all the way out to Ft. Leavenworth where he caught a bull-team to Santa Fe. It was actually there in a card game he lost his eye proving the knife was faster than the derringer and now was the stage company's fastest man with the double Fargo by as much time as the wink of an eye.

Standing in the Headquarters' shadows are the adjutant and his lady and Maria with her "hanky" at the ready, and the sergeant-major giving a respectful salutation to a former warrior from the Great Cause (war records — like birth marks — are never lost or forgotten) and the old sergeant can now assure his colonel (brevet), whom he served with through the Campaign of the Shenandoah Valley, that his lady

Looking south, Ft. Selden in 1900.

is in good hands, at least through Magdalena Gap, Goodsight, and Cook's Canyon, on to the Timmer House in Silver City and possibly as far west as Knight's Ranch and Doubtful Canyon Station.

Coming out the corral, past the Quartermaster's quarters is the escort lieutenant, hoping action will give him his captain's bars before forty, to lead the coach up river to the ferry. Here the sgt.-major had made a midnight inspection of the ropes and rigging with 12-year old Ferry-Master Caesar Brock, stepson of civilian Royal Yeamans, post butcher and ferryman — just after the dispatch rider from Ft. Craig had come in — stomping more Paraje River Crossing-mud from his boots than dust from Martin's Well — with the word the river had crested there two days before.

And so it's on to the ferry at the San Pedro Crossing — if Cochise's renegades haven't cut the ropes. Then it's only 40 miles and a "whoop and a holler" into Lowell — to a Lady's holiday and a ball at the post more to a lady's liking.

And so the old colonel, who has given his years to the service, will go back to his quarters — to his pipe and dog — assured, with his permission, that the Adjutant and the Sergeant can run the post.

There to dwell on his up-coming retirement along the tide waters of the Potomac — of campaigns in the past— knowing well that his young wife, Betty, — the army brat — will somehow get through with her luck and a few soldiers — come Apache Hell or high water.

FOOTNOTE: If my memory serves me correctly, there was a retired sergeant who coached the Ft. Bliss Cavalry Troop baseball team from 1926-29, whose father was a Top Sergeant at Ft. Stanton in the early 1880's and who knew the Seldon-Lowell.

Fort Seldon looking south, during re-building in 1975.

The mud wagon loaded with Xmas baggage in front of the Hotel Victoria (Wilson's), where it was reported that Fred Mister was on the box with the ribbons (wrong). Jim and Mike Moffett assisting the big Concord's passenger, whose mere presence put "electricity" in the air after 43 miles from the steam-cars at Goodsight Station — through the snows, hills, mountains and canyons.

Second floor, third window from the right is the man who changed her life. He's upper class, not common variety, as on the ground floor.

THE LADY-IN-RED

       Shown here is the driver on the "box" handling the ribbons to the mudwagon having just arrived in front of the new brownstone Wilson Hotel, one jump ahead of the big Concord, from which walked the Lady-in-Red, on a snowy evening before the grand opening of "Pretty" Sam's Casino. It was a Christmas to be remembered in this silver-crazed bonanza of a mining camp — Kingston, New Mexico Territory, 1883.

       The Lady-in-Red put "electricity" into the air, and into every living man-jack of a man with goatee or horsetailed beard, for the land may have been booming with silver, but there was a dearth of pretty ladies with class in this land, the one thing seldom off a miner's mind while he "dreams" and blasts his way hopefully into bedrock.

Looking northwest over Kingston in the mid- 80's. The Victorio Hotel is in lower right foreground. Sam's Casino is probably the center of the three large buildings, on the right of the street near the left center of the photo.

The photographer appears in the left center foreground. It would be nice to know who he was; I'm sure he had something to do with making this a pleasurable event.

Credit to the Rio Grande Historical Collection, New Mexico State University.

The lady stepped lively, her nose elevated, in a way of setting the "hawkers" — leering from the hotel windows — to thinking she could be straight down from Laura Evan's Tenderloin Queen, or Jennie Roger's House-of-Mirrors on Holladay Street in Denver City.

Saloon talk, the miner's telegraph, had it that a certain San Francisco investor of mines, banks, and railroads had been seen recently in the best Parlors along busy Holladay Street. Thereafter their "Long-Stemmed-Rose" had disappeared.

The Lady-in-Red glided into the Wilson (later Victorio) as smoothly as a snake into water, knowing full well that every man there, who had ever seen a horse race, was comparing her long, slender legs to that of a race mare prancing past the grandstand. And, if they be right, only the most wealthy developers of San Francisco and Denver City could afford her— for this Lady hadn't forgotten the late war!

The first Lucy family settled on the upper reaches of the Tombigbee on the Alabama side, shortly after the Indian Wars. Their grandmother, Lena, settled a "ways up" the Tombigbee from my great-grandparents in Fayette County. The mother soon became a young widow with two small boys, one of which was my great uncle William Shadrock Humphries, Lieutenant of the Southern Cavalry, who was bushwhacked in the late war year of 1864.

Then, sometime-cousin Lena was developing into a beautiful long-stemmed variety of an Alabama rose. It was rumored she was a teenager who could clear a cotton cart without breaking daylight in an English sidesaddle. Then the ravaging scum came through — raiding the outer fringes, far out and beyond the military skirmishers of Grant's approved, Sherman's "burning" march-to-the-sea. My great Uncle William (home on convalescent leave) put Cousin Lena (after the attack on her) into a canoe and

Sadie Orchard sometime after acquiring her husband (left). He was a man reportedly good with horses and stage coaches and the photo depicts them sometime before she shot at him and ran him off (a boozer).

Mina Lucy, in summer side-saddle clothing. Gift from Sadie Orchard (Hillsboro, 1929-41).

shoved her out into the Sipsey, saying, "Go on down to the Tombigbee, on to Mobile — nights only — on the river. Take the night-run — the mudscow to Nu'awleens."

Lena was a "kissin" cousin — his last. The bushwhackers got Humphries the next day.

Her brother Bob said Auntie Jones, when she heard that Cousin Lena had been ravaged, called Grant names — words he had never heard before. She just threw a fit! Eyes flashing, frothing at the mouth. Had the South another infantry division like her, the war would have ended at Second Manassas or surely with Shiloh or Chicamauga.

In New Orleans the trail led to Bourbon Street, then on as a hostess on a river-gambling boat, the Delta Queen or the Robert E. Lee, up to St. Louis. Then from there, west on the steam cars out to the end of the line at La Junta. Then the stage on into Denver City. A Kingston mining man, on seeing her dance at Sam's Opening, Christmas '83, said he was positive he'd seen her dance on top of Jennie Roger's tables in Denver City. (The Lucy's admitted to being parlor dancing people — not on table tops.)

Few today remember the Kingston's Whittlers Club of 1928 to 1938, or the "ins" and "outs" of this early silver camp, save those that lived it in the turbulent years from '82 to the silver bust of '92. According to the club, the best time to remember the

Narrator's grandsons near the grave of Mina Lucy as pointed out by Jim and Mike Moffett in 1929-37 (in Kingston Cemetery).

beginning was the opening of Sam's Casino, a year after the smallpox plague of November-December, 1882. But what a year, after the beginning, as many will find in McKenna's excellent classic, THE BLACK RANGE TALES.

From as far north as Socorro — southward to Chloride, the Placers of Gold Hill, Hillsboro, Lake Valley, and on down this ore-laden Black Range to the "Gopher Holes" of silver called Cooke's Camp, to the railroad at Deming Town, saloon talk (the core of

Mina Lucy walked thru door, near the three, Xmas Eve in 1883. Original building had three stories as shown in color illustration.

the Whittlers Club) had it that the Lady-in-Red had been seen in each camp. "Such seeing," huffed Billy Bates, who drove the stage between Silver City and Georgetown and reported, "She was a 'Looker' all right, just waiting out there, as in every prospector's dream, for the big "strike" that would bring her into reality."

Frank Priesser, co-packer and scout with Bates during the Apache Wars of '79 and '80, said in his quiet way, "She, the Lady-in-Red, couldn't have been better known in such a short time had she come by swimming down the river at flood stage. Then, as sure as shootin', ten cowmen would have happily drowned —plunging their horses into the raging river at Tonuco Trail Crossing — just to save her."

But she did come down from Denver on the railroad, changing from the steam cars at Goodsight Siding to the Kingston stage. Some swore it was the train whistle, and not her scarlet coat, that sent the prospector's burro bucking off into the greasewood, banging coffee pot and frying pan, braying and kicking to the high heavens. "The only red that burro had ever seen," said Jim Drummond of the Club, "was on an Apache head-band, and then just missed being Apache jerky."

The Lady-in-Red's date for Sam's Opening was a gambler that didn't show, so she came on the arm of a nephew of one of four "colonels." They seemed more plentiful after the killing of the War — just sprouted like mushrooms.

The lady came not as one of "Dog Face" Connaly's Girls of the Orpheum or Shady Lane, as told by some.

None of the Lucy family will ever know if Cousin Lena was Kingston's Mena Lucy, for all who knew Lena have long passed on. But does it matter? To me it does, for I have dug into past illusions, fantasies and most of the folksy folklore of this wild and turbulent land. All the facts, the history, even down to Ellen Garrett's theory of clairvoyance (the communication with the dead), that these two — Lena and Mena — might possibly become one, the Lady-in-Red, in the hereafter.

A big mining man from San Francisco left Kingston for the new strikes at Chloride, Fairview and Winston, and was later seen taking the mudwagon (mail hack) eastward to Cuchillo, crossing the River at Fiest's Ferry on to the railroad at Engle Station.

106

Gig Griffith standing on site of Sam's Casino. Looking east, 1982.

Fred Mister, hosting Gov. Merritt Cramer Mechem (NM) in Sadie's Orchards Mountain Pride stage, near Oak Creek Station on way from the railroad via Lake Valley to Hillsboro. Sadie said the Governor was outside the coach but not too far away.
Gift from Sadie Orchard.

The saloons in Kingston had it the Lady-in-Red also took the stage to Hillsboro and Lake Valley, and was seen boarding a club car on the main line at Goodsight Siding. And, was never seen thereafter.

Fantasy, folklore, history or facts beyond the average imagination, make up Cousin Lena. But as Sadie Orchard, of Hillsboro, long-time Madam and owner of a stage line, hotel, saloon and a couple of "Houses," and oft times known as Sadie-the-Lady, for the fine clothes she wore, said, "Spell it Mina Lucy," pointing to the back of the picture. "Just change it a little, see," and gave me one of her most cherished pictures.

Later, on one of our last days out to the cemetery on the ridge behind Kingston, Sadie knew she was looking for the last time. When I asked,

"Sadie, what name shall I put on the picture - her married name, I mean?" She fixed me in one of her torch-like stares and said nothing, for I understood well.

In 1938 Jim Moffett showed me the grave site, long after the marker had been removed by her daughter and taken back to San Francisco and thrown into the Bay. Jim said he was back in Pennsylvania when Sadie and Fred brought her here for burial.

Out of respect for her late husband, the train stopped in the night at Goodsight Siding (Nutt) where stage driver Fred Mister was waiting for the coffin. The Mountain Pride (now in a Santa Fe museum) recently removed from its Hillsboro storage, stood with six well-groomed horses with plumes and in newly-shined harness. Fred would have taken the

107

Kingston, NM. Jim Moffett is left of telephone pole (in the big hat on the right). In buckboard is Col. Hopewell, manager of Las Animas Cattle Company (Brand J+ [John Cross]) in town from Las Palomas (on river).
Gift from Jim Moffett to narrator. Hopewell in small hat.

casket with a cortege befitting a queen through Lake Valley at high noon, and on to Hillsboro, had not the lady written Sadie she wanted to go quietly — on the stage in the night with no "mourning at the bar", to the plot behind Kingston — back to the beginning— the best thing that ever happened to her — back where she met the greatest man in the world.

Fred took the stage through Lake Valley and into Hillsboro in the night, where they held a wake all the next day so that a boy rider on a fast horse could take the word to the few remaining "gilt-edged" old timers that their "Lady Had Come Home."

The next night Sadie drove the Mountain Pride — with those well enough "who remembered" — with their LADY up the nine miles of the Percha Creek Road to the Kingston Cemetery. Fred later said that every spring flower seemed to stay open in the moon glow that night.

In one of our last conversations, Sadie said, "Don't go swimming in the bay looking for names on the grave marker, for there were only two words on it — A LADY — and the dates. I wouldn't have this fine woman's name desecrated for all the newspaper trash (stories) in the world. Her son was one of the first volunteers in the flying Lafayette Escadrille, and shot down over France early in the war (WWI)."

My Uncle Bill Harris came through Toyah "Cowtown," Texas in 1911 stopping by the ranch.

Here is where I could have heard her "name" while he told of the great San Francisco Fire (he worked for the city), after the earthquake of 1906.

He told of a great lady from Knob Hill, dressed in a plain gingham dress and sunbonnet, who would come down with her driver in a rubber-tired carriage behind a span of white horses to deliver food and help with the needy.

A saloon keeper on Market Street told him she was a lady from "way back," from a mining camp in New Mexico Territory. The name and the territory was meaningless to a boy of four.

Had I known then (in the 1930's) what I know now of my family in Fayette County, Alabama, I'm sure Sadie and I could have done business. She died in 1943 during my WWII years.

And, as I remember back to 1939 in Hillsboro, when Sadie gave me Mena's picture withholding her married name, she said, "If you must write something, say something GOOD, for she was a good woman.

FOOTNOTE: Most of this story came from Jim and Mike Moffett, Mike Drummond, a Mr. Wilson (Victorio Hotel builder); also Uncle Jim McKenna, who I'm sure most all were at the opening of the casino. Why not? Where else was there to go?

Looking northwest across California Street at Grand Central Hotel in which Joel A. Fowler and wife Josie were registered and where Fowler stabbed James E. Cale in the saloon about dawn, Wednesday, November 7, 1883. The building to the right is Socorro National Bank which fronts on Manzanares Street and in which Fowler deposited $52,000 in drafts from sale of his cattle and ranch, the Bear Spring property some 10 miles north of Magdalena. Here, first owner John Miller, with a large family, built a low 4-5 room adobe, surrounding a patio — topped with parapet and slots to discourage raiding Apaches and Navajos.

> *Picture Credit: Edward Bass, photographer, later Joseph Edward Smith's photography and studio which was in front and across the street from the Hotel. This excellent photo, as with many others, depicts the history of Socorro and Magdalena and were the works of Edward Bass, 1880-84, and Joseph Edward Smith, 1884-1908.*

HANGED IN THE SIGHT OF GOD

> *The narrator knowingly acknowledges that certain information appears both in the captions to the illustrations and in the main story. Basically, both are correct. Since so much has been written by some writers as sheer fabrication, a little duplication of fact should not bother the reader.*

This picture-story began at dawn on the 7th of November, 1883, in the barroom of the Grand Central Hotel. As a newcomer, James E. Cale, while assisting in the removal of Joel A. Fowler's six-shooters — still smoking from dancing an old man around the room, was stabbed with a pocket knife by the drunken cowman Fowler.

The only law was Colonel Eaton's "Committee for Safety," a hooded vigilante group of the town's best businessmen.

This barroom illustration shows about what Estevan (then age 10) and his father saw from the back door at dawn in the Grand Central Hotel on 7 November, 1883.

At the bar is Emile Wills. The first man left, in center four, represents Cale holding Fowler's right gun arm, then Reed, then Fowler (short man kicking). Fourth from the left is Collins.

The old man at the center table has been dancing to Fowler's six-gun music. Estevan tried to sell me one of the empty cartridge cases and a copy of the back bar picture while I was living at the nearby Home Court (1933) that was behind and west of Cook's garage, which was on the Hotel site.

Tweed is leaving through bat-wing doors. Brooks, the night clerk, is to his right.

Estevan, age 10, and his father, the hotel janitor, watched the stabbing from the west and back door entrance.

George Cook's father was in the bank next door when Fowler deposited drafts for $52,000 from J. D. Reed, a Ft. Worth buyer of his cattle ranch. Fowler then went to the Sun newspaper to place an ad that any claims against him must be submitted, as he was leaving town soon.

Fowler and his wife — a young, pretty, card-dealing, saloon-trained woman — were staying at the hotel. Shown here, at the bar, is Emile Wils (Wills). From right to left is Cale holding Fowler's right arm. Reed is holding Fowler from the back. On his left arm is Collins, his partner in the bar-room revelry of the evening before. F. M. Tweed is leaving through the bat-winged screen doors for the sheriff. To his right is hotel clerk C. H. Brooks.

At the right foreground table sits a newshawk, sharing a whiskey with a gambler. To their left sits the old man who had been dancing for Fowler.

The room is pictured too wide and the bar should be rotated ninety degrees right.

The street scene on page 112 shows Fowler being escorted from the jail cellar, out the courthouse's back door (south end) to the hanging tree midway between the jail and the Methodist Mission (far left), where a light burns in the parsonage of Preacher Potter, who is up and stirring.

The courthouse was actually 200 feet to the right, and the disarming of the jail guards was done inside, but for aesthetic reasons was illustrated as shown, as was the positioning of Socorro Peak, shown to the right of that photographed by Joseph Edward Smith, an early photographer to whom history owes much.

Famous Death Alley's old adobe wall ran between Park and Grant, later to become Church Street.

"Kiko," a 14-year old apprentice fireman, homeward bound, is standing by the broken ore wagon, having come off the midnight shift (smelter's), and who recognized — by his voice — the merchant-banker Brown, there to guard the south entrance road from Fowler sympathizers.

The men at the tree untangling the rope are Morrison, O'Neal, and Munroe. The man running toward Fowler with upraised arm is his attorney, Niel Field — oft-times reported as being present.

The tall man to his right is Andy McClusky, saloon owner, with the rope just unwound from around merchant Art Goebel's belly.

Fowler did shout and scream when the vigilantes appeared at his cell door. His legs were shackled and he was chained to a stone embedded in the earthen floor. As Fowler crossed the dusty street he pleaded passionately, but as he neared the tree, full realization took over and he changed his tone to that of bravado and jest.

Only a few vigilantes — for their reasons — could "remember" the names of those escorting Fowler. Some thought they were McMahan and A. McDonald, with a third, unnamed, and not shown here.

There have been many variations in describing the jail-to-the-tree scene in its highly-charged atmosphere of intense drama. "Kiko's" word picture of the doctor's buggy racing down Garfield, undistracted by the hanging, was the high point in his story.

The best account of the removal of Fowler's body is in Hardcastle's letter to Kyle Crichton, in which he stated that Sheriff Simpson, he, and three others removed the body at dawn on the 23rd of January, 1884, to Texas Ed Rousseau's plaza saloon, "where it lay in state" under a fog of stale whiskey, "to be viewed by 3000."

Cale died three days after the stabbing and was buried in the Catholic cemetery — today an unmarked grave.

George E. Cook was a boy of 7 running around on the streets picking up all the news on the great events of 1883-4. His father owned the site after the Grand Central burned (1890's). It was Cook's garage east of the Home Auto Court, where I lived in 1933. He led me to the people who were at the stabbing and the hanging. He separated the chaff from the grain, and detoured me from the "Windies."

FOOTNOTES:

This research began in 1927 and lasted through 1949 when most of the old timers were gone. In 1934, while living at the Park Hotel, north of the hanging tree, I surveyed and drove a Model-T axle in the site, which by 1942 had disappeared.

While living at the Home Auto Court, George Cook sent Estevan, then about 60, to my room with an offer to sell an old photo — shown (on page 110) behind the bar — for "train fare back to Los Angeles," and at the

time gave me his version of the stabbing — almost 50 years before — and a .44-40 six-shooter empty brass, one of the eleven he swept up from the bar floor, he said, after the sheriff had taken Fowler to the jail.

While a member of the NM A&M (NMSU) basketball team and on returning from playing NMU, we'd stop at the Socorro School of Mines. That's where the Fowler story got started. It was A. C. Torres, owner of the El Defensor-Chieftain, who led me to "Kiko" and his story.

The hanging scene in moonlight, looking west. From left, C. Brown; next is Kiko; (visible over the broken wheel) and the men at the tree are: Morrison, O'Neal and Munroe. Running in the street toward Fowler is Attorney Neil Field. The tall man to his right would be McClusky, saloon owner. The men shaking down the prison guards (next to the jail—a one-story adobe) would be vigilantes who still do not trust the guards — not until Fowler is dead. On top of the surrounding buildings are vigilantes, guarding against any takeover from Fowler's cronies. In the center street is the doctor leaving the smelter (a midnight accident) for a baby debuting into this sordid world on the eastside of town.

The tiny light in the room behind the Spanish Methodist Church is Preacher Potter stirring in a world past saving. Whether he knew or never wanted to know has never been contested. Fowler was hung until cold-dawn, when they cut him down and displayed him in good Socorro saloon style — in Texas Ed's saloon — under a fog-cloud of stale whiskey. Some say they ran out of whiskey but the bar-keeps just poured five gallons of water into each empty barrel, sloshed it around, and sold it again. The 3000 viewers (reported) just ran over to the bier, looked at Fowler's size five foot in a new pair size ten boots, and ran back to the bar for another shot of that diluted whiskey.

Note: Kiko, a man of 63, back in Socorro in 1933 (visit), helped position some of the named parties in the hanging scene.

Footnotes:

(1) The distance shown from the courthouse to the Hangmen's Tree was compromised to get the courthouse into the illustration. Hangmen's Tree was in Death Alley on a tree-lined ditch that brought spring water down to the town. The Hanging Tree, as shown, should appear about half-way between the courthouse and the Methodist Mission.

(2) One writer, an Englishman, who wrote glowing accounts of the event was proven to be on a boat enroute from England to Socorro County where he ranched. He saw it all. Some "seeing."

(3) Note light in annex room of the Methodist Church.

Socorro stories have it the reverend was aroused by the noise from the courthouse area but elected to return to a warm bed knowing the corpse would need a good refrigeration before lying in state in a saloon where a saturation of pungent whiskey was sure to preserve it to its destination (Ft. Worth, TX).

Credit: Of the many contributors to Fowler's demise, I owe most to: George Cook, Montague Stevens, J. E. Smith (photographer), <u>Reminiscences</u> by C. Potter, A. C. Torres (newspaper editor), and Col. E. W. Eaton's heirs.

Joel A. Fowler on his favorite horse and with his favorite gun, a double barrel shotgun with buckshot in each barrel. One or two six-shooters never conspicuously shown. Fowler, a 5'5", 130 pounds of treacherous, educated (some law), quick as-a-cat and twice as cunning. Small with lots of guts and an eye for beautiful women; offering marriage for fidelity, insanely jealous. A known two-time loser and crazy when drunk. Shrewd in business trades and oftentimes given to civic mindedness. If tampered with (stealing his cattle), would go to any end for restitution. Such is Fowler, who came from a good family in Indiana, reportedly born about 1849.

Credit: Photo made about 1881-3 by Edward Bass, Socorro photographer, who sold his gallery to Joseph Edward Smith in 1884, but continued with very important pictures.

Fowler Ranch site (north of Magdalena). In 1971, first home of John Miller, on north side of Bear Springs arroyo. Fowler bought from Miller and sold to Reed at Ft. Worth. Below the large adobe house (not shown) was the Fowler corral built of juniper post — set like sharks teeth in a row — held his cattle and sometimes others. After his demise, several skeletons were dug up. Miller, a man with a large family, left because of a rash of cattle thefts (miners liked beef).

The Baca Store building, which began about the time of the Fowler event and continued in use through 1971, located near and on a short street running north from the original courthouse and north to the plaza. From the courthouse cellar jail to the hanging tree one would pass to the left of the lower left building. It's doubtful this building was there in January, 1884.

Col. Ethan W. Eaton. Prominent early land and mine owner. Officer in New Mexico Volunteers (Civil War), organizer of vigilantes who instigated the hanging of Fowler and others.
Credit: Palace of the Governors, Santa Fe.

Blazer's Mill — site of the opening fight in the Lincoln County War

You are looking just south from the roadhouse erected by Dr. Blazer (dentist) and rented to Major F. Godfroy, agent for the nearby Apache reservation, who used it also as a Travelers' Inn.

Blazer retained a room as office and post office (at the near left), just behind "Buckshot" Roberts. To the center across the ditch and beyond the trees are the barns and corrals where the 13 "Regulators" had stabled their horses. The Regulators, led by Dick Brewer, were the opposite faction from the posse Roberts served on in the murder of Englishman John Tunstall in the start of the Lincoln County War that February past.

The Regulators were having dinner when Roberts rode past the corrals - not seeing the horses because of the high, slab-sided board fence, tied his mule near the ditch and started to the post office for an expected check in the mail. Dr. Joseph Blazer was feeding the horses when the fighting broke out and remained there (as a smart ex-1st Sgt. of Iowa's First Vol. would).

The log pile where Brewer was killed is in the forefront. The immediate right is the Blazer home. Between the mill and this house ran the road to Las Cruces. The road to the agency and Ft. Stanton ran in front, along the south side eastward to the left.

THE FIGHT AT BLAZER'S MILL

I first heard this story 70 years ago. It wasn't an old story then to two of the on-scene players I met on a snowy December day in 1927, when the N. M. A & M basketball team stopped its two cars to water-up a steaming radiator in a snowstorm at the Blazer sawmill (at the ditch shown here by the trees). Almer N. Blazer, son of the owner, came out to offer assistance. I ran up on the nearby hill to see the graves of the victims of this fight that had been churning over in my mind since 1911. Here is where "Buckshot" Roberts took on Dick Brewer's 13 "Regulators" at high noon, April 4, 1878.

Detail of the opening of the fight from close up and from in front of the post office where Roberts was going.

    Roberts is shown as he rose up from the door step to Blazer's office, where he and Frank Coe had been talking. Coe was trying to convince Roberts to surrender. Bowdre and four of the Regulators came around the building, Bowdre demanding of Roberts "throw your hands up." The results are shown here. George Coe, as he described it, was close behind Bowdre, taking Roberts first bullet after it glanced off Bowdre's belt buckle. Billy-the-Kid shown here running for the protection of the logging wagon — took no active part in the initial firing. John Middleton shown here running toward the wagon (to get behind Roberts) and was shot down there by Roberts.

    Billy-the-Kid, after seeing Robert's six-shooter and belt hanging on his mule's saddle, sneaked along the building wall — out of sight — and fired as Roberts, who jabbed violently — bayonet style — his empty Winchester into the Kid's belly. The Kid's shot went wild, into the door facing, and he ran like a scalded cat.

    Roberts got the door open and found Blazer's Springfield and .45-70 cartridge belt. Wounded, he dragged a mattress to the partially opened door facing the mill.

    There is a good possibility that Waite, Brown, MacNab, and Scurlock were in the initial firing, though only two are shown here. The other six of the thirteen covered the east side. George Coe, stunned by the first shot, ran dazed toward Roberts and around the north end of the building. Frank Coe, (shown here, unarmed, clearing the line of first fire) passed the post office-store front, from the east side, near the kitchen.

    These illustrations were developed from going over the site with A. N. Blazer, who was in and around the building that day, as a boy of 13, smart enough to stay out of sight.

    George Coe, who had a "hand" in the fight, also went over this site showing me where to step the distance, as did Blazer, — from Roberts to Brewer. (A 100 and 120 steps or about a 100 yards — somewhat short of the 250 yards some "Windies" have reported.

Blazer's Mill after a grist mill was added, 1882.

Our next stop was at 4:00 P.M. for lunch at the Bonnell's ranch on the Ruidoso, where George W. Coe, at a vigorous age of 71, came in wearing a snowy sheepskin that covered all but his full graying beard. I had at last found a living hero of my story.

Four hours later, the coach, student manager and six players (the college ran a tight budget) staggered across the N. M. Institute gymnasium floor just as the officials were cancelling the game.

I first started hearing these stories from the cowboys and passersby at Casey's New Mexico Hondo Ranch (the center of the Lincoln County War), coming to their Texas ranch, south of our Nine-Mile which straddled the old Ft. Davis-Ft. Stanton mail road.

These drifting cowboys would turn their saddle horses into our horse trap and "ride" their war stories until they got the wrinkles out of their bellies, then when you showed them a shovel handle their horses would be gone come first daylight thereafter.

With these stories came my first thoughts of the "Fight at the Mill" inquiry, a fascinated boy of four with big ears in Buster Brown boots. Years later, I stood on the spot at the mill site one April 4th with old George Coe, where he stood as young George 54 years before in a cloud of cordite and black powder gunsmoke. He walked from the car saying, "It was right about here — no, right here," and he paced two steps toward where the old foundation of a building

stood —there in the middle of the gravel highway from Las Cruces to Roswell. "I was a farmer of 22 then," he said, "green as spring wheat." Then he paused and ran his tired old eyes of 74 along the foundation to where the door had been; where the wounded Roberts had retreated and fired the last shot of the fight. Then he looked down at the old sawmill door by the logs where Bowdre and Brewer had gone (that day long ago) for a better look at the Robert's door. Bowdre fired over Robert's head as he lay wounded inside the door, watching in pained agony, with Dr. Joseph Blazer's newfound .45-70 Springfield rifle (his Winchester was empty).

Brewer came from the roadhouse by the corrals (below the hill and out of view of Roberts) to the log pile by the mill. Thinking Roberts dead, or about so, Brewer crawled out on a log and after a spell raised his head up like a curious turkey, not sure the "bobcat" was alive or gone. That did it! The top of his head just disappeared.

Old George's eyes went from the log pile back to the graveyard hill as if following Brewer's body, trying to reason the sense of it all. Why the need for why it happened? A tired old man, beginning to stoop, living it over again, in his youth and in his time.

He then looked down upon the ground where he once stood, as if looking for something — something of flesh and bone, a part of him left there years ago. To take it with him wherever you go from

117

here. Back to the hill he looked as if to say in some forgiving way, "Neighbor, I'm glad you stopped me before I fired . . ." For Roberts was a neighbor of Cousin Frank Coe on the Ruidoso, and it was he who, unarmed, sat in the doorway trying to reason Roberts into surrendering.

Andrew L. "Buckshot" Roberts' (sometimes known in Texas as Bill Williams) first shot glanced off Charlie Bowdre's (in red shirt) belt buckle, taking George Coe's trigger finger. Bowdre said later, "I dusted him on both sides." It was the most feared, horrifying wound, an unmercifully slow way to die. This five-foot seven, 140 pounds of sheer guts added 24 more hours onto his 46 years.

Grandma Williams (Mrs. J. W.), our Texas neighbor, died in the early 1920's before I'd found Bill Williams' grave. Grandma, an admitted spy for the Southern Cause, said one time outside Vicksburg, in the dark of the moon, she heard the command, "Halt" and just squatted for a moment with her basket of biscuits — putting her dispatch, rolled tight in fishskin — up where only a woman could best find it, and smiled with a twinkle in her eye.

I knew then she must be kin to this Bill Williams, who left Texas on a half-dead mule, two jumps ahead of a posse; leaving two carpet-baggers, who never seemed to learn you don't walk up and arrest an ex-member of Hood's Brigade, not in Texas — not "in" or "out" of the law.

George Coe in 1940.

Charlie Bowdre, neighbor homesteader to Dick Brewer, killed by Sheriff Pat Garrett (Southeast of Ft. Sumner, December 23, 1880, with his wife and wedding ring purposely showing, a native of San Patricio.

A. N. Blazer in 1939.

Looking east, moon rising. The fire burning out in McSween's home. Time to go, thought Billy- the-Kid, shoving Morris out the back door toward the gate where Morris fell.

THE FIRST TO GO

The First to Go is a picture-story based on what was seen by George Coe from an upper warehouse ventilator behind Tunstall's Store in Old Lincoln Plaza on that fiery night, July 19,1878.

Harvey Morris, shoved out McSween's door by Billy-the-Kid, the first to go (a patsy of the time), drew first fire of the eight eager guns hoping to be the first to put a bullet into the Kid — whose gun they feared most. Morris (as shown) made it to the gate before going down riddled by several shots.

Followed closely by the Kid (before they had time to reload), he leap-frogged over the fallen Morris and disappeared into the underbrush of the acequia and the safety of nearby Bonito Creek.

He was followed closely by O'Follard, who then turned back and became a man among men, no longer a mere boy, not yet 18. He ever-so-gently raised the dying Morris's head, and yet, not one gun fired — not then and after as he more gently laid Morris back down again. He respectfully disappeared into the darkness of the Bonito. What higher honor can a warrior receive?

You are looking west. Here O'Follard is bending over the dying Morris.

This man-boy act should live for always in the memory of man — to be counted among our great — not buried in some forlorn, forgotten grave.

"And who says," in the immortal words of Gene Rhodes, "New Mexico has no heritage!"

The fourth to go was Jim French, bursting out this same door, streaking through the cross-fire, dodging through this yard of deadly fire into the darkened circle of Dolan's men awaiting there, eyes eager and aglow, to shoot down all who remained cowed behind the last of those fire-riddled walls. The last of the McSweens — huddled like sheep before the wolves, so helpless in their final hour.

At this point, George Coe abandoned the warehouse for the safety of the Bonito. To prophesy from here on would be sheer speculation — dare not desecrate the history of that day.

Remarks:
On June 19, 1936, George Coe and I stopped by old Lincoln where this same McSween gate had been, where young Harvey Morris fell that night 58 years before. There old George stood, an old warrior crowding 80 years, and I, concerned, desperately trying to read his thoughts as he went back to age 22. His tired old eyes went down to the ground where Morris had lain, O'Follard bending over him. From there his thoughts drifted back to the adobe wall, some of it still standing; then along where the paling fence once ran and on up to where the gate once stood. Then, there was a long pause, as if he were unraveling the past, but saying nothing, just silently living those days over again. I dared not break his trance, for his world he was now living in was not for me, only his, in his youth.

Then his eyes went quickly out to the old acequia and to the brushy trees along the Bonito, as if he'd found his old comrades waiting out there. Not gone, still living only in a mind far out into the nothingness-of-time, out there where no man can ever bring them back again.

But for sure he was living over again the events in this picture-story, as he had told it many times before, and now on the same spot, I would like

The famous adobe wall behind McSween's from where the Dolan gang massacred some of McSween's men. The chicken house and gate is to the far left.

to believe, was his last trip back into a world gone forever. And I, seemingly, had the experience of being here.

And for all these years since, I've been thinking that, if only for a fleeting moment, Harvey Morris didn't see by the fire-glow the concern on O'Follard's bent-over face, and wondered just why the guns had suddenly stopped firing. Or, was he just slipping away into a Norseman's funeral pyre, with some old Viking taking him away, off onto the Sea of Eternity.

Just one of those things we will never know. An unsolvable mystery of our historical past. Not to be found in the files, lest writers go crazy looking. Not even in books. But to remain locked up forevermore out there somewhere on the sea with young Harvey and the old Norseman.

Louise Fritz Ferguson, granddaughter of Col. Emil Fritz, whose insurance policy (money) was the fuse that blew open the Lincoln County War. Money, greed and cattle kept it going. Gunpower ended it.

You are west of and looking east over the base of the grave markers of Bob Beckwith (died July 1878) and the nefarious Bob Olinger, who died in Lincoln Plaza (May 1881) from a face full of buckshot from his own shotgun in the hands of Bill the Kid. Olinger was a phrenologist of the worst order. His own mother said on learning of his death: "If there is a hell, he will be in it."

*Frank Gomez, employee of McSweens', was behind the store when the heavy gun-fire broke out, 17 July, 1878. Shortly after, the home was ignited to burn slowly all day, while Lt. Col. Dudley, a habitual drunk from nearby Ft. Stanton, **did nothing**.*

Robert Beckwith (age 28), a deputy sheriff, was killed a few minutes after the event, while coming inside from the back wall to take McSween's surrender near the chicken house (shown in the upper right corner of illustration.)

Robert was reported to be engaged to Viola Howell who, a short time later, married John Slaughter, a widower and wealthy cowman moving a Texas cattle herd to Arizona.

122

This illustration was made from on-site photos and measurements; details were from Cherokee Bill's version. He was in the bunkhouse doorway just behind Olinger, who is aiming his six-shooter to take out Beckwith, who is blowing away his son-in-law's head. Son John is too late to stop him. Camelia is to the far right.

A SAD DAY AT SEVEN-RIVERS

It gets to you — when you start to draw. This illustration of a young woman of 21 with her 16-month old son in her arms — not ten steps from her husband—seeing him blasted into eternity by her father's shotgun.

In the wink of the eye, her life changes from love and hope into tragedy and despair. You want to help. But there is no help! Only tragic hopelessness.

You stop drawing. It's gruesome. But history is for those who come after. How do you show a pretty face — changing from full life to horror?

I stopped drawing this scene of a Saturday evening, August 17, 1978. I'll just put it on hold for two weeks, I thought. And, for ten years this story stood still.

Hugh Beckwith, of English peerage, shown here in his Spanish dinner jacket that he sometimes wore, was born in 1826 in Florence, Alabama, near where my great uncle, a casualty of the Civil War, was born.

'Tis said of young Hugh, when enraged his nostrils snorted fire and he was as determined in cause as was his South, when stormed into a winless war.

This photo of Camelia Beckwith Johnson Olinger was taken of her by Fieldman's in El Paso, 1903, at age 46.

CHEROKEE BILL, an Oklahoma Indian, who worked for the cattle partnership of W.H. Johnson and J. W. Olinger, was standing inside the bunkhouse door when the racket started. He stepped outside just as Wallace (Olinger) shot a part of Beckwith's chin away. Cherokee Bill said "Johnson came by where Olinger was working on a saddle, said the Ole Man was mad as a wet hen. Olinger said Johnson was just like a bedpan, always there when you needed 'em." Cherokee Bill was age 84 in 1940 in Pecos, Texas, when I last saw him.

Beckwith lost his eldest son, Robert, in the five-day fight at Lincoln Plaza ending July 19, 1878, and it was his belief that his son-in-law Johnson's influence was the cause of Robert being there.

I'll just draw son John, show him coming from the dining room to stop his enraged father. I'll draw Wallace Olinger at the bunkhouse saddle shop, with gun in hand, defending John and himself from the crazed Beckwith. Wallace Olinger, brother of dubious Bob, sometime Deputy Marshall, later got a full charge of buckshot from his own shotgun at the hands of prisoner Billy-the-Kid.

Beckwith ranch had several related cattle owners, including Wm. H. Johnson and Wallace Olinger, according to Cherokee Bill, an Oklahoma Cherokee who worked for Johnson and Olinger. The owner, Hugh — according to gossip, had turned "hen-pecked" since the demise of his son Robert (age 28), who had actually run the business without the advice of Johnson and Wallace Olinger.

The romantics might call it chasing a fantasy that can drive you insane. I had to find this woman, somewhere, someday. It had become an obsession

since Ella Frazer of Toyah and Ft. Stockton, Texas, my nurse through the flu epidemic of 1918-19, had told me the story of how her sister Anne had befriended Camelia Johnson at Ft. Stockton in 1879. A pregnant woman with a small boy enroute east on the stage to her late husband's father's (a Civil War surgeon) home in Ohio. Johnson, the surgeon's son, also served in the Union army. Beckwith learned of this just prior to this scene.

By 1930 I had traced Camelia Beckwith Johnson Olinger to the home of Preacher Hunter Lewis' home in Mesilla Park. Now, at 22, I had come to the end of my story.

There on a recliner under a large tree was a graying, beautiful woman of 73. I was tongue-tied! My story was here, not even 30 feet away.

Lee Myers, a noted southwestern historian, standing at the grave of William H. Johnson in old Seven Rivers Cemetery. Pecos river is at right. The graves were removed in 1988 to nearby Artesia, New Mexico. Myers went with me and told me what he knew.

Her dark eyes saw right through you in some pleasing, demanding way, and an understanding, faint smile belied her tragedy of long ago.

I stood like a second grader in a school room corner, afraid to look. She looked as if she knew I was unraveling some burden, but not knowing how much I knew.

Or, was she living over again her happiest day in Santa Fe, a church bride of 18 in 1875 — just 2 years 8 months prior to this tragedy.

While back on leave in 1944, I visited her grave. Obsession will eat away at you until you "write it out" and file it.

FOOTNOTES: Camelia married Wallace Olinger, older brother of the nefarious Bob, and they divorced in 1913. Camelia's mother, Refugia y Rascon de Pino (Beckwith), once owned the land where the Las Cruces Masonic Cemetery is until her passing in 1892. Camelia is buried there. Known to Preacher Lewis' daughters as "Grandmother Olinger," it is they who marked her grave with dignity and simplicity:

CAMELIA OLINGER
Mar. 30 1857 - July 18 1939

Her "Paso por Aqui" (she passed by here) is a Gene Rhodes' logo and especially fitting for some of this book.

I was in school with her grandson and granddaughters and with the Lewis' girls.

Myers standing at grave marker of John M. Beckwith at old Seven Rivers Cemetery. The marker that was placed here remains. The body (it is believed) is still interred in Pierce Canyon 7 miles southeast of Malaga, New Mexico. The grave marker was stolen from the grave, recovered in Carlsbad and returned to the old Seven Rivers burial ground.

Myers standing in the kitchen of the old Beckwith home. He is facing east toward the public road from Ft. Stockton, Texas to Roswell / Santa Fe and the Pecos River. The nearby tree is in the old acequia ditch leading from the diversion gate in North Fork of Seven Rivers. The main house, bunkhouse and home of Camelia and William Johnson was enclosed by an adobe wall. The only gate opened east.

The aerial photo taken shows the ditch head a mile from the house shown to the right and one-half mile from the large group of trees in the center. The river is just to the lower right. Note house in lower left which was a part of old Lakewood.

The bearded man is the author's grandfather, Jackson Wiley Humphries. Standing is Eugene Alfred Humphries, the author's father, and Nancy Melissa Hamm Humphries (author's grandmother.) Photo made about 1881 in Dew, Freestone Co., Texas.

William Shadrock Humphries (1838-1864), the author's great uncle, with the photo taken when he was about 23 years young. He was a lieutenant with the Alabama 16th Regiment, killed in 1864 during the Civil War.

Notes on the Humphries and Beckwith Families

My great grandfather settled in the upper right fork of the Tombigbee, known as the Alabama part of the Tishomingo River, coming thereto from Virgina, where their forefathers came down (through the years) from Boston Colony in 1640.

My grandfather, Jackson Wiley, was born in Tishomingo County in 1837, as was my great Uncle William Shadrock — a friend of the Beckwith family who lived on the north side, and across the Tennessee River, then known as Florence Landing, Alabama. It does not matter if Hugh M. Beckwith was born there in 1826, or in upper Virginia. Nor does it matter

that another young Beckwith swam his horse across the river to join up as a young Lieutenant of the Confederate Cavalry at Courtland, Alabama.

What does matter is whether or not both made it out of Shiloh, Pittsburg Landing and Chickamunga. Uncle William (it is believed) was wounded at Kennesaw Mountain and was sent home (Fayette County) to convalesce.

The Carpet Baggers surrounded the home to take Humphries' Troop Commander, a Captain of Cavalry. They fled on horseback in the darkest of nights. William never made it to the woods. Family folklore has it that he was not the "wanted" man which always goes with the telling. Others think the Captain was a Beckwith — a demanding and driving man.

ROBERT OLINGER, in the garb he wore out of Oklahoma, hit Seven Rivers saying, "Call me Pecos Bill!" This rooster had hardly quit crowing before Hugh Beckwith told him "he'd eat with the boys and roost in the bunk house."
Credit: The Lincoln County Heritage Museum, Lincoln, NM.

THE REAL OLINGER

From a sketch map provided by Lee Myers of Carlsbad, NM, I flew from Pecos, Texas, up the Pecos River in 1978, past the Ross Ranch and Pope's Crossing just short of the "goose necks," dropped to 200 feet on the river's east side where I should find the scar of the old NASH choza — on the north side of Pierce Canyon and seven miles southeast of present day Malaga, New Mexico.

The early small ranchers (1877-80) banded together because of Apache thieves; all were partisans in the Lincoln County War— all were antagonistic to Chisum (sometime overlord to 175 miles of river grazing).

Looking south from the Andy Boyle/Milo Pierce cow camp at the junction of Pierce Canyon and the Pecos River, some 7 miles southeast of Malaga, NM, on 26 August, 1879. Near the corrals and river, John A. Jones and John M. Beckwith, partners in a cow camp a short distance down-river, had an argument over the filing of the cow brand. Two young hot-heads, both with the gun-itch. Jones wanted to settle it by sale and dividing, although he was the fastest gun. Beckwith (like his father) wanted guns. The duel was fair, said all, and Beckwith lost. They buried Beckwith behind the choza (rock-dugout hut). Note: the choza was purposely set on higher ground to tell the story in one illustration.

Three days later (29 August), Jones (after moving his cattle farther down river) decided it best to give himself up to the nearest Justice, probably Seven Rivers, about 30 miles upriver. To show he had no animosity, he stopped by the Pierce camp. Olinger saw him coming, gave Pierce (lying on a cot outside) his plan and ducked inside.

Jones tied his mule and went over to shake hands with Pierce, who grabbed his gun-hand with both of his. Bob Olinger, the "brave" phrenologistic killer, put two bullets into Jones, one glancing downward that lodged in Pierce's hip.

To the stage and the Army surgeon in Ft. Stockton, Texas, went Pierce, in a wagon followed the Beckwith surrey carrying Camelia Johnson, pregnant with her 2nd, going to take the stage east to live with her husband's family.

At Ft. Stockton, Annie Frazer Johnson and her mother, Mrs. George M. Frazer, took care of Camelia until the Concord came through, going east.

Later, in 1881, after Billy-the-Kid blasted Olinger from the upper Lincoln County Courthouse window (about two years later), with Bob's shotgun — both barrels stuffed with buckshot — the story came out that Olinger had said, "If it were not for Bell (also an assigned guard), he'd throw the little Rat (the Kid) out the window — handcuffs and leg irons — shoot him double-dead (both barrels) before he hit the ground — just for trying to escape!"

Olinger was reportedly seen in the five-day McSween shoot-out in Lincoln Plaza, July 14-19, 1878, wearing two six-guns with full cartridge belts, cradling a late model Winchester. His name never appeared in print in any report of action for July 19, 1878.

FOOTNOTE: The good people of Lincoln County like to think they buried him in Ft. Stanton (cemetery) as ignominiously as he lived — the real Bob Olinger.

Only the base of his headstone remains at the grave. His mother, in so many words, said "He was a born killer" and implied he "had it coming". She lived with the Beckwiths.

JOHN M. BECKWITH (born 1855). Strongly favored his mother in appearance. Unlike his older brother Bob (after his death in Lincoln Plaza fight, 19 July, 1878), John was unable to run the ranch and went down-river to ranch with his friend Jones below the Pierce/Boyle camp. He was buried behind the choza. The grave headstone was recovered in nearby Carlsbad. It definately was near the W. H. Johnson grave in 1971, in the old Seven Rivers plot.

The grave marker of ANDREW BOYLE (a tubercular) and strong participator in the Lincoln County War — known as the Pecos River Bunch. Was buried near Beckwith.

The Sunset Mine on ridge-top showing windlass and foreman, the big man (left) in checked shirt, who "Fat Annie" said was big enough for her to "cuddle."

GHOSTS AT COOK'S CAMP

It Took Sporting Women To Do A Good Deed

Years later, cowboys would tell how, on stormy nights, you could still see their ghosts by lightning light — riding out, still fighting back — dying men on screaming horses, stacked up on one another - riderless mounts racing back hysterically into the pass, hopelessly caught between an orgy of Apache fire pouring into their ranks from ambush, high up on the rim — up almost to the skyline, in Gavilan Canyon, 13 miles north of Cook's Peak, the cock's comb of the Black Range nine miles west of Lake Valley, NM.

But it is only the wind you hear and not the echoes of gunfire, long ago absorbed by boulders and gnarled old juniper and oak, still lasting it out up there on the mountainside. Still hanging there on Gavilan Wall. For dead men don't cry aloud, nor do dead men ride again.

Family going out. Had enough. Too much liquor, too little water. Gambling day and night. Note stove strapped to center burro's back. The name of this family was lost with my historical records during WWII as a result of vandalism.

Story Spreads

Others used to tell in barroom and by campfire, from Del Rio to Nogales, how it was only the cries and groans echoing down the stairway to the desert floor from the riders on the Lake Valley stage, fleeing Cook's camp, only an hour behind two surreys of Sadie's girls — outbound from Cook's, inbound for Lake Valley, where a new strike had blossomed. Luscious silver ore — the fabulous Bridal Chamber, embedded with millions — hornsilver, at grass root.

Word reached Cook's Camp by a Negro trooper, recently turned white, stuttering the news that old Nana and his Apaches were heading their way after sinking their teeth deep into the tender flanks of Lieut. G. W. Smith's Troops B and F of the 9th, colored — killing the lieutenant and others, and how their fire had "drained" the whiskey from George Daley and six cowboys "just tagging along to see the fun." The fears of man are many, and so it was with the Business Men's League and the Home Guard of Cook's Camp who went into action like a battery of

howitzers. "The lieutenant don't matter," they said. "He's paid to die, but . . . not George. He's home folks." So nodded 20 or more ruddy faces, long in whiskey and short on foresight.

Men of Distinction

The men of distinction were in the league and in that day it was those of the soft hands, poker faces, stray fingers for loose pockets — men of beards and goatees, all gentry of the saloon and gambling trade — patrons of the "arts," they said. For art to them was women and all women are beautiful, properly mixed in their proper setting — roulette, monte and poker tables, singing and dancing girls, showing the monied-men a sleazy waist, velvet-smooth, wasp-like and small, a garter black from the cancan and a sizeable square of fair skin. To them all men were silver and silver was their business.

The guard was of the more permanent type-freighters, cowboys, stage buckers, drummers, and miners.

Picnic group up on Cook's north ridge. The man on the left burro was a cavalryman. Note the hind legs of burro. Both are on their last legs.

Cooke's Mining Camp water system. Originally it was at a spring half-way down the mountain. In the driest of years, it may have had to come from other sources. Water was distributed to each mine.

Burro's with feed-corn probably raised on the Mimbres or came up from the railroad station (March 1881), of Florida, NM. Ore was hauled to Deming railroad for processing by long mule teams after earlier ox-teams became obsolete.

Cooke's Camp Stage Station and water system is far left, facing south, and the stage road going out — but Cooke's Peak does not show.

The water system owner and wife — the motivating force of this story. Note well dug to far right. Burro's were the "pipe" lines. This man's name was lost with the historical records. (Texas, 1942-46).

The Business League commissioned Poke Lovejoy's stage before it had hardly come to rest, but the guard, long on beer, said `We'll stand and fight!" The league, smelling to high heaven of whiskey, shouted, "No, we'll run and fight! Save the girls out yonder on their own!"

Drinks Flowed

Drinks flowed. Arguments ran high. "Stand and fight?" . . . "Run in shame?" So bobbed the "needle" between guard and league.

A half-dead Mexican sheep herder settled it all, quickly. Scalped and bleeding, he stumbled into camp, groaning incoherently, "Los Indios! . . . Nana! . . . 'paches!" pointing down into the Mimbres Valley. The word spread fast. The coach loaded faster. They left a trail of cards, bottles, and beer bottles. A fight broke out for seating space - 27 on a 15-man coach — not counting girls.

Then gunfire from behind the big saloon tent! From around it came flying a miner in underwear — two jumps ahead of his wife. On his overalls she had detected a strange and sweet odor — a feminine smell — and so had "decontaminated" them in the stove with the pockets full of .44 cartridges. Six horses bolted, already eager for oats and the curry comb at Orchards Corral at the end of the line.

Off at Fast Speed

Off the mountain into a big night and moon tore the stage — at fire-engine speed — rocking fore and aft on its thorough braces, groaning, dipping into the downgrade, slewing on the turns.

Unaware and to one side rode Jim McLaughlin and Bill Reeves, two cowboys decked out in their hunting best — dodging Nana's scent, hoping to find Sadie's girls.

From the coach a drunken leaguer shouted,

Looking north at stage office, store and water system. The event of the day was the arrival of the stage. With it came the mail, whiskey and groceries — in that order. The water was as necessary as all three. The "girls" as important, but came with — and sometimes went with — the whiskey (as in the story).

COOK'S CAMP grew from tents that came by muleback, to rough lumber that came by ox-train. The ore went out first by ox-trains. Later, mule teams, 8 to 10-span with three wagons trailing.

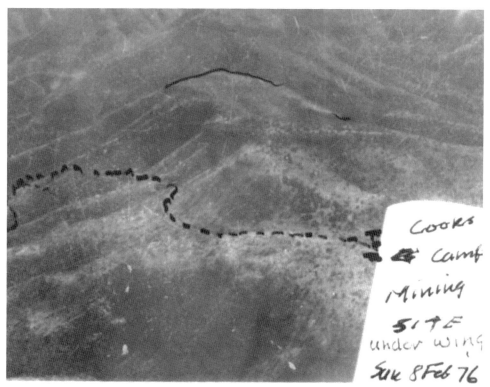

Aerial picture of the camp looking south. Camp under the right wing. Road to center left winding down the east side of the mountain.

"Indians!" and opened up on them with his derringer and got back for his eagerness a .44 slug through his derby. Gunfire broke out in earnest — two cowboys — too much rye - "two hundred Indians." The coach started skipping a step, hopping and bobbing on the snaky turns. Bottles were lowered and revolvers raised.

Straight into the valley followed the cowboys, firing over the coach, waving for identification.

Shotgun Guard

Later Dave Crowe said he was only riding shotgun guard and didn't see just how it all started but thought he heard Sally Sue cry out, "Indians!" and knowing Sally, figured she was just going into another man's pockets. He said he was minding his own business — just upending a bucket of beer - when the stage spun in on the turn and rolled over, the bucket "grabbing" him around the head. Still heavy on liquor and light on bullets, they emptied their final rounds at each other. Bill Reeves finally caught Newt Buntline a mile farther down the road — still running, firing back, saving his scalp with space and speed.

Skirted Camp

Nana and his Apaches had skirted Cook's — to the west — going down the Mimbres and into the Florida Mountains this 1881 night.

Poke Lovejoy brought the injured into Lake Valley the next day on a doorless coach and with a half-team. Dad Gromatch's tin snips fixed Dave so he could see again.

A Bible woman said Sadie, the Lady, did more in one business move to clean up Cook's Camp than old Nana could have done working full-time in a hundred years.

Showing road at its steepest section and believed to be above the early Graphic Mine.

Jim McLaughlin and Bill Reeves featured in the stage ride dressed "fit to kill." Story and photos were gift, it is believed, from Jim and Mike Moffett, miners who came from Ireland, who first prospected at Cooke's, then Lake Valley and settled in Kingston. They knew everyone and were generous to a fault with their time and information.

The Apaches driving the troopers into Cuchillo.

THE WAY BEYER'S TROOPERS CAME INTO CUCHILLO

Victorio's Apaches bit deep into the "tinder flanks" of Captains Beyer and Dawson on the headwaters of Cuchillo Creek, September 30, 1879 and harassed the limping Troopers all the way down, just short of Cuchillo Plaza, where Beyer went to lick his wounds. (As seen through the eyes of young scout Billie Bates.)

Shown here is Captain C. D. Beyer coming off the north mesa, before sun-up, just west of Cuchillo (9 miles NW of T or C) in late September 1879, after a night of harassment out of the mountains — bringing his wounded and dead; leaving Captain Dawson with Victorio's Apaches on the headwaters of the Cuchillo.

Old Bill Bates (87 in 1937), with drooping handle-bar moustache, balding, a fringe of grey, misty blue eyes that can "look" through you — way on out there where he, as a cavalry scout and packer had been before — now here with me in the late 1930s on a dirt road west of present day Winston.

137

He got out of the car, slowly, raised a gnarled old hand — from years of hard work — pointed shakily up to the timbered slopes and into the east canyons of the Black Range at what is now known as Beyer's Run. Here, where once it was the heart of Apache Land.

Old Bates was also the young Billie who rode down three good horses from the Placers (north of Hillsboro) to Slocum's (Station) to warn the night stage to Silver City that 60 or more of Vic's best were raiding south-bound for Mexico.

ANDREW A. SCHMIDT, assayer, who came to the Chloride mining district as it was opening up (1882) and before the Black Range had been completely deloused of the Apaches (1886). He showed Bates and me the fight area on upper Cuchillo Creek, where Victorio "put the breeches" on Major Morrow's command and where the military blazed the trees (for the Washington Brass to review) so that the military might study the Apache's fighting tactics.

Two officers of the campaign, September, 1879, cogitating on Victorio's next move. The officer on the right is believed to be of the 9th Cavalry.

Part of Captain Beyer's Troop of the 9th Cavalry resting somewhere between the arroyos, Seco and Cuchillo, 1879 or '80. Gift to narrator from old timer and owner of the Buckhorn Saloon, Hot Springs, NM (now T or C).

The Butterfield's mud-wagon from Franklin (El Paso) changed teams at the stage corrals in Mesilla, NMT, and is shown leaving the stage office on east side of Calle Principal westbound. Some say they blasted their way out of the Overland Street corral (El Paso), taking the money and records — leaving a fog of manure-smelling dust for Baylor's oncoming, snorting Confederates.

SEVEN BRAVE MEN

The story of the "Seven Brave Men" in the Cooke's Pass fight in New Mexico first came to me as a boy-victim of the influenza epidemic of 1918. My nurse, Miss Ella Frazer of Toyah, Texas, daughter of the late George M. Frazer, when I asked her for my books on Kit Carson and Daniel Boone, told me the story of how a "handful" of brave men from El Paso — braver than Kit Carson and Daniel Boone together— fought many Indians for many days until all were killed, and how her father had to go "out west of Mesilla" to bury them. I did not know this story would haunt me all of my life.

After visiting with the late Judge O. W. Williams of Ft. Stockton, Texas, who drew me a sketch map, I had no trouble in the 1930's finding the site. In the center of the parapet about six inches under the soil, I found a bottle neck of the type used in Mesilla for bottling wine for the sutler at nearby Ft. Fillmore.

The stage at the crest of Cooke's Pass and the west end of Cooke's Canyon. Driver Roescher has seen three pine trees across the road and is wheeling for the rock pile shown beyond and just to the right of his face in the illustration. John Wilson reported as a stage hand with a fancy gun who knew the route, was put on top of the coach coming up the two-mile canyon with narrows in it. The mule-shoeing delay at the stage station aided the Apaches with more daylight. The gamblers, who boarded at Mesilla (Aveline and Champion), were both excellent gun-men. The illustration was made from photographs taken at the site. Ella and Anne, daughter's of George M. Frazer, in telling their father's story always mention the dead Apache bodies — rock covered just west off the road.

About this time I also acquired the .40 caliber Sharps shown on the parapet (on page 143) from "Judge" George Bisby of Pinos Altos, New Mexico, whose father acquired it in 1867 from a former member of the Walker party, gold-seeking miners of that district. The first owner of the gun supposedly acquired it from a Mimbreno Apache for two sacks of corn, who on being asked where he got it, stood up on the ridge, puffed himself up like a frog in a churn and pointed with pride to Cooke's Peak, saying he took it off a brave man in the big wagon fight before the soldier came many moons ago (the California Column came in the summer of 1862). It is believed he traded it from a Chiricahua brave who was the last to leave the fight under Cochise, taking his loot to Janos for sale.

Another story has it as being bought from Cochise's band in Janos, along with some gold watches by two Americans who brought it to Pinos Altos and it came through the saloon trade into the Bisby family.

If you could go back to a twilight evening (Saturday, July 20, 1861), and stand on top of an adobe building later to become John Lemon's mill on the Acequia Madre of Mesilla, and look over the stage company's corral on the property of Cristobal Ascarate at the Overland Stage office in the Sam Bean block on Calle Principal, you might have seen the coach as it swung out of Lemon's corral. On top of it, in it, and boarding it would be seven men — boys, stage hands and gamblers —on their way out under a rising moon-out in front of John

Grist mill and stage corrals on John Lemon's property (1860's) on the west side of Calle Principal and across the street from the departing stage.

FRANCISCO MADRID, who sold the apples to young Mills on the departing stage.

Baylor's Texas Confederate Volunteers, whose hot breath was blowing ominously up the Mesilla Valley, and who were all too eager for the blood of Union sympathizers.

The two gamblers aboard — both good men with cards and too good with a gun — were especially anxious to be out of Mesilla and to dodge the Apaches into Tucson. The outcome of the Civil War was to them of little concern so long as there were plenty of games, girls, and gold (in Tucson).

On the coach was the oldest, Freeman Thomas, age twenty-nine, conductor and shotgun guard; on the box was driver Joe Roescher, age twenty-six, cracking his whip over the back of Lemon's Yankee-fed mules, seemingly eager to be on their way from this hot-bed of secession sympathizers.

Five days later, in Cooke's Pass, under a hot July sun and a circle of buzzards, the seven were found and buried.

Once on a plane trip from Tucson to Alamogordo early in the World War II, we passed over Cooke's Pass — in a tangle of brown hills — and I couldn't help thinking of those valiant men who so long ago fought against such odds for three hot July days and three long nights. By the standards in which they fought, our odds in the upcoming war didn't seem half bad.

Each time during the ensuing years as I would fly westward, low and slow through this same pass, I could not help but look down as if I might be seeing the wounded young John Wilson, wildly shooting his way out of the rock parapet in the full moonlight amid the gleeful shouts of swarming Apaches scrambling in their lust to be the first to run a lance through his bleeding body, ravaged with exhaustion, crazed with thirst, and down to the last caps and a few "linen" cartridges — the last of the seven.

This hero of my boyhood would drag his bleeding body around the hill from one stony protective point to another, fighting back against such hopeless odds, as if in one vain, lasting hope he might somehow reach the safety of the barricaded stage station two miles down the canyon.

It has been said by the four stage hands at Cooke's Springs Station, two miles east, and the last to see the party alive, that had Joe Roescher, age twenty-six, not stopped to hook in another span of mules, or had those mules been properly shod, not needing re-shoeing, the coach would have gotten through the pass in the dark of early dawn (Apaches do not attack in the dark) and they would have missed the combined forces of Mangas Colorado and his son-in-law, Cochise. Nor would they have encountered them, as expected, in either Doubtful Canyon or Apache Pass. And there would have been no legend to haunt the Southwest for thirty or more years thereafter — everywhere men "good and true" met in saloons; nor would I have this gun.

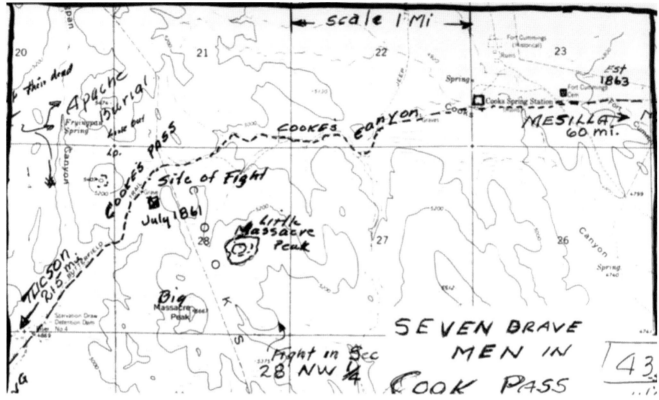

The coach came westbound up Cook's Canyon, made its run and pulled up near the rock mound (shown with dog depicted on page 143) in the northwest quarter of Section 28. The coachmen were aided somewhat by the Apaches having the sunlight in their eyes when they fired their opening shots at the coach.

FOOTNOTES:

The story information came from notes and interviews with the following persons who had heard it or lived it first-hand:

William (Billy) Bates, in El Paso in 1938 — a civilian scout with Major Morrow's command in the fight with Victorio in 1879 and 1880.

Jim Parks of Duncan, Arizona, who with his father and mother in their wagontrain, passed through Cooke's Pass and visited the graves and the parapet in October 1879.

Agnes Meader Snyder of Silver City, New Mexico, who with her father's wagontrain, passed Ft. Cummings, Cooke's Canyon and Cooke's Pass and saw the parapet in the pass in November 1879.

O. W. Williams, in Ft. Stockton, Texas, in an interview verified the location of the parapet and two of the graves scattered around the area. This parapet was pointed out to him by the stage driver in April 1880. On later trips through the Pass, he reviewed the battle scene.

Eugene Van Patton's reminiscences as an employee from 1858 with the Butterfield Stage Company, who was at the station when the celebrity

wagon with the seven departed Mesilla on Saturday, July 20, 1861. He was twenty-four years old at the time. He died in 1926 at Las Cruces at the age of eighty-nine.

Francisco Madrid, who died in Rodey, New Mexico, sometime after 1939 and after his 94th birthday. He was born south of Mesilla at Santo Tomas. Maybe I put words into his mouth and turned his mind back as I recounted the story of Cooke's Pass Fight, but it sent him mumbling back toward his duffel in the corner of his one-room adobe, scrambling for a copy of an old newspaper he had nursed for so many years but could not find. His story, as I recall, went about as follows:

He was a boy-merchant of Mesilla, met the stagecoaches and the muleskinners - selling them two stolen apples for one copper, and for which he got to-boot, a swat across the seat of his breeches and all the fresh mule manure he could run his bare feet through as he scrambled out of the corral and out of the way of the incoming, thrashing teams — thirsting for water, corn and curry comb — amid the shouts and the cussings that only a muleskinner can give.

142

Photo depicts where the over-turned coach passengers fled to fight behind this parapet. Looking south over the parapet at Massacre Peak. The Sharps gun points to where the two men fled up the slope in their last desperate stand to hold out until someone came along. The poodle dug up the wine bottle from the windy silt of 115 years inside the parapet. He wasn't looking for story relics, just being a dog. Here he hears the coach ghost coming from the west.

His last sale, he believes, before the coaches stopped running, was to a young boy-man who tossed him a handful of pennies for a straw hatful of apples — catching the stage on the fly amid shouts from the saloon trade as the coach tore down the dusty street westward to Pichacho. I couldn't help wondering if his last apples didn't go to Emmett Mills, age nineteen, the youngest of the seven; and my last and best link to the story of the Seven Brave Men.

The location of the fight was the NW 1/4 of Section 28, T 21S, R 8 W NMPM. It was reported Cochise lost forty-four men, which is questionable. Mangas Colorado, who pulled out of the fight on the second night, did not reveal his losses. It is possible that all Apache casualties did not total forty-four, although a number of Apache bodies were found, rock-covered in a crevice, high on the west side mountain.

I have, I like to think, a Sharps rifle patented in 1849, with a serial number that is similar to those issued by the Butterfield Overland Stage Line, 1859-1861. I also have the wine bottle dug up inside the barricade.

The gun and the bottle are a comfort to me, a tangible link to Seven Brave Men.

143

Ruins of the Mimbres River Crossing Stage Station (had the coach made another 20 miles).

Mangas Colorado, in red shirt, with his son-in-law Cochise (holding his wounded son from the stage fight in Cooke's Pass — story Seven Brave Men) are going to the doctor. Padilla's father is one of two home-guard men on the rooftop who Mangas is giving a mean eye to, shown here as a "Mexican Standoff". (He had 40 or more hidden braves in the trees at the east end of the village.)

Mangas dangled the gold watches (from the stagecoach fight victims) in front of the peep-hole of the door. The doctor's door came unbarred immediately.

Once inside, Mangas placed his knife across the doctor's throat saying in unmistakeable Spanish, "He dies (his grandson) — you die!"

(A California-bound gold-seeker wrote in his 1849 diary: "Janos is a poor, destitute, held-in-captive and servitude village that has lost its will to fight.")

A DAY IN JANOS

Janos from the air —1977 photo looking southeast.
  P-1. Where Natividad Padilla was born. His father featured in stories 19, 31 and 50.
  P-2. In front of church where James J. Johnson was greeted after Apache massacre at Juniper Springs, April 22, 1837.
  P-3. The main street to doctor's office in his home.
  P-4. Rooftop where Padilla's father lay — not the same building shown in photo.
  P-5. Original part of Janos in front of and on the creek. Here the ore-packing mule trains from Santa Rita del Cobre Mine en route to the furnaces at Corralitos always stopped for rest and feed.
  P-6. Route to Fronteras, Bavispe, Bocachie, Magdalena, and Moctezuma.

Janos left foreground shows church plaza (in front) and early camp-ground of arrieros.

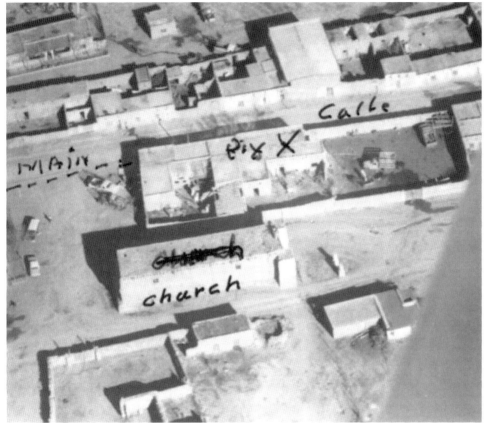

*Janos shows church, main street (1861) and possibly the same building upon which
Padilla's father watched.*

*Natividad Padilla, who was born at point 1 in air
photo at top of page 146 at far right.*

Charlie Batchelder going for the scrub oak tree (top left), October, 1878, in the head of Corral Canyon.

CHARLIE BATCHELDER

A year before this story occurred, Victorio's band of Warm Springs Apaches had been transferred from the Warm Springs to the San Carlos Reservation in Arizona. That had put "electricity" into the air. From Silver City to Globe, Arizona Territory — two blossoming mining camps — lay 170 miles of mountains and uninhabited canyons, and few dared to ride the stage when Apaches began to mumble, lost their appetites for government beef, and issued guns and ammunition ceased to tally in the years of 1877-78.

The gates to Warrington's Corral swung open. Charlie was on the box, see-sawing the reins, shouting, "So long!" The empty mud-wagon (hack) rocked on springs, then tore down the street — canvas curtains flapping in the fresh autumn air.

In the dust Charlie pulled up in front of the Exchange House. Louis Timmer called out, "No business today, Charlie. Everybody is a-feared the Apaches are a-raiding." There was a moment of deep silence, then he wheeled out and rattled on up Yankie Street.

In front of Higbee's General Merchandise the rig made its last stop. Soon it was stacked with bottles, a keg of whiskey, cigars, extra guns, cartridges and mail consigned to Globe — all entrusted to gallant Charlie and his sturdy team.

The jacal-type house stood about where the gate (left side photo) stood. The barn/hayloft was beyond where the negro soldier was stationed in the hayloft to guard the mule in the picket corral. Near midnight, the Apaches came for the mule and were unwiring the gate when the trooper fired his gun up into the moonlight, before falling out of the loft shouting, "I seed 'em!" The men were waiting in the shadows of the jacal just for this chance. Brock said he felt like "shooting that 'nigger'." Brock was born in Texas.

Charlie, young and tall in black hat and boots, with his .44 Colts hanging loose and businesslike, climbed onto the seat. The "whittlers" and other "onlookers" noticed an unnaturalness in his action and their silence reflected their concern.

"Just a minute, Charlie." It was Joe Hull, in store apron. "For months I've been a-wantin' to go to Globe. I'll change my duds."

Charlie answered, "No, Joe! Can't explain it, but somehow I know the Indians are "out." You'd better stay home this time. You got kids and a wife."

Three miles west of Silver City, Charlie topped the scrub-oak crest of the Continental Divide, weaving between yucca and bear grass — to enter into that vast stillness of Apache land, tiny and seemingly unafraid.

Thirty minutes later, Charlie broke out of Wind Canyon and ran with loose reins through rabbit brush and desert willow, crossing the Mangas Creek bottom. His .44 Winchesters snuggled more closely

— the mountains would be getting steeper and the trees denser. They hit the north fringe of the Burro Mountains — a long, heavy drag through juniper and oak to the pine crested top. Every rock, every tree, an ambush to an Apache's making.

On top, he pulled up his team to blow. Their flanks were lather white, their sides pumping like bellows. He sat ever alert, watching behind, in front, and to each side. In this dead stillness each tree took shape, each jay's scream was an Apache yell. Every see-saw of a horse's ear could be the signal of death lurking to the front, just waiting for the snort as the signal for Apache shots to break out.

It never came and Charlie kicked off the brake. The team was eager for the start. The rig dropped over the high divide westward — down Mulberry Canyon, heavily lined with juniper and oak, the wheels slewing on the turns — sending up thick sprays of sand, and on to Burro Springs Station farther down the canyon, a long two miles to safety,

Present Burro Spring showing road leading southwest to Verdin, NM (old Guthrie's Station).

hay, grain, and water.

That mid-afternoon Peter Hansen, Royal Yeamans, and his stepson, Caesar Brock, were standing at the corral gate when Charlie came in. Mrs. Yeamans and the two little girls waved from the jacal (a juniper post and mud hut) as the coach rattled up to a stop. "Was kinda worried, Charlie," said Yeamans. "Didn't know if you would try it."

Sliding from the box, Charlie threw the lines to Yeamans while Pete chopped the traces. "Thank God." he said, "Them mountains are behind me. Swing in a fresh team, Pete, I'm goin' on."

"Not goin' to stay the night?" asked Yeamans. "You can make the flat tomorrow by daylight. From there on it'll be good sailin' into Guthrie's." They walked toward the picket jacal.

"I calculate," said Charlie, "to pass Ash Springs tonight, while it's dark. I've a hunch 'paches will jump me there tomorrow. Should be in reach of the Fort Thomas Scouts by sun-up." They passed on into the house.

Mrs. Yeamans said, "It's ready, Charlie," and they all crowded in to the table. Someone started kidding Charlie about his girl back East. His usual response was lacking; the jesting was flat.

During the meal Charlie overturned the pepper box. Pete spoke up, "That's a bad sign, I always heared."

Charlie flushed. "I know it, folks! Had a hunch this morning 'fore I left. Had it all the way over. This is my last trip. I'm quittin'."

"Ah, Charlie, we'll be a'seein' you in three or four days, for sure," Yeamans said reassuring him. But this fear caught and grew on the group.

The mail hack stood ready. Pete was holding the leaders' bits. Charlie adjusted his rifle on the seat, then rolled up and tied the curtains to cut the wind resistance.

"Better come along, Pete," said Charlie. "Could sure use an extra gun."

Pete answered apologetically, "I reckon not this time, Charlie. Too much hayin' and waterin' to be done around here."

"So long, folks," yelled Charlie, as he let the fresh team out. The family stood waving goodbye and good luck as the rig tore across the canyon bottom to the west side. Once out of the canyon and on the mesa top, Charlie turned to wave — then faded into

150

Caesar Brock, who showed me Burro Springs and the site of Batchelder's demise in Corral Canyon, the ambush of the McComas' in Thompson Canyon and all the history of the west side of the Burro Mountains. He lived at Burro Springs at the time of these events.

Photo: Courtesy of his daughter, Mrs. Marie Brock McCauly. Cliff, NM

the head of Corral Canyon.

The next day, Jesus Duran, mail courier from Clifton (Arizona Territory), rode into Burro Springs on a half-dead horse with nerves like a Mexican jumping bean—eyes dollar-round — shouting, "I seen heem! Et ess Charl-ee. There he ees under a tree, hee's han's folded like thees." He made his gesture in full pantomime. "I theek hee ees a-sleep. Theen I see thee wagon. She ess over-turned, an un caballo ees keeled een the harness. Apache tracks all over. Mi Dios! Hee ees just three miles down thee road."

They brought Charlie's body in and buried him in the old Silver City cemetery.

FOOTNOTE: Caesar Brock took me to the site. The scrub oak on the hill that Charlie ran to. It was still there in 1934, through 1939.

Had Charlie stayed under the wagon he could have fought them off said Brock, until someone came along the road, as there were only three renegade Apaches from San Carlos Reservation this 1878.

Site of Apache ambush of Judge H.C. McComas' family in lower Thompson Canyon, while they were enroute from Silver City to Shakespeare (near present Lordsburg, N.M.).

MRS. McCOMAS

Caesar Brock said he was on his way back from warning the Knight's Ranch that the Indians were off the reservation when two mounted Apaches jumped him — waving and pointing to the red headbands saying, "Me Scout! Me Cavalry Scout, See!" —maneuvering him into Thompson Canyon where the main body of Chatto's band of 18 were laying in ambush for the next stage from Silver City to Lordsburg that March 28,1883.

Not taking the ploy, they fired on him. He fired back de-horsing one, then mounted for the run home to Burro Springs some three miles westward.

In 1934-35, Brock took me down Thompson Canyon a mile below his ranch home. He showed me the old walnut tree near to where McComas fell, where they picked her up — her beautiful face bashed in by a gun butt-stock. Her body was nude, for squaws had stripped her. Little Charlie, age 6, had disappeared.

I stooped to scoop up a fruit jar of sand where Mrs. McComas had fallen. Brock said, "What do you want that for?" "For my grandchildren," I said, "This gallant lady should be remembered some way." Brock grunted, "You are the only one I've known who lives it."

Looking north up Thompson Creek past the big walnut tree, under which Judge McComas' body was found, below present Ceasar Brock's ranch. Mrs. McComas' nude body was placed into a buckboard, along with a dead horse, in the area marked by the "x" at the far right.

Since then, I have gone back to the site with Brock and twice to check the old tree lest some woodcutter had destroyed the spot where Judge McComas fell. I was again "seeing" Mrs. McComas "standing tall" in defense of her womanly instincts. Survival!

A hopeless moment. Any kind of death is better than life ravaged in a slow, wasting life of slavery. Unfortunately, not one of these stories ended with the Cavalry charging to the rescue. True stories don't make movies.

FOOTNOTES: The Connors dressed and made them ready for the stage to Silver. Little Charlie was killed in the Sierra Madres of Mexico by a squaw when crowded into a losing fight. All Silver City turned out when the McComas' were sent back to Kansas for burial.

How to put together the many stories into one — such old timers as Mrs. John T. Muir, James Parks, Billy Mauldin, Tom Wood, Liege and Anthony B. Connor? I used only Brock's. He was there just before and many times after.

While on a basketball trip to New Mexico Military Institute sometime between 1927-31, we stopped for radiator water (auto) at Blazer's Mill. A. N. Blazer pointed out Chato to me. I was then deep into the Lincoln County War so it didn't mean much. This story sprouted in 1934 at Brock's Ranch.

Brock pointed out in the arroyo sands where McComas led the attackers away that Mrs. McComas

153

The buckboard in which the McComas were riding was traced to Silver City's Elephant Corral and displayed for a time, then sold to Meeson-Marriage Corral, who sold it to a homesteader on Mule Creek, who sold it to a small-time rancher on Little Dry Creek, where it rested at the County's Old Pioneers Home. I photographed it there — ending a long search.

might turn the rig around. A lucky head-shot downed the horse that spun the buggy in.

During WWII, some patriotic soul broke into my story-file trunk — sold my brass (cartridges from this site and my collection of Apache fights), and the jar of sand.

It was not until 1959 when Apache Jason Betzinez's book came out that I learned where and how little Charlie's life ended in the Sierra Madres of Mexico by an enraged Apache. I again had to visit the site for a last look-see, hopeful this obsession would end.

Knight's Ranch was established in 1874 by R. Knight in Knight's Canyon, less than a mile from the ambush sight. The scalped victim crawled up to the door.

THERE'S A NAKED WOMAN AT THE DOOR

Early afternoon on September 9,1877, five ox-drawn freight wagons from Cohen's Silver City warehouse passed Knight's Ranch enroute to Clifton and stopped to rest and graze their oxen where the tree-lined canyon road turns out upon the high, flat plain — all 20 miles of it in yucca and gramma grass to the Gila River.

Waterless, treeless, wide-open and feared. Feared most by travelers to Globe and Clifton of being seen by the Apaches crossing their travelway from the San Carlos Reservation to the Sierra Madres of Mexico.

One doubtful story has it that the Mexican freighters had unyoked their oxen to graze in anticipation of a night jump across that wide and forbidding land.

Soon the Conners, at their ranch, heard rapid gunfire not long after the train had passed. One said, "It was only the freighters jumpin' a bunch of deer."

Shortly thereafter, a rider came tearing in at a whipping gallop, shouting, "*Los Indios! Los Indios*!" and incoherently jabbering all were killed but him. (As narrated by one who was at the house at the time.)

The dogs in the corrals became restless the following predawn. After the wagons had passed, Conner, Sr., alert and cautious — as was the rest of the fear-

A portion of the 4 room adobe (in a square) is all that remained in 1935-9 photos. Cottonwood trees have grown up around and almost taken over this once proud stop that withstood all Apache threats since 1874.

stricken household, moved about in the darkness from window to window, quietly surveying the outside, the corrals and livestock washed in glowing moonlight. No animals moved. The horses, every Apache's desire, were quiet. The milch cows, good only for meat, were quietly lying down and chewing their cuds.

But there was an ever present, death-like stillness about, a sense of mystic gloom building in the air outside and a chilled feeling of cold fog "working" its way into the house. No one could sleep.

Then came the stirring near the corral of whining dogs. Soon, at the door, came a pained, whimpering voice, followed by broken sobs and intermittent scratching at the door. The distressing cries of a desperate person.

Cautiously, Mrs. Conner cracked the door, saying "There's a naked woman at the door!" There stumbling, she fell upon the floor, sobbing, the horror of a scalped, naked woman.

Mrs. Conner and her daughter, Mrs. Knight, washed, clothed, and made her ready for the Silver City Stage.

The Greeks had their Thermopylae; the Texans their Alamo. Silver Citians . . . ? I doubt if one can find this WOMAN'S grave.

The men of Knight's ranch buried the three Mexican freighters. But there were five wagons? One man galloped away. Sheriff Whitehill reported a wounded Anglo-named man and a Spanish-named woman. This makes five men of record.

Folklore has it that the scalped woman's husband tried for a reconciliation, but was rejected because he ran.

I last saw this woman in 1934. To me, a stranger, she was still shy, reticent. She did not remember me. A woman of all women, I thought in respectful silence, back through all those years . . .

What more is there? I turned from her, a kindly soul, still standing wonderingly there in the door as I unknowingly walked down the hill to Broadway, still hearing the screams of the dying in that canyon fight of yesterday. The feelings stayed with me until I got to my rooming house west of the Elks Club.

Joseph Elijah Connor (at age 15) was one of three boys at the ranch when the naked woman crawled up to the door at dawn. Connor is buried south of the old Gila River Ranch/farm and 2 miles up-river from Red Rock He was one of the better of several story contributors.

Air photo of Knight's Ranch, looking northeast toward Silver City and Santa Rita copper mine El Cobre. The road west leads to Guthrie's Station (on Gila), Clifton and Globe. Also road to Ft. Bowie, Arizona. The road fork's 1/2 mile below this picture in the canyon (lower left). Here the Mexican "flour" train had stopped for supper and rest (to graze their oxen) before the night trip to Guthries (Gila River).

The stage and freight road from Silver City, 300 yards short of Knight's Ranch, to the left of the large rock.

Ma Meader, the last of the Meader family to go to the Robert's cabin. At age 19, Agnes was the last of two girls seen entering into Mrs. Roberts arms.

You are looking northwest, up the Frisco Valley. The two Meader boys went into the corn crib with their father. Apaches that killed all the livestock were beyond the cabin, upon the hill to the left and over the roof of the corn crib roof. Note absence of cottonwoods, shown in all later photos. The cabin, in the old photo, was not more than one year old in April, 1880.

MA MEADER'S RUN FOR ROBERT'S CABIN

Chief Victorio and his Apaches, 40-50 Bucks and 50-60 women and children (having been run out of the San Andres Mountains between T or C and Mescalero Reservation), worked their way through the Black Range — crossed into the highest of the western Mogollons at Mineral Creek that empties into the 'Frisco River near Alma and Roberts' cabin.

Victorio made known his presence (April 28, 1880) and the news was brought into Cooney by George Williams and Eli Mader. On their arrival they notified the settlers that they had been fired upon and two men killed.

In relating the event of their coming, John Lambert, one of the original old-timers, stated that at first he thought and believed that Williams and Mader were unduly excited. Continuing, Mr. Lambert said that "by common consent we took a position on the hillside, enabling us to overlook Mineral Creek. We had but just reached our point of vantage when the Indians came in sight, where the upper, or main portion of the town of Cooney was situated. A short consultation was held

Corral adjacent to the cabin in which all horses were shot down from Apaches nearby on the west mesa.
Gift from Agnes M. Snyder, Silver City.

The Robert's family some time after the fight (note tree to the far right). The cabin is to the right out of field-of-view.
You are looking east at highest Mogollon's. Victorio was on far mesa about mile on a white horse with a long Yucca stalk flag directing his Braves on the west mesa behind the cabin and corn crib.

and Sergeant Cooney was for attacking them then and there. It was urged by some of us that we were not only short of rifles, but the people of Alma and Pleasanton should be notified that the Indians were out and protection should be afforded the women and children, and besides, the miners on Copper Creek were presumably ignorant of the impending danger. It was then arranged that two should go to the valley. "Jim" Cooney and my partner, Jack Chick, went to Alma, gave the alarm; another party went to Clairmont, on Copper Creek, and George Doyle and myself remained on the ground and looked after matters as best we might, all of us believing that it was a small party out for pillage and plunder only, and did not intend to attack in force the valley settlement. The next day this illusion was dispelled. Doyle and myself made the best of it. During the night the Apache scouts prowled around us and came quite close."

"It was a long, cheerless night. At daybreak I determined to visit the cabin. I worked myself to within fifty feet of the door. A slight noise on the hillside caused the appearance of two Indians at the doors of two separate cabins. Seeing that the camp was strongly garrisoned by the Indians, I cautiously made my way to my hiding place, and enroute I heard a signal up the canyon, which was followed by the appearance of a medium-sized, spare-looking Indian, mounted on a fine-looking bay horse, whom I recognized as Victorio. Riding into the midst of his warriors, he addressed them in a few impassioned words. At the close of his speech, every warrior set off on a trot down the canyon to attack the settlements on the 'Frisco. Victorio remained and was soon joined by two other chiefs, whom I believed to be Nana and Geronimo.

Death of Cooney and Chick

"They remained in consultation but a few minutes when Victorio took the trail of his fighting men. Up to this time but three or four mounted

159

Maurice Coats, old-time merchant in Mogollon, scouted the Apaches before going to the Cabin-Crib for the fight. He came with the Roberts from Arizona-Utah, the year before the fight (Mormon pioneers).

Agnes Meader Snyder (in hat) was taken at age 79 to the site of the fight. The photo with the .45-70 Sharps rifle was made in 1950 in Silver City, age 89. They came from North Texas for new homestead land and passed the Mexican massacre site shortly after it happened.

Indians had been seen. Now the pack animals in charge of the squaws, strongly guarded by the bucks, made their appearance and immediately appropriated three wagon loads of supplies we had received the day before. Following the pack train, there came about sixty young bucks, in reality mere boys, but all armed with the old-fashioned store gun. Some were driving small flocks of sheep. Most of the band passed my viewpoint, leaving but forty or fifty at the cabins, now headquarters for the different encampments. At this time, about eight or nine o'clock in the morning of the 29th of April 1880, I distinctly heard an irregular volley of shots, which was followed by a few single shots, which convinced me that Cooney and Chick had been ambushed, murdered and mutilated without being able to make a defense of any kind. But a few minutes elapsed when a courier brought news to the headquarters camp of Apaches, which remained quiet and decorous. At the outer camps the scene was different and, in these camps, pandemonium reigned supreme. Every demonstration of savage joy was indulged in to the utmost. About noon a mounted messenger came to camp and presto! What a change. The cabins were stripped of everything they contained and set on fire. One of the bucks entered my cabin and stole my looking glass, suspending it on his back, followed

160

by a string of squaws who were yelling, wrangling and fighting among themselves to obtain a glimpse of their dirty faces. At dark the entire outfit marched down the canyon, and under the cover of darkness, I made my way by a difficult and circuitous route to Clairmont, and I assure you that the crowing of chickens and barking of dogs was the sweetest music I ever heard."

Besieged and Besiegers

"The arrival of Cooney and Chick at Alma on the night of the 28th of April with the terrible news that Victorio and his band had killed Brightman and another man, name unknown, caused some excitement. A messenger was immediately dispatched to Pleasanton. The balance of the night was devoted to strengthening the Roberts' cabin, on the west side of the river, and only when every available piece of timber was used was it pronounced well 'forted' by those old and experienced Indian fighters, Keller, Elliot and Coates. The young men of the settlement put in the entire night corralling horses and strengthening the corrals. About nine o'clock on the evening of the 28th of April, Cooney and Chick visited the Meader home, now a part of the W.

S. Ranch, and gave the alarm. Mr. Meader did not credit the news, and at the close of the day's labor said to his wife 'that now the garden was planted, old Victorio could come if he wanted to."

"Mrs. Sarah Roberts, Mrs. Agnes Snyder of Dry Creek and Mrs. George Warden of California are the only women survivors of the siege that are known. Mrs. 'Grandma' Roberts is hale and hearty at 76 years of age and bids fair to round out a century. Mrs. Meader, deceased, with her womanly judgment and intuition, did not agree with her husband and immediately began preparations for the following day, one of the most eventful in her life's history."

"From 10 p.m. until 1 a.m., Mrs. Meader busied herself in moulding bullets for her son Edward, who was loading Winchester shells for the fight, which opened at about 10 a.m. the following morning. Early on the morning of the 29th, Cooney called for volunteers to join him on a trip to Cooney. Chick alone responded. Mrs. Meader vainly tried and expostulated with Cooney and Chick, begging them to stay, but, believing the force in the valley was strong enough for defensive and offensive movements, they started alone. Between 9 and 10 o'clock, their animals came back riderless. Potter and Mottsinger rode up the Mineral Creek valley on a scouting trip and were fired on within 3 miles of Alma, Potter receiving a wound in the hand. Mottsinger escaped uninjured. On their return the Pleasanton contingent came in sight. The party consisted of Williams, Wilcox, Thomas Carpenter, Robert Sipes, Meadows and Foster. When Cooney's and Chick's horses came in sight, Maurice Coates turned to Jim Killer and said, in his quiet way, "Jim, we're in for it now.""

"The Pleasanton party immediately proceeded to the fort, picketed their animals and took an active part in the preparations for the impending battle. At 10 o'clock, the Indians appeared on the hillside west of Roberts and opened fire on the 'fort,' which was filled with women and children. The fort was Robert's cabin and corn crib barn. As the Indians appeared in sight, Mr. Elliott, a brave and fearless frontiers-man, hastened to the Meader Ranch and called out to Mr. Meader and his family, 'There's no time to lose. Get over to the fort.' The team was in readiness, but it did not require a second invitation or warning for Mr. Meader to start with his wife, two sons and two daughters for the Roberts' cabin."

"When nearing the cabin, the Indians concentrated their fire upon Meader and his family. One bullet from the Indians passed through the cape of Mrs. Agnes Snyder's bonnet and the same bullet clipped a lock of Mr. Meader's hair. Mr. Elliott succeeded in housing the entire party and a second time the heroism and foresight of Mrs. Meader was in evidence as to what might happen if the settlers lost the day. The women and children occupied a hollow square within the fort, weeping, as well they might, for none could guess as to what the outcome of the siege would be. In a few kindly, reassuring words she quieted their fears. Mrs. Meader told them that while only one side of the 'fort' was under fire, they would fill an empty barrel with water, and all of the empty tubs and buckets, before the Indians turned the ditch. They responded with a will and every vessel that would hold water was filled to overflowing, and not a minute too soon, as within a few minutes the water had ceased running in the ditch."

"The firing now became general, the men occupying the space between the center and the walls of the cabin, and as opportunity presented, taking long range and often effective shots at the enemy on the hill. This continued for some little time, when five men took up a protected position in the rear of the fort, which enabled them to do greater execution. This lasted but a short three-quarters of an hour when, without warning of any kind, Coates and his party were fired upon from the rear. A hasty retreat was made to the cabin, with the loss of a belt of cartridge and a six-shooter belonging to Mr. Coates, which was recovered during the afternoon. One of the attacking party of Indians took it into his head that he could creep up to the cabin in broad daylight and steal a horse that was picketed within thirty feet of the fort. If he had continued lying flat on the ground when he reached the horse, he might have escaped, but rising to his feet to cut the rope, offered too good a mark for Jim Keller's .45 caliber, 120 grain Sharp's rifle. When he had fallen and it was safe to examine him, the identical pistol and belt which was lost in the morning was buckled around him. The pistol was removed and for many years Mr. Coates regarded it as a priceless relic."

"After the death of the Indian, Wilcox, for whom the mining district of that name was christened, needlessly rose up in full view above the barricade and an instant later fell with a bullet through the heart, the only casualty of the day. During the night, which was very dark, the Indians succeeded in removing the body of their comrade and made their retreat in good order."

"At about 2 o'clock in the morning after fighting all day and on guard during the night with no food or water, 'Skelt' Williams, who, with the Pleasanton boys occupied a corn crib or barn about thirty yards from the fort, went over to the main cabin and, knocking, Mrs. Meader inquired in a low tone of voice, "Who's there?' Williams replied, "It's Skelt, and I want a drink of water for the boys." Mrs. Meader recognized the voice and said, 'Come in, Skelt; don't strike a match; be careful; the water is in the barrel in the corner and don't step on the dead man.' Wilcox, who had fallen in the afternoon, had not been removed. With all the danger which beset them and the impending massacre in the morning, Mrs. Meader took in the situation and its attendant horrors calmly and quietly."

"Williams returned to his post of duty and the succeeding hours from 2 a.m. until daylight were long and tedious. Every one in the little fort was wide awake and each one expected that at the first streak of dawn the fight would be renewed. The majority believed that a renewal of hostilities meant a charge on the fort and the massacre of all."

"Day broke and every foot of ground was thoroughly and anxiously scanned, and as the sun rose it was found that the enemy had broken camp during the very early morning hours and left for parts unknown."

Footnote: The above is as reported by several in the Roberts' cabin and corncrib to the editor of the <u>*Mogollon Mining Journal*</u> *dated 1915, some time after the fight of April, 1880, and will differ from the remarks of Agnes Meader Snyder, whom I visited the site with during my Silver City years. The remark under the illustration and the photos are from Mrs. Snyder.*

Looking east across (Rio) Frisco Valley at high Mogollon Mountains from where Apache Victorio and his band came. The Apache group that killed all the livestock (in corrals behind the cabin) were on the hill and west of the corn crib.

Victorio, squaws and main band stayed on the far east-side hills.

Aerial photo made October 23, 1977, flying south along the west side of Frisco. Note irrigation ditch still in use. Apaches were on center right hill top marked "X". Trees came after the fight.

Looking west at York's home. Knox, on seeing his lead horse shot down, bailed out of the wagon, to die in a volley of rife fire. His wife came back to the wagon for a last look at the children. Her mother and grandmother ran for the house. In the wagon was Mrs. Knox's father and a hired man, and possibly her younger brother.

FELIX KNOX

I stood on the ridge a quarter mile north of the old York ranch and looked down upon the old Silver City-Clifton road and the spot where this brave man, Felix Knox, fell, throwing himself between the Apache horde and his family's wagon under a barrage of rifle fire that April 22, 1882. I thought of all the orphans and widows these renegades had made and the many ranch houses they had burned and gutted in their sweep from the San Carlos to the Sierra Madres of Mexico.

Then those moments of the past began unraveling as I watched below me, a day in 1934, when Jim Parks, W. H. Mauldin and friend, Hick Hames (also a Gila River cowboy working for the 24-Circle), as they pondered, argued and beat the mesquite for the exact spot where Knox fell.

Knox lost his head — as any father would — bailed out of his wagon, charged the Apaches on the ridge-top, irresponsive of his military training and judged by some as foolish. We do know that one of the women was his wife, as were at least two of the children in the wagon. The other two women are believed to be Mrs. Knox's mother and grandmother.

The wagon driver, on hearing the warning shots from York's corrals — saw the Apaches and wheeled for the run back. The lead horse went down — gut-shot at first fire. (Mrs. Knox's letter, two days after the fight, said they were attacked by 20

163

Mrs. York is at the lower right window. In the upper window is a Twenty-four Circle cowboy. Lower center window: Mrs. York's father. Left lower window: believed to be George Musgrave (who was living in Sufford, Arizona in 1935), and who brought the word from Clifton that the Apaches were raiding -burning and killing — in a wide trail, southward to the Sierra Madres of Mexico. (At York's Ranch, past noon, 22 April, 1882.)

Indians and gave only the number—not the names of those in the wagon). Mrs. Sara Butler York, widowed by the Apaches the October before, and with five small children, wrote in 1928, "the hills on both sides were covered with Indians" — actually about 75-100 Bucks — "of which about 30 were firing at the wagon."

South and across the river moving southward were about 150-180 squaws and children driving their commissary — the stolen cattle of murdered settlers and freighters.

Shown on page 163 is the left lead horse to the Knox wagon as it floundered and struggled in the harness. The women, all of Mexican descent, jumped — running from the wagon. The second woman, a grandmother familiar with early Sonoran Apache raids, is shown struggling to keep up. Mrs. Knox is shown back near the wagon.

The man at the rear of the wagon wheel supposedly would be Mrs. Knox's father, and the boy of 18 on top, her brother. They fought off the Apaches until the horse struggled to its feet.

An animal of devoted endurance (as horses can

and will) rose up in its harness and the wagon was off and running. Overtaking the women, the men threw them in, as if they were sacks of straw.

The eight men from the house and corrals began shooting over the wagon at everything on a horse, said Hick Hames later at the Old Timer's Reunion at Jim Parks' home in Duncan, AZ in 1934. Jim East's Sharps rifle could be heard booming above the Winchester fire as the Apaches came crowding the wagon in the yard.

FOOTNOTE: They buried Knox with the three Apaches on the west side of the house. These same Apaches were fresh from a daylight killing about 4 miles down river, having killed Francisco, the 21-year-old wagon master. His father, Barbaro Lucero of Las Cruces, was owner of the ox-train of twelve wagons. Francisco was the oldest brother of the late sheriffs of Dona Ana County, Felipe and Jose, who still have heirs living there.

George Riley York and Charlie Moore, his foreman, an 18-year-old boy-man, were killed in the Doubtful Canyon ambush the October before and are

FELIX B. KNOX: Ex-military (band). Saloon owner: Silver City, Globe and Clifton. Married upperclass Mexican woman, Tucson. Children: two. Family: mother-in-law and grandmother-in-law. Mrs. Knox re-married Jesus Guerra, died in 1916 in Ruiz Canyon, Globe. Knox's daughter, Merceda, married Frank Diaz, who died in Ruiz Canyon, Globe, in 1925 (according to historian John B. Woody, Globe, Arizona.)

Picture credit: Clara Thompson Woody Museum, Globe, Arizona.

Sara B. and George Riley York. Sara B. died in Los Angeles at age 95 in 1939. She was one of our GREAT women. York died chasing Apache horse thieves. They hang white men horse thieves; Apaches just kill the owners.

Credit: The Clara Thompson Woody Museum, Globe, Arizona.

also now in unmarked graves at the ranch house site.

I often wondered about this Jim East who was reported at Gettysburg. Was he the sniper who, from McPherson's barn, "took out" General Reynolds high and in the neck at 400-500 yards - a lover of horse flesh?

Mrs. Knox died in 1916, her daughter in 1925, both now lost in the old Globe cemetery.

The tall Apache on the white horse (page 163) represents Nachez, son of Cochise. Others reported there were Chato, Loco, Geronimo and some of Ju's Mexico band, all perpetrators of the outbreak.

After lunch there, Knox refused to stay at the York Ranch after repeated pleadings and warnings that the Indians were raiding their way. He drove on hoping to make the little settlement of Mexican Flats four miles down river.

Why was this so important? Saloon rumors have it that it was the embarrassment from whiskey and wine in the wagon that sent Knox to his death

(also confirmed by Louis Abrams, in Silver City, whose father owned a saloon business in Clifton).

How times change! Were the fight today — after the Indians had gone — they'd brought out the whiskey and wine and there'd be singing and dancing at the Yorks'.

Others say that Knox passed the circuit preacher above Purdy's Ranch (above York's) where he gave him a drink of water. Folklore has it that he always made generous donations to the Silver City and Globe churches.

Shown at York's grave site is Harvell Coster (b-1910), lifelong native, well-to-do Gila River farmer, who lives a short two miles below the York Ranch. You are looking west from the former front yard of York's ranch over a plowed field, through cottonwoods, to the Gila river.

George Riley York was killed 13 October, 1881, in west Doubtful Canyon at the spring (lower right corner). Also killed was York's ranch foreman, an 18 year old boy-man from Kansas, who was working to support his widowed mother and children. Doubtful was the main stage and freight road from Las Cruces and Silver City to Tucson and the west coast.

Site of York's ambush. To the right is the windmill in the desert willows where the posse rode into the spring after a 40 -mile, hard dry ride from the river.

Natividad and wife in Bavispe in 1935 — visiting relatives for the first time.

Natividad and wife visiting in Fronteras in 1935. He was age 100 in 1930.

THE SACKING OF NORIA

Natividad Padilla

Padilla, born in Janos, Chihuahua, was a lifetime freighter for military cargo and charcoal for the Clifton Smelter in Arizona, first using oxen and then mules as corn became available.

Padilla's father, Anastacio, known as "El Senor", was head arriero for an ore-packing mule train before the Apaches shut the mines down in the late 1830's. He then joined the home guard as a scout at Janos, where he met Pepe Martinez, also a scout for the *milicia* at Fronteras, and father of Natividad's first wife.

When the word of the sacking of Noria reached the Commandante of Janos and Fronteras, Senor and Pepe were sent scouting south to Nacozari (10 miles north of Noria) to report the Apache strength and direction on the trail of travel, with El Senor reporting back to Janos.

The scouts turned eastward at Nacozari, going through the pass into the valley of the Rio del Bavispe, where they cut a large Apache trail going east into a large canyon.

Juan Jose marshalling his Noria captives into El Cajon de Las Mujeres Muertas 18 air miles west of Bavispe.

After passing the canyon some distance, the scouts went into the timber to camp. The next day came a dust cloud-galloping bucks crowding their stolen herd. The squaws and children riding double — Chief Juan Jose was pushing a good "harvest" of Noria mules.

The scouts followed discreetly northward where this group was joined by another under Juan Diego (brother of Juan Jose), whose renegades were moving a cattle herd from Rancho San Bernadino.

Apaches Meet

The two groups joined north of the pass. The scouts waited until dark. Pepe went home to Fronteras and El Senor to Janos.

The two Apache parties joined and went north to camp at Juniper Springs.

Natividad Padilla was married to Pepe's oldest daughter in Janos in 1849. Pepe told this story to his son-in-law and old friend, Anastacio Padilla, of the "*Cajon de Las Mujeres Muertas,*" which was

the canyon they had passed on their scouting trip to Nacozari and had been known for years thereafter as "the Canyon of the Dead Women."

Here the Noria raiders went into the canyon for a drunken orgy, to ravage their captives and show disdain for the *Rurales*.

". . . The Apaches drove the herd into a dead-end canyon for the squaws to guard, while the remaining squaws stripped the older girls and women down to their bare feet.

". . . The warriors, not needed at the canyon entrance, were then shown their huddling victims amid giggling and screaming of sheer delight.

". . . The more active girls fled up the canyon to throw themselves under the trampling horse's hooves. The older women crawled bear-like up the slopes to the top, only to be lanced back into the canyon.

". . . The Apache camp and livestock moved restlessly about to the sobbing and moaning of the victims. At daylight, the braves on guard were shown their victims to further ravage into their death-like stare in this land where the scalp-bounty was a way of life.

Looking Southwest at Juniper Springs and the distant Guadalupe Pass near Section 34, T33S, R19W, where Lt. Col. St. George Cooke's Mormon Battalion camped, November 24th,1846, with the remaining 321 men (and 5 wives) and their mule-drawn wagon train, California bound. South 4.5 miles is today's southern Hidalgo County (NM) border. Here, through this San Luis Pass, is where John Johnson's men (23) escaped from the Playa (sometimes dry lake) Apache fight (3/4 miles West) —fighting their way 45 miles SE to Janos (Mexico), leaving another seven determined Apaches dead. Above right is a Brigham Young University (BYU, Provo, UT) senior (Mormon) researching the trail of his fellow brethren on March 14, 1992, late by 145 years and 110 days; here where their spirits still live on in the juniper trees on the juniper-studded hills.

Pepe's Story

Such was Pepe's story that Padilla told me in April, 1937, at his jacal on Whiskey Creek, my real-life link into the history of a forgotten hundred years.

I asked Padilla how many victims there were. He stared in shocked surprise: "Eet ess better theeese things (the records) always get lost een the garrison," and gave me one of his whimsical go-to-hell grins. "There ees no way you can breen these peoples back ageen."

On his birthday in 1937, I drove him for the first time, back to Janos, a present for 6 years of my prodding.

His old home was still a live-in adobe and appeared to be outside of the old walled-in village. He showed me where the priest stood who rang the church bells announcing the coming of the 17 American trappers (with five-mule packers) who had fought a large encampment some two days north at an Apache waterhole.

While the Commandante and the Alcalde were unwinding long speeches of glory of how the *milicia* would drive the enemy from the land, John J. Johnson, the leader from Montezuma, posted a letter to the Governor of Chihuahua and a note for the Commandante at Fronteras (who had offered no help for the fight) as to where he could find his cannon.

169

Looking south at the playa; over the crest and beyond is Guadalupe Pass, through which Cooke's battalion departed in 1846 and through which Johnson's men (from Montezuma, Sonora, Mexico) came on April 20th, 1837, to overtake Apache Chiefs Juan Jose's and brother Juan Diego's horde camped here with an estimated 600 head of Sonoran horses, mules and cattle (a year's commissary) and other loot from the sacked Noria 100 miles SW. Testy Juan Jose accepted Johnson's wine supper, his "last supper". The following day, a small cannon roared — blasted through the horde picking over a pre-set feast of their favorite pinole (wheat flour) — leaving dead about 20 braves and 3 squaws. This tree, a full grown "witness" to the event, long gone — dead, more alive than the Apaches buried here. The tree is standing tall for the BYU student, whose hand is above where his brethren left their markings "11/46" in 1846.

Johnson's Reward

John J. Johnson, who had promised his men payment with half the horses and mules, had lost his money and the herd (but did save their "hides"), was in no mood to give the Commandante at Janos his scalps for his Governor — not after risking the lives of 22 men, riding 265 miles and being away from home for over a month — for a Governor's award of 100 pesos or four and one-half pesos per brave killed.

Johnson and his riflemen (trappers and mule buyers) overtook Juan Jose and his renegades at Juniper Springs, an encampment of 75 well-armed braves and twice as many

women and children, where he was immediately challenged: "If you have come to fight, we are ready."

Johnson professed to being lost — he and his 22 undesirables, now that America was at war with Mexico in Texas.

Johnson observed squaws hiding a young captive Mexican girl and offered trade. Juan Jose replied: "She make a good squaw," and traded for gunpowder, which further assured Johnson that trouble was abrewing. The 12-year-old girl — sharp and observant — told Johnson that runners had already gone to outlying villages, so Johnson set out a feast of wheat flour within the pre-set range of his cannon.

170

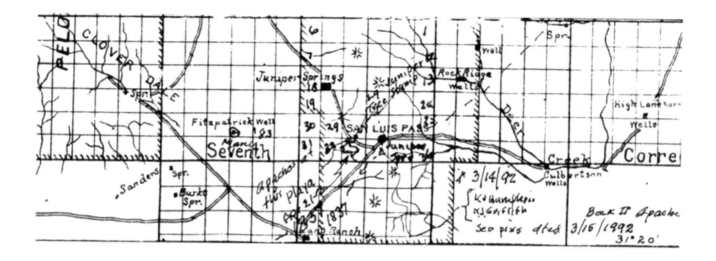

The Big Boom

Amid the scrambling and jabbering of the braves dominating the squaws, Johnson, from his hillside, touched off the fuse of the cannon (a small tripod mounted mule-packing gun) with his cigarillo. The BOOM reverberated from the hillside — dying into the screams of the maimed and wounded whose abject stares ranged across the swath-of-the-dead at each other. The braves frantically scattered to regroup again.

One of the American trappers at Janos, before Johnson's party departed for Montezuma, said to Padilla's father: "I only wish that cannon boom could have reached to Noria."

Johnson showed the scalps of Juan Jose, Juan Diego and Moreno around Noria before presenting them to the Governor of Sonora. Only Johnson should tell of the joy of the girl's family. She married and lived another 42 years in the Montezuma area.

Pepe Martinez and Anastacio Padilla, as far as Padilla knew, never saw Noria.

FOOTNOTE: Sometime after June, 1907, Charlie Johnson, a Harvard Mining Engineer from Silver City, N.M., was locating mining claims east of Cloverdale in southernmost Hidalgo county.

In the playa a quarter mile west of Juniper Springs where some Mexican ranch hands were building fence, Johnson was told there appeared to be a brass mounted cannon barrel in a pool of water.

Johnson set his transit up but the soil was too soft for accurate bearing readings. A cloudburst came and drove him from the area. On his way out, he stopped at a prospector's mining claim. The prospector told him he came there with the Clantons in 1881 and stayed there after the fight with the Mexican smugglers in Skeleton canyon. The prospector also said the Apaches used to come up from the Sierra Madres in Mexico and dance and chant around the spring to scare the bad spirits away from their ancestors who were killed there in a Big Fight maybe "viente y viente anos hace" (20 and 20 years ago).

Charlie Johnson (no relation to John J.) gave me his rough notes and his Powell & Kingman map in 1935, hoping I might prove his location of the "Johnson Massacre of 1837" — the one then touted at Santa Rita, east of Silver City, N.M.

As a high school researcher on the Maggie Graham story, I met Rex W. Strickland, a teacher in the public school at Van Horn, Texas, in 1924-5. It was there he gave me my best tip on the story "Re-creation of Maggie Graham."

On my last visit with Dr. Strickland, who became Professor of History at the University of Texas at El Paso, he showed me a paper he was preparing — THE BIRTH AND DEATH OF A LEGEND — which answered many of my questions in THE SACKING OF NORIA, after a search of five flights into the areas between Juniper Springs and Montezuma.

To Mrs. J. Paul (Mary) Taylor of La Mesilla, I am indebted for her research through church files throughout Sonora and Chihuahua for the names and dates of people important to the period of the 1830's.

171

Rosa, her kids and the boy from the Lyon & Campbell Cattle Co., squeezing through the "box" trap set by Nachez between Mud Springs and Guthrie's Station.

ROSA

Rosa's grandmother came from a family of Spanish stock raisers on the southern slopes of the Pyrenees mountains. The family came to new Spain in 1800 for a land grant and to raise cattle in the new world, settling in El Rancho Presidio de San Bernardino, 10 leagues northeast of Fronteras and southeast of the present Douglas, Arizona.

Rosa's grandmother was born in about 1808 in the Presidio where it took four eight-pound cannons, a firing cannister and cut chains to clear the outer walls. It was manned with only ill-trained Rurales and flint-lock, muzzle-loading rifles firing one shot to the Apache's five arrows.

Rosa's grandmother was saved from the burning Presidio in 1838. Here, the successor to Chief Juan Diego—who was killed in the Johnson massacre of April, 1837 — captured the Presidio by tricking the commandante into a parley inside the only gate.

About 1840, Rosa's mother was born near Bear Creek on the Gila river. Rosa was born in 1861 on a rancheria in the Sierra Madre Mountains, east of Bavispe, while her Apache father was raiding on the Butterfield stage road.

Rosa's Apache husband (a son of Cochise) and their son Blas, born in this house about 1897. Picture believed to have been taken by Zane Gray on his visit about 1910-12. Copy made from Blas's copy 1935, when Blas worked in the Clifton mine. Shown here is the wooden bathtub Blas said his mother used twice-a-week in nearby Blue Creek, while her husband Neme, with gun, watched on nearby ridge. Muleshoe cowboys always were nosing around. Barrel with tub cover was their domestic water. Sheep and goat pens to right of hut in the distance.

Rosa's father was wounded in a costly stage fight, but it is not known if he was wounded in the April ambush of the stage near upper Doubtful canyon, or in the Cook's Pass fight in July. Both were costly to the Apaches.

Rosa's mother took her to a Mexican family in Bavispe for adoption, returning immediately to her rancheria. When her warrior came home wounded and demanding to see his "new son," the toothless squaw said in broken Spanish, "You have no son." She then cowed inside the wickiup (ocotillo boughs and skins) waiting for the worst, while he searched the rancheria and outlying bush. Rosa, many years later, learned from the Bavispe family who traded with the Apaches, that her mother was thrown out into the snow and died of the "coughs" (pneumonia).

As Rosa neared her 14th birthday, her adopted parents knew she must be sent away before some "buck" picked up her scent. Nachez II, the disowned son of Cochise, had been waiting for the right moment. A big fight broke out with knives between Cochise's sons in the tapia portion of the walled-in section of the village. Only with guns was the family able to drive off "Nachez the Warrior," the perpetrator of the fight.

The family quickly hid Rosa under blankets in an ox-drawn carreta — a two wheeled wooden cart

and sent her on the night road to Janos with their son Nemecio, age 17, goading the steers and Nachez II trailing behind as rear guard. At Janos, the family's cousins took them in, hiding Rosa in the wine cellar; their plan was to take Rosa and one man out north to Dog Springs to wait for the first freight wagons going north to Santa Rita del Cobre. Rosa chose Nachez II over Nemecio, knowing that Nemecio would never survive either Nachez in a knife fight.

At Cow Springs, Rosa and Neme — Rosa's name for her new man whom she would make into anything but an Apache — caught the freight wagons of Tulley and Ochoa going west as far as Soldier's Farewell. From here they could walk into Knight's Ranch.

At Knight's Ranch, Mrs. Sara Conner Knight fed them, put them beside the fireplace for the night, and the next morning sent them on their way to Burro Springs. At Burro Springs, Mrs. Royal Yeamens fed them and started them up Mulberry Canyon where Neme hoped to join a woodcutter (charcoal) camp. Only the night before, the mail hack driver said "Come on, Reverend, let's get the knot tied!" The priest hesitated, looking at Neme, a young, strong, six foot two Apache heathen with a bland look on his face, patiently waiting to take Rosa's "hand-in-his." The priest did not know that he was uniting a half

173

Another picture (believed) by Zane Gray. Note the arrangement of the picture. Blas is shown in the center beside the hut. Gray was noted for taking many photos of his story sites. He visited the Double Circle cow outfit north of Clifton. This story was never published.

Mud Springs where Rosa's girl was born. Here was her first real home. It is now the Charlie Martin Ranch (son of the founder), who ranched here in 1935.

Here is where Rosa passed away. The tree she watered as a seedling is shown 22 years later (1935). Here a small Spanish-English dictionary (believed to be used for education by his son, Blas, who was good in both languages) was found sealed inside a gallon Karo syrup bucket.

Spanish, half Apache with a 15 year old Catholic girl who needed uniting right soon, and who was even more Indian, being 3/4 Apache and 1/4 Spanish. "Hurry up, Reverend!" shouted the driver. "We gotta get to Ash Peak by midnight or your soul and my hide will be lying under a circle of buzzards by noon tomorrow!" By mid-afternoon the next day, a boy rider from the LC's (Lyons-Campbell Cattle Company on the Gila) came in on a sweat- lathered horse shouting "Paches off the reservation!" Yeaman put his stepson Ceasar Brock on a horse, shouting "Get up the Mulberry and get our Mexican bride in here fast!" That evening the renegades struck, killing 10 Mexicans from a group of traveling musicians in Mulberry Canyon.

Believed to be a photo of Rosa's twin boys and girl taken at Mud Springs by George Musgrave before the Apache raid of April 1882, and before Rosa's run.

W. H. (Billy) Maulding holding a .40-70 Sharps Buffalo Rifle used in keeping the Apaches (under Nachez) on the west mesa. Guthrie's station is east of present Verdin, New Mexico. Maulding held the gate open for Rosa.

Hijos

Next summer at Burro Springs, Rosa "bingoed" with twin boys. The next year they moved 12 miles west to Rhiels Ranch on the Gila, where Neme was to herd goats and sheep "on the shares." After two years with a start in goats and sheep, they moved to Mud Springs, an "open" spring 9 miles northwest of the Gila. It was here that she started a new home and birthed a new daughter. Rosa also began her trade of making cowboy's deer-skin gloves, which she traded at Guthrie's Stage Station on the Gila, famed as Schriever's Ferry by writer Ernest Haycox in his epic story "The Stage to Lordsburg."

Rosa's Run

On April 22, 1882, the dogs left Neme, the sheep and goats came whining into Rosa's jacal (hut); she knew that the Apaches had jumped the reservation. Rosa had the kids and horses ready when she looked down the wide arroyo and saw a boy-rider breaking out of Blue Creek. The 9 year-old boy-rider from the LC's galloped passed shouting "Paches are coming up the river! The settlers are gathering at Guthrie's!"

Rosa knew that Nachez wanted her and the kids alive — to torture. With 9 miles to Guthrie's and Apaches appearing off the right-front and left-rear, Rosa knew that every minute the "box" would be closing tighter. Rosa knew the best canyon into Guthrie's. She snapped the bullwhip, putting the twins on the grey mare in the lead and kept her horse's nose right on the mare's tail — the boy's race mare had no choice but to follow. Had the boy lagged behind the Apaches would have "gut-shot his horse and tortured him later." Nachez wanted his victims alive as only an Apache can. The horses came off the west mesa, near the old Mexican cemetery. The Apaches opened fire with long range rifles, shelling the station walls as Rosa stormed through the opening gate.

The three children passed with diphtheria in about 1885 as Rosa searched the river valley from Red Rock to Duncan for a doctor that existed only in Silver City or Clifton.

The cemetery on west mesa at Guthrie's where Rosa's children (the three tots who made the run) are buried in unmarked graves. The George Guthrie Stage Station is the site to the left of the distant buildings. You are looking southeast over the Gila River valley east of Verdin.

A Mexican oxen carreta of the type used to convey Rosa from Bavispe to her cousin's (merchants) at Janos. Wheels were larger in the mountains of Mexico. It is believed this type cart was used to transport the widow of Don Florentino Samaniego, Bavispe Commandante, who was killed in Apache ambush west of Bavispe in 1838. The smaller wheels were seen in the valley around Oposura and Noria, Sonora, in 1935.

Site of the fight where Rosa's Apache father was wounded April 28, 1861, one mile west of Stein's Peak on the Butterfield Stage route. Here John James Giddings of San Antonio was among those killed.

The Apache era ended in 1886 with the surrender of Nachez and Geronimo. The little cowmen were crowding the "big boys." Texas' John Alexander Martin filed on Mud Springs in 1887, causing Rosa to move her sheep to the Gila between the LC's and the Trofers — only to be "hounded out" because of the sheep. They moved their small herd 12 miles northwest of Mud Springs to the head of Blue Creek. It was a sad day for Rosa to leave her first home. In the words of W.H. (Billy) Maulding, who opened the gate for them to storm through amid the rifle shots at Guthrie's, "If I live to be a hundred, I'll

never see anything like it again." He died in 1955, at age 91.

About 1911, a writer from the Double Circle Cattle Co. came into Rosa's sheep camp in a two-span mule team buckboard with a driver. Blas, her only son, later said he didn't know what to think when

176

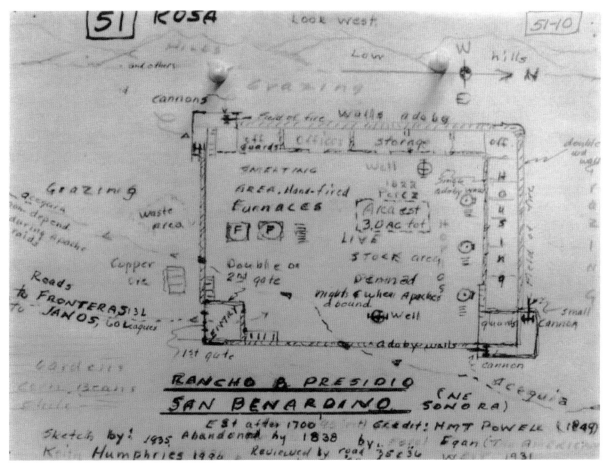

A sketch map of the Rancho and Presidio San Bernardino as was in one of the diaries of the gold rush emigrants of 1849 period. From the Journal of H.M.T. Powel. Rosa's grandmother was, it is believed, taken captive here by Juan Diego in the (possible) sacking of the Presidio about 1837.

the big man in knee pants, wool socks, shoes and a cap, carrying a camera and a beautiful, engraved rifle said "My name is Grey. Do you have any wolves that needed killing?" Could this be the writer Zane Grey? There were some Greys around Ft. Henry about 1776-82, who were hell on the Indians and winter wolves. He took some pictures and later sent them back, but when the book "Riders of the Purple Sage" came out there were no "Riders of the Double Circle."

Time

The little cowmen were spreading from the river to the Forest Reserve. On a trip to Clifton to sell wool and gloves, Rosa and Blas topped the ridge a few rods before getting home; their cabin was blown into rubble. The sheep scattered, the dogs shot and there sat Neme on the rubble. With head in hands, the blank stare on his beardless face was one that only an Apache can make. They gathered the remnants of

the herd and moved 5 miles farther up the Blue to the Forest Reserve.

Rosa was beginning to show her years now. Her beautiful face was still unwrinkled and firm, but lacked its old determination. Her dark hair was turning grey-white in streaks, enough to make any middle-aged bachelor cowman wish. Maulding once said "There isn't a cowboy in all the river- drinking ranches who had seen her trading her gloves at Guthrie's that wouldn't have traded his horse and saddle for a lottery ticket to marry her." The way he told it, made me wonder if he had really married at Wahl's ranch the week before.

Rosa began watering the little oak seedling behind her new home each day. Something was bothering her. Blas said, "I caught her looking southward, down the view at her first home where she buried the Little Ones; I suggested we go see the Little Ones." Her eyes watered and she replied "We'll move them to Guthrie's on the west mesa." After they had finished, Blas helped his mother back into the wagon and Neme said "We'll take the long road back down-river past Duncan to the old York's Ranch." Rosa just sat there, saying nothing. She was living it all over again, just as she told it to Blas — from Bavispe to Janos, Knight's Ranch, Burro Springs, Rhiels and up to Mud Springs where she left the best part of her life. She just stared at the mules as if they were taking her to some foreign land. She climbed down from the wagon, picked some blooming yellow turpentine weeds, laid them tenderly upon their grave and said "I wish there had been a priest."

Nearly home, at the head of Butler Canyon on the divide between Bathtub Draw and the Blue, Rosa pressed Neme's arm and said "Wait!" The sun was sliding down behind Mount Graham, splashing streaks of crimson on Ash Peak; farther south on Animas Peak, farther to the right and deeper, a tinge of gold claimed the Sierra Madres with her mother and her grandmother.

At dawn the next morning, Neme slipped out of bed, dressed, shook Blas and went outside to the crisp mountain air into the yard of jumping dogs. He turned the sheep out and returned to start the breakfast fire while Blas milked the goat. An eerie feeling hung in the early quiet of something foreboding to come. It came over Blas as he took the milk to the house. He stepped inside. His father was standing at the bedroom door, tears streaming down his stolid, beardless face. His eyes were of a middle-age man, turned into child-like pity — reaching out for help — where there was no help. Rosa, at 52, was gone. Too soon, but it is always too soon.

They buried her upon a point behind the cabin where she could see southward over Guthrie's, the children, and onto yon horizon — Gold Hill, Pyramid Peak, and "forever."

Photo: *Nachez (left) and Geronimo (right) taken by Army at Ft. Bowie, 1886. Nachez's mother was Rita's oldest daughter. Story 52.*

Life After Rosa

Neme sold his sheep and boarded up the cabin. In Clifton, Blas worked at the mine and Neme at being a janitor in a saloon. Soon after, Neme was killed accidentally by two drinking, "pay-day" cowboys who had left their brains outside and wore their chaps and guns inside. An argument began when a bar-room senorita smiled at both men. The stupidity switch ticked in both of their heads and they went for their guns; only Neme was killed. They got the hole-in-the-rock jail and the sheriff got eight dollars and thirty cents. Twenty years later, I saw a piece in the Globe paper about a San Carlos Apache being killed, nothing more — just killed.

High in these Sierra Madre Mountains between Bavispe and Fronterias, Rosa was born of an Apache father.

By Land and Air

I last saw Blas in Clifton. He gave me some pictures from a New York man to copy and said that now that his Mother and Dad were gone that he was taking a job in the Globe (AZ) mine.

Next, I picked up his trail in 1935 in Douglas, Arizona. Mrs. John H. Slaughter said that he had been out to the ranch and had gone down to the old San Bernardino Ruins — "Maybe he wanted to see where his mother came from."

Historian of the Globe (a town in Arizona) area, Mrs. Clara T. Woody, wrote "that Blas Duran had died in a mining accident in 1939 and was buried in the Mexican cemetery where Mrs. Felix Knox is buried."

While stationed at Douglas AFB, I chanced a half Sunday off and drove the 22 miles to the old San Bernardino Presidio site. Having read some expert's theory that ghosts come back to haunt their victims every 100-plus-five years in the month of the crime and it being mid-August and the correct month, I stayed the night. The next morning I awoke having seen no ghosts, stiff from sleeping in the car and late for work, but still determined more than ever to try again on a chance coming up. The writer did say "ghosts prowl best on stormy nights."

An air force cadet, ready to graduate, had to make up a "round-robin" night flight from Douglas and I asked if I could go along. Soon we were off runway 9, passing through 6000 feet over the Presidio site, eastbound for CP #1, Animas Peak, when the cadet turned to look me over. He saw my age but said nothing. Any company is good company on a night flight over mountainous, strange country. His weather checked ACVU. What he didn't know was that I had a single-engine rating and had worked over, as an engineer, all of the mountainous country we were to fly over.

From Animas we turned north and soon the Santa Rita Mine's dump lights came up, behind which showed a dark, ominous cloud bank running from the Mogollons westward. Here at Santa Rita is where Mangas Coloradas (before 1837) took a Mexican child-bride; their first daughter going to Cochise, the father of the notorious warrior Nachez.

We passed over Knight's Ranch and then Burro Springs where Rosa married and had her twins. Then the squall line hit. A blast of rain lurched the AT-9 skyward. We bumped, then dropped back into a swirl of hail and rain. The nose dropped ready for a spin, the wings were iced and the yoke was in the cadet's belly. I said without thinking "This is it. No, not yet!" The junction of the Gila and Frisco came through the rain and "she" cushioned. I pointed down the river through a hole, it looked VFR over the river.

We had passed over the Gila, Mud Springs, Rosa's grave and then down-river where the lights of the Clifton mine began to show. We went to half-flaps, gear down—tiptoeing down the river—easing us into the east pass and into the lights of the Globe mine dump. Circling tight, climbing to altitude, and into the clear. It was "chicken-and dumplings" from there on into Williams. We passed Marana, over Davis-Monthan (Tucson) through the Pedro Crossing and came upon the final leg — the Dragoons — in a full moon. I asked the cadet if he would begin his "let-down" earlier as I would like to look into Cochise's Stronghold. He nodded, looked at me and grinned "You old rascal. You knew all along." What he didn't know was that just across that river was Mt. Graham, at 10,700 feet in the clouds. I have often wondered if he made it out of the war?

In the Dragoons, in a rock-filled crevice is Cochise's crypt. According to the abuelos (grandparents) of Bavispe and Fronteras, it was here that his second son Nachez II (Neme) was born of a Sonoran-Spanish child-mother.

This story began in depth in 1934, on my meeting with Natividad Padilla born in Janos, then living on Whiskey Creek (east of Silver City). His first wife was born in Bavispe; his second and third in Fronteras. Their grandparents predated the sacking of Noria. They vowed that Rosa never got over her choosing "Neme" over her adopted brother Nemecio. This part of the story was withheld from Blas, who was born in their first home at upper Blue Creek in 1886-7.

The last time I flew over Rosa's grave was a low, slow fly-over in 1979. The knoll was grassed over and oak bushes grew up the slopes. The jack pine with 66-plus-years had been struck down by lightening. It had been 42 years since I had "walked-out-on-her" in a snow on my last deer hunt. I spent the night in a storm on a Brushy Mountain near Rosa's grave — next to a dead log tending the fire — with plenty of time to think. If there are any ghosts of Rosa, they are there on the mountain somewhere among the trees.

MANGAS COLORADO AND HIS CHILD BRIDE returning from their Gila River Hot Springs honeymoon (Summer, 1832) — that could have lasted until she conceived — passing the torreon (her parents' home is to the left). The mine priest is turning his back upon her as he sees she is wearing the traditional feather, which means she accepts her master's right to choose his conjugal partner, now that she is pregnant. He also sees heathens, not Catholics. It will be her last trip home.

THE LEGEND OF THE KNEELING NUN IS THE LEGEND OF THE DEAD

High in the Pinos Altos Mountains, northwest of the Santa Rita del Cobre mine (Spanish since 1803) and east of the gold placer mines of Pinos Altos (since 1859), is an adobe rock house in the middle of juniper and pine where Diego "Pepe" Garcia lived in 1935, in a house his father Don Arnulfo Garcia, built in 1830. Having just read Comfort's APACHE, I was directed by George Bisby whose father came to the area in 1867.

I showed Pepe an old 1900 map of del Cobre mine, whereupon he slowly traced the old church site, the third since the original with the flat roof, and it was here where Rita Gonzales-Melendrez's Spanish family lived before she was born in 1818; where she prayed and was admired for two years before being taken, as a virgin of 14, for the third squaw of Mangas Colorado (Red Sleeves). He was a big 6 ft. 5 in., strong, determined Apache who as yet had not reckoned with the two brothers of his first wives in the tribal knife duel to the death; nor yet had he become chief at age 42 in 1832. He ignored the mine priest and the pleading of her family.

181

Kneeling Nun today. Most of the rock (the Nun) has fallen away.

Diego "Pepe" Garcia, whose father Arnulfo worked at the mine during Rita's life and knew her family well. Pepe shown here in 1934-5 at his father's home where he lived before Mangas closed the mine in 1838.

It was Mangas's belief that for the Apache race to survive they must intermarry with the Mexicans and Americans.

Mangas captured his new squaw under a blanket in a two-wheeled carreta (cart) at Apache Tejo (where 31 years later he was to be killed), a spring some ten miles south of her home, which was a square of adobe in the center of the mine area with a small open placita in the center for storage, an horno (bake oven) and a haven of safety for a passel of milkgoats that would at night go up on the roof with the dogs — for like dogs, the goats could smell an Apache — thus allowing the family the needed time to flee to the triangular adobe walled-in battlement (150 ft. on a side), built with a torreon on each corner and manned by a rifleman on guard — who, sometimes was awake — not that it mattered — for the Apaches could take the village with its 25 families at will or leave them bottled up inside the bastion to starve.

The Church's Influence on the Apache

Del Cobre mine became Mexican in 1822, American in 1848 and Mangas became chief of all Gila tribes after April 22, 1837, when Juan Diego and brother Juan Jose died in the Johnson massacre at Juniper Springs. On receiving the word by runner, Mangas asked Rita to pray for their souls to her new God who reined over her at Bear Creek and Mangas Springs, since she was ostracized by the church. He no longer trusted the Men-of-the-Cross, never the Mexicans and by 1860 the Americans were crowding the country and, as he was convinced that the Juniper Springs massacre was perpetrated by the Americans, they could no longer be trusted.

Mangas succeeded Juan Diego and Juan Jose.

Where Arnulfo Garcia died (about 1889) on west side of the Mimbres across from Brockman's Mill.

He admired Jose for his ability to speak and write Spanish (who was taught in the church schools and by the good Elias Gonzales family of Arispe and showed his gratitude by perpetrating the rape and sacking of Noria and died, to no one's surprise, as he lived — a determined heathen!)

The Baptists Made Their Move

One day when I was young and filling out between the ears, I met a self-ordained "Hardshell" (Baptist) circuit rider coming into the ranch on a gaunt, half-dead horse — with bullet holes in his long coat and a shot-up saddle cantle. He stopped by for food and water with an outward appearance of hastily moving on. Then I thought "This fool has been across the Rio. No less an idiot! That's Catholic country!"

He said he'd crossed at Presidio (Texas)/Ojinaga (Mexico) and his looks showed it; not long from a fresh self-imposed mission into Chihuahua where no doubt he'd heard the "Juan Jose Story" with its many modifications of how the Men-of-the-Cross (priests) hadn't made an Apache convert in over 150 years, and how he was destined to be the first of the Men-of-the-Cloth to go up-river to an Apache (Bronco) rancheria and break that record come hell or high water in the nearby Rio Grande.

Mining Engineer K.V. Harris at the site of the torreon after it was rebuilt (not according to some old plans). Photo 1940. This site has disappeared long ago into the Hurley mine (waste) dump.

Rita meets Lt. Emory, General S. W. Kearny's cartographer, on the south side of Mangas Springs encampment. Rita is challenging him as to his need for a small cannon (his sextant). She is the leader in charge of Mangas' herd of stolen Sonoran (Mexican) trade mules, shown coming off the foothills of the Burro Mountains.

Rita decides to trade mules with Emory and brings a pair of her best, shown behind her, being led by her Mexican slave-boy (age 13 — a captive since age 4). Emory is passing the remainder of a bolt of scarlet trade goods. His striker is holding his worn-out mules.

A Legend is Born — 1838

In the shadows of the Kneeling Nun is a tumbled down rock that lays crouching below a bluff, an altar of piled-up rocks, the ownership of a legend born 20 years after Rita. Here the besieged miners slipped out in the dark to the mountain top to watch for the coming of conductas, carretas and mule pack trains — anything with food and help.

The Mexican Rurales started from Janos to their rescue, ran into an ambush, lost some men, hightailed it back to celebrate their victory behind the presidio walls, saying, "Our friends will be coming manana (tomorrow)."

The miners and their families, starved and gaunt, assembled in the village plaza. Some on foot, on burros, on mule back, and stragglers of barefooted women and children. A ghostlike procession that file out before dawn, "crawling" their way southward for Janos and the nearest soldiers, knowing the inevitable was not far away — just where and when would the carnage begin?

Some of the more destitute began dropping at Apache Tejo. The stronger made it to Ojo de la Vaca (Cow Eye Springs). The strongest made it to Dog Springs before coming down crawling on their knees. There were those with hopes of reaching Janos, more than a day away, when the Apaches closed in. To those crawling, they cut off a hand; to the yet standing, a foot — thus ending their hopes in a slow, "grateful" death.

Before he'd gotten his Bible out of his saddle pocket, he was jumped by a bunch of gringo-hating Mexican Rurales. He came fogging back past Ojinaga, jumped his horse upon the slow river ferry, amid a volley of gunfire, prudently jumped off into the river — taking their concentrated shots around his bobbing head, knowing their disdain for shovel work and their reason for his water burial.

While I hung a feed-bag of corn over his horse's head, I overheard him say to Mother, a nearby Baptist: "Sister, you can pour coal-oil over water all day long, but they won't mix." I was old enough to know his kingdom lay farther to the East, deeper into the Bible belt. The old paisanos had told me the Apaches and religion "no compadrar" (never got along).

Pepe's father said Mangas spared Rita's family when he shut the mine down in 1837-8. He saw Rita once in the plaza near the church with two little ninas (girls). The abuelas (grandmothers) on the plaza said: "Ella esta muy feliz y contenta." (She is very happy and content.)

The few families who would not leave or were tied to their church remained to starve with the abandoned dogs, a ghost camp until opened by the Civil War's need for copper and gold.

Natchez, grandson of Rita by Cochise, who fought with his half-brother, Neme, over the hand of Rosa. Disowned by Cochise (for cowardice) from his first wife, a Spanish (or Mexican) child-bride and taken captive near San Lazaro, Sonora, 20 miles SE of present Nogales, AZ. Photo credit: U.S. Army and Arizona Historical Society.

The Kneeling Nun - The Prayers Thereof 1837-8

A few possible relatives of Rita hid upon the mountain and in the bluff that made the altar and the Kneeling Nun. Here the Apaches stripped their captives, hanging their naked bodies from the rocks to wither away in the winds of time, that those who were responsible for the Juniper Spring's massacre would know the wrath of Apache land.

Pepe's father, Arnulfo, a relative of Don Antonio Garcia, wealthy mine owner of Organ Mountains mines (1810), missed all this while visiting relatives, the James Kirker's in Janos; left the furnaces at Corralitos which closed with the Cobre mine siege. He disappeared into the farm lands below 'Paso del Norte to reappear in Pinos Altos placers in 1859. From there he went to Georgetown in 1873, retiring on the Mimbres (across from John Brockman's grist mill). He died in 1889 leaving six smelly milk goats, a half-acre of chile, corn and frijoles, a mint of stories and the old adobe-rock house to his son.

Bill Eaton, freighter from Silver City to Mogollon at his Pinos Altos home. He carried Rita's grand-daughter from Alma to Mangas Springs. She gave him much information on Rita's life. She wore a copper ring made by the Navajo girl as her mother's deathbed gift.

Rita's Navajo Captive Slave-girl

Mangas' two older squaws treated the young captive as most squaws did — Rita cared for her as one of her girls — knew her to be a talented coppersmith who made bracelets for her and Mangas and rings for the girls.

Pepe's father, Arnulfo, first noticed the bracelet on Rita at a church mass soon after the Apaches fired the church (1838) to show their contempt for the priest who, according to Arnulfo, would have married Rita standing inside the church door and the heathen (Mangas) outside; and prayed to God the Americans came before any half-heathens popped out.

186

Not far from this Spanish arrastra in Pinos Altos is where Mangas made his fatal mistake, "wishing to see General West." Not far from the home of Bill Eaton and George Bisby, the arrastra crushed ore by a mule pulling the long arm off the center pole, round and round. The center pole with a short arm attached to chain and heavy rock in the pit, crushing ore-laden rock. Pinos Altos reported 50 such rock pits.

Lost Camp, October 19, 1846

General S. W. Kearney's packtrain (mules), with about 100 troopers from Santa Fe, entered the deserted El Cobre mining camp where they found about 25 empty, walled-in adobe huts arranged in three quadrangles between the presidio and the mines — bisected by the church that stood roofless, blameless, vandalized and desecrated. The twenty or more gaping, open-mouth mining shafts looked down from the foreground of the ever-present Kneeling Nun (first an Apache God before it was transformed into a saint that went with the land.)

All of this was of no importance to the California-bound muletrain scrambling to be a part of the California acquisition. Herein the need for the fresh re-mount mules — expected to be at the mine which surmounted all else. It mattered not that they were stolen from the Sonoran Mexicans, where the Apaches held a "lien" — an acquisition tax over them for over a century. Mules or captivity!

Kearney's troops went the 13 miles to San Vicente Springs (today's Silver City) to wait. Dark came and no mules, October 19, 1846.

The following day, Kearney camped 20 miles west at Mangas Springs, the main rancheria of Mangas Colorado. In the twilight, in stormed a herd of dusty, thirsty mules. A consternation of mounted bucks, squaws, kids and Rita's family, mounted in singles and doubles, screaming in delight at the snorting, stampeding mule herd. Unwatered since daylight, they waded out into the lake —chest deep — to see which animal could drink from the innermost portion of the clear, cool, crystal water. That's mules when hassled hard all day (from the Cienega Springs, near the AZ/NM state line south of today's Lordsburg.) Mangas and his scouts were trailing 10 miles behind to see that no Mexicans got foolish ideas. But they stayed smart, most always did, even when women and children were involved (which were also traded as a commodity).

This barn standing near where James K. Metcalfe established his ranch and forage station at Mangas Springs in 1872, according to a letter from his daughter, Mary (Molly), dated Nov. 19, 1933, in which she states: "The Indians had some superstition about the Mangas (I dare say because of the old burial ground) and never harmed nor stole from us." Near this barn Bill Eaton divulged where Rita's granddaughter said Rita was buried.

Mule Trading at Mangas Springs - October 20, 1846

Rita trembled aghast at her own temerity on seeing, for the first time, a handsome young white man in uniform. She fumbled her answer to Lieutenant Emory's offer to trade mules, saying in incoherent Spanish that she "had no use for his money", and rode around the lake to her family's wickiup more confused than ever.

Later in the evening she came back in fresh buckskins, her hair let down (for she instinctively knew why the Mexican senoritas did so). She came to Emory's tent, her slave-boy leading two of her finest mules.

They traded with a bonus in scarlet cloth, enough for the girls. When she took the bolt of goods she purposely passed her hand over his and noted the reddening in his face, as all women know, and went on the offensive. Her large grey eyes atwinkle, a whimsical smile slithered across her olive tanned face, a perkish chin dropped to allow these Spanish words to come out: "You poor Americano soldier, a long way from home, what would you give . . ." and turned away with the air of a wanton minx for him to wonder what she was really thinking. She was a lithe, beautifully hard-trimmed 28, with three daughters and 15 years of unromantic living in a rancheria — wondering her lifetime what every Spanish girl

dreamed of — and had. What she now saw for only a moment and had been denied. Saw it teasingly pass her by.

A femme fatale can break out in the most unsuspecting places. Not foreign or uncommon when the mind and the gene instincts revolt as one to over-reach the surly bonds of matrimony.

Pacheco II, years later, said his father told him this: "He theenks Rita lak thees Amer-i-cano sol-ger veery much. Eff-een Mangas had seen heem he would have keel heem queek!"

There were no cut-off noses in Mangas' rancheria, the penalty for infidelity. This site is still here today, west of Silver City. The spring still flows, but the lake is dry meadow. The giant cottonwoods grow up and die every 100 years, and will as long as there is a spring, and it will last. (Only if we stop absorbing the world's trash.)

The other squaws made no trades. They demanded too much in trade goods; they knew only the methods of trading with Mexicans where the two wishing to trade placed their goods on a common table. From opposite sides, they pulled their knives, sticking them in the center of the table, handles up. The one believing he was cheated had the opportunity to go for his knife — if he had the guts. Mangas made all the mule trades, accepting red shirts for Rita and the young daughters and the American money with which he would buy contraband guns and powder from the profiteers, who, knowing the Mexican law, were willing to chance the firing squad.

The tulies in the foreground are part of Mangas Springs today. The lake, now a vacant dry meadow, appears to the left in the illustration (see drawings on page 184) with some wickiups around it. Here Rita traded with Emory.

Rita's gravesite where Pacheco, the Navajo girl, and the Bronco Apaches (reportedly) buried Rita, according to Pacheco II. The headstone marker (rock) aligns perfectly with Sacaton Peak, the highest peak to the right of Mogollon Peak (flattop). Vegetation usually grows denser around where a body has been buried. Eaton said Rita's granddaughter told him they buried Rita four body lengths eastward from the gravestone, toward the rising sun, on the month of her birthday. Pacheco II said his father (who was at the burial) also confirmed this. (Note the bushes in the photo). East is to right of natural rock — site selected by El Pacheco.

Warm Springs Apaches Fight to Survive

In 1852, Cuchillo Negro was chief of the Warm Springs tribe and was among the few who escaped the invitational fiesta party of mescal and aguardiente by their "good" and "friendly" Mexicans of Ramos, most of whom lost (in their dull, predawn stupor) their scalps to the Mexicans' bounty knives.

Cuchillo called in Cochise and Mangas Colorado saying, "Now comes the time to visit Ramos," and sent ahead his trusty scout to feel out the enemy's strength. He felt, and fell "in" with a pretty senorita with plenty of aguardiente.

He never returned to report the enemy's strength. Nor, to lead his men in the valiant charge. No-oo! Nothing like that! He died in his sleep, in bed — painlessly with a belly full of aguardiente — not spoon-fed by some Mexican woman captive, but with his own knife. She opened him up like a watermelon. He uttered only a faint "ug-ugh".

With the death of Cuchillo Negro, Mangas had only the support of Cochise, whom he "bought" with the marriage of his first daughter. Together they shut the freight and Butterfield Stage lines down in 1861, but not before he had taken a .58 calibre rifle ball in his body, necessitating a long travois mule ride to the Janos doctor.

Mangas Surrenders, A Ploy and His Death — January 18, 1863

Mangas, before going into Pinos Altos for a peace talk with the Walker Party (a bunch of mining prospectors), rubbed noses with Rita and gave her his copper bracelet, as if the treaty talks carried some bad omen. Pacheco II, son of the Mexican slave boy in Mangas' rancheria since 1838, told this narrator in his home at Pueblo Viejo (up river from Safford, AZ) that he never learned why Mangas was living in upper Walnut Creek (near Pinos Altos) in midwinter or why he agreed to meet with Walker's men in Pinos Altos.

Mangas, old and tired, seeking peace for his people, was duped into going to Apache Tejo with the soldiers of General West's command (California Column) to meet with their Chief of the White Eyes, who had left word with his men at Apache Tejo to "not let that old rascal escape." The guards summarily heated their bayonets in Mangas' tent fire and probed him to rise, then shot him for trying to escape.

The Army report read: "Only a few trinkets were found on his body." This confirms Pacheco's story of the gift to Rita.

Mangas Springs today. This is probably the second or third growth of cottonwoods.

Rita Dies at Home, Mangas Springs, Late January, 1863

Rita escaped down Bear Creek aided by her Navajo slave girl, stopping at the sandstone ledge altar to nurse her wounded leg, to pray for Mangas and the last two daughters who, like the first, never came back to visit after marrying into another tribe.

Soon she broke down crying, pulled the bracelets from her arms, flung them into the ledge, sobbing loudly, "There is no God! I'm still cursed!" She collapsed in front of the altar, her body trembling in silent grief. Pacheco, who unknowingly to Rita had escaped from the soldiers, stepped out from the dark into the firelight, looked at the Navajo girl, who only shrugged, showing a bland stare of hopelessness. Pacheco kneeled down, placed his arm around Rita's shoulders, saying in consoling Spanish. "Mama mio." Rita, had she been Apache by tradition, would not have looked up or shown any manner of affection, but not for the first time since his capture at age four and

her capture at age fourteen had she needed someone to lean on. They had not been permitted in the same wickiup or allowed any form of friendship during the 25 years they lived in the same rancheria, but apparently some caring friendship had developed. Rita's eyes filled with tears and she, now a woman of 45, pulled Pacheco, a now-small man at 29, to her and said: "Te amo como mi hijo. (I love you as my son.)"

Mangas' prophesies were unwittingly working. Rita's leg turned gangrenous without her native herbs. Pacheco made a litter-travois for Rita's 5 foot 8 inch form and 125 pounds. The Navajo girl stocked it with pinons and water for spirits who would be following, as they pulled it for the two nights and three days through ten mountainous miles southwest to Mangas Creek to complete her burial wish: to be placed upon a hill where she could look down upon the site where she raised corn and squash and the three little girls that played and romped the hills, learning to ride Mexican mules before the eyes of their proud

Horace Hooker, who came to Silver City in 1876 and established a ranch on lower Bear Creek. He said the Bronco Apaches always came from upper Mogollon Creek, camped at his place and went on to Mangas Creek on their annual pilgrimage to Rita's grave. They never bothered his stock or stole a thing.

determined father. He saw in them the unity of three additional Apache tribes that would hold the Mexicans longer in bondage until his concept of intermarriage might save his nation. Rita, too, saw inside them, as all mothers do, be they Spanish, Mexican or Apache.

I never told Horace Hooker, Bill Eaton or Molly Metcalfe that I found the sandstone ledge from which the Broncos built Rita's altar.

The Old Timers have long been gone. Let's leave the Legend of the Kneeling Nun to those who died in the mine debacle. Nor did I tell them I spent all my deer hunting seasons (1934-40) hunting the upper reaches of the Cherrie, Walnut and Bear Creeks for the mythical bracelets. For all those years the only deer I saw were those running from other hunters.

Fantasies and Folklore

Mystic stories. Fantasies of illusion. Gone are the folklorists and Mexican storytellers who told those stories best while smoking cornhusk cigarettes in the twilight when the evening cools and you can almost hear the whispers of history fading into the past. When the old paisanos said Rita never left the church, the church left her; when they tell you again to look along the sand and gravel bars of Bear Creek below Rita's altar, then you become a believer and go back to looking again.

I've heard these old folklorists for over 79 years. They don't stretch a story as do the news hawks. What for? Their stories came from many captives — relatives — that were forced to live for years (and many grew up) in the Apache rancherias. Folklore now, someday history. Who knows?

On my second trip to Mogollon with Bill Eaton, we stopped at Mangas Springs near the old Metcalfe barn to brew a pot of old fashion black coffee. I sensed he was going back in time when he stopped drinking and began staring into the dying embers. Then I made my move and asked which side of the canyon Rita was buried. He was old and I was young. He said he had promised her granddaughter he would never tell, then looked me in the eye and stood up saying, "When I begin to count and reach ten, I'll be looking at her grave." Now you guess which way he was looking.

Pacheco, Rita's slave-boy, after her death left Mangas Springs for a new home and goat ranch on the Gila River above Solomonville. He lived his life out in this adobe. His son, Pacheco II, buried him under a slab rock with the initals "PG" on it, for Pacheco Gonzales always believed he was kin to Inez Gonzales, (age 15) captured by the Apaches between Santa Cruz and Magdalena, Sonora, Mexico, in September, 1850.

Rita's Hereafter

In 1935, I borrowed a horse at the Jack Hooker Ranch on Bear Creek to ride the 10 miles from the altar to the hill top at the junction of Blacksmith and Mangas Creek, where nearby had been Mangas' main rancheria for many years. How Pacheco and the Navajo got Rita's litter down all those mountainous bluffs, I will never know. I flew over it (1963) to stare down into the rough "to find them," but it all happened too fast and I was 100 years late.

In 1937, I stood at the gravesite where Pacheco, the Navajo girl and four Bronco Apaches (who managed to escape the slaughter at Mangas' rancheria) had buried Rita in her cryto-wickiup, that her soul might pass on in the first full moon from beneath the earthen floor to her God. A moon later, they removed her wickiup and burned it, that her remaining spirits might find their way back to her in the "Land of the Waiting" when all would be there together again — as it was before the Spanish, the Mexicans and the Americans came and took it away.

192

A Summary of Life in that Day

All this came from Pacheco II, the slave boy's son at his adobe near Pueblo Viejo (above Safford/Solomonville on the Gila River. His father said Mangas was smart in "governing" and in "war." Rita would have made a good priest had she not been born "upside down." I thought of what I had heard of her . . . "a priest"? With her lust for life? And I couldn't help remembering what Pacheco had said of how she made Lieutenant Emory lose his rationale, for the moment, when he started leading his new trade mule up to his sextant case as if to put the mule in the box.

Rita's spirit was strong at Mangas Springs. I sensed it most in the moonlight evenings. For 6 years — every time I drove by Mangas Creek Springs, I would wonder what I would have done had I been Emory.

When I asked Pacheco, the son and the philosopher, he said: "She would mak-a you put thos two mules een thee box. She mak-a all me-ens go c-r-a-zee!"

This is Pacheco II between Santa Cruz and Magdalena, Sonora, Mexico — still seeking more on the Gonzales family. He was past 60 in this photo — still a wood hauler.

Epilogue

APACHE LAND began as "Sabres, Sunbonnets and Sombreros, from the Pecos to the San Pedro."

As a small boy, I sat a grullo pony in the shade of an Eclipse windmill, looking far off into the desert stillness over a burned-out, drought-stricken land, shimmering in the heat-hazed horizon, I saw a cavalry troop trotting, Apaches waiting, stage coaches running, freight and covered wagons crawling, all westward — then and there I decided these peoples' stories must live on.

My wife typed and corrected them. My daughter, strong on religion, gave the legend her sharpest eye. A lifetime on the north side of the Rio (Rio Grande) was motivation enough to find the last of the earliest settlers and friends with their stories. A search that began in 1912 ended in the late 1940's.

MOTHER, in 1910, drew a picture of herself riding sidesaddle in a sunbonnet, going for the mail (an 18-mile ride). She was the beginning and the most important reason, years later, for the following remark: had I the artistic talent and the time, I would like to have done MAGGIE, ROSA, and RITA, victims of their time, in color, that they might live on in their Apache Land.

Footnote: My last story from Pacheco II, son of Pacheco, the Apache slave-boy, came in 1935 at his Pueblo Viejo (above Solomonville, AZ) adobe where he told of his father's last visit with Rita's middle daughter, which was as follows: "Some soldiers from Ft. Craig came down the Gila (river) to his place looking for a 'very intelligent Apache woman' who wanted to surrender some of the White Mountain Tribe to the U.S. Military" (in late 1863, several

193

Pacheco II died in the late 1930's in the small adobe near the main house (air photo Feb. 1943), near Santa Cruz, and probably is buried in the same cemetery with Inez, his father's cousin, which gives him the same "Gonzales" name he had long sought. Pacheco, who at 16 was only 18 miles from the Santa Rita Copper Mines when the U.S. Army freed Inez from the Mexican traders, who had bartered her from the Apaches with whiskey and to sell her into prostitution at Santa Fe.

Inez, at 27, during her second marriage to the well-to-do El Alcalde of Santa Cruz, raised four fine children and was the most gracious lady the village had ever seen. If all the children went by her last husband's name, the trail would end there. The priest (1935) said he would check the church records — then in Durango — for her name and her death notice — believed to have been about 1900 and age 65. No letter of record ever followed me out of Tucson. (The vandals that took my coin collection during WWII destroyed many notes and most all of the Mexico photos.)

months after Rita's death). His father took them up Bonito Creek, crossed over into the Eagles and on up to the headwaters of Black River, to the daughter's rancheria — some 30 miles east of Ft. Apache.

This daughter's daughter (Rita's grand-daughter) gave the rest of the story to freighter Bill Eaton (Silver City to Mogollon) of how her mother went to Ft. Sumner with the soldiers and found the military mixing Navajos with the Apaches, who don't mix — they fight. Here she learned of her younger sister's desertion at Ojo Caliente to live on her husband's rancheria in the mountains west of Bavispe, Sonora, Mexico.

The second daughter lived her life out,

according to the granddaughter to Bill Eaton, on the San Carlos reservation. The oldest died in the Dragoon Mountains (east of Benson, AZ) in early 1880's and was buried in the canyon near her husband, Cochise. The third and youngest faded into the Apache "past" under a rock crypt in the highest of the Sierra Madres, between Bavispe and Esqueda.

This was "their" land before the Conquistadores brought the settlers, the priests and the soldiers with their bastions and wall-mounted cannons.

They came to save them from the Devil, "they" said — but gave them Hell on earth with their firearms; the Spaniards, the Mexicans and the

You are looking down Mangas Creek at the confluence of Blacksmith Canyon and about 4-5 miles above the junction with the Gila River. The Metcalfe Ranch is in the area of the original Apache burial grounds. Rita is buried on one of three mountain tops in the general area. It's doubtful if any Apaches were buried in this area after Rita (late January, 1863), which was only seven years prior to Metcalfe's moving to his homestead.

With the establishment of military posts and Apache reservations, the country exploded with mining, ranching and farming.

Americans — they drove them into forgotten graves in their Apacheland.

The priests converted one "good" Apache — Juan Jose — who rewarded them with his sacking of Noria.

ACKNOWLEDGMENTS

1. Without the help, letters and pictures from Mrs. Vera and the late Yancy Barnhart, grandson of Mary Little, younger sister to Maggie Little Graham and the late Douglas Little, son of David, brother of Maggie, whose time and site tours put the "heart" into this lifetime collection, the Maggie Graham story could not have been complete. It made the years of search throughout the country more interesting and worthwhile.

2. My visits to and the writings of the late Judge O. W. Williams (of neighboring Ft. Stockton), along with the writing of his late son, Clayton W., were an inspiration for me to try on my own.

3. The visits with Lee Myers, Southwestern Historian, were helpful.

4. The late Maude L. Sullivan, El Paso City Librarian, who made available to me endless files of newspapers and documents which were just across the street (west) from my YMCA home on Oregon Street during high school years, 1925-27, and the college years through 1931. (A few years back I went to the City Library for a last look-see. I couldn't find a thing. The information had all evaporated into Books — the Eastern-born writers had found our trove.)

5. I thank the late Juan-Jose (a nickname from the Easterners wintering in the YMCA); also the janitor shown in the upper left corner of the illustration, leaving the scene of conflict (on page 43) as any prudent, burro-cart tamale peddler would have. He said he always parked at noon in front of the Pony Saloon. The first bullet by Dallas Stoudenmire killed the hapless Mexican (purchaser of peanuts in front of Zack White's store) and spun itself out in the dust in front of his burro. He said he then remembered that his mother had some wood to chop and he took the shortest and fastest way home.

   Sunday, past noon, when he'd finish cleaning the gym and washrooms, I'd walk south with him along South El Paso Street to the picture show near the Hotel Paso del Norte,

and he would recount the story from those who told it to him over again through the years.

6. My visits with James Gillette at his clothing store on the north side of Railroad Street in Alpine as I passed Sul Ross Sub-College in 1925. He gave me his version of the "Six-Shooter's" story. When you saw the morning passenger train stop and an old ranger cowman-dressed man got off and "streaked" for Gillette's store, it was time to cut class or you'd miss a good ranger story.

   As I recall, he said he was one of the Rangers in front of the State National Bank, or possibly at the corrals in back of the Central Hotel shown at the north end of El Paso Street, about where the railroad is today.

7. To Louis Abrams of Silver City, NM, and Clifton, AZ, I owe much of the "Six-Shooter's" and "Felix Knox at York's Ranch" stories. He gladly went over the sites, although he was anything but a gun-loving man.

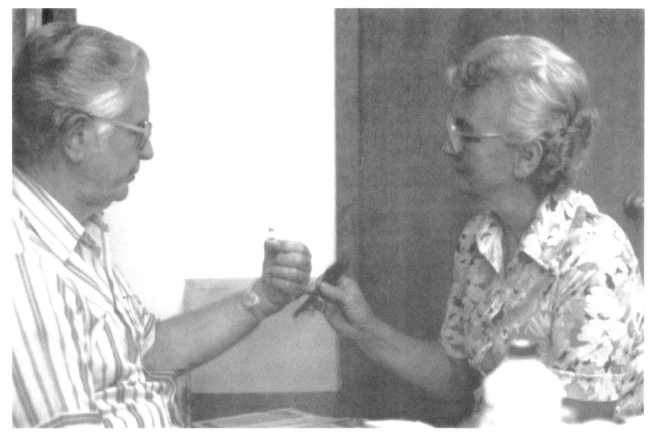

Yancy and Vera Barnhart holding Maggie's lock of hair and ring. The late Yancy was Mary Little's grandson.

ASSEMBLY, EDITING, AND TYPING CREDITS

To Bob Beck, owner of The Printing Corner on Yandell in central El Paso, a master printer; his maps and years of expert training made it sound even easier. As always, he gave it his best. Many thanks.

Credit for bringing this book to the forefront goes to Vicki Beck-Drennan and Sandi Kahn-Hammond, two talented co-workers. Sandi, with a major in English and an eye trained to key the words in "word processing" (words I never heard before), "washed it" cleanly (when I let her), changed some colons to semicolons and G— knows what else; returned it to Vicki to shape and carve, to trim and garnish with maps and put into her "oven" (presses) to bake. WOW! What women can do in their "kitchens"! Special thanks also go to Geo. B. Drennan for overseeing the final stages of this book. His knowledge of the history of the area and his appreciation of a good story helped put the finishing touches on the book.

Leaving all the levity aside, how grateful and indebted I am for the graciousness that comes to so few in their sundown years — an experience that is without words. How do you say "thank you" for a job well done? God bless them for keeping alive the memory of these "Three Women" dear to me and the backbone of this book. All but Maggie left heirs, some scattered and most lost. Had she been two months further along and only two miles farther down the road . . . there'd be no history of the other two's wretched lives — unremembered and unknown to the printed page — for Time leaves little to remind us of the saddened years gone by.

NOTE: The source of this "thank you" note can be traced back to 1640, when King Charles II decreed the Humphries brothers' heads to the guillotine for slander in book printing. Down through 350 years from a Boston (Massachusetts) colony to a West Texas ranch in 1907 again bloomed the gene of a book.

197

ILLUSTRATIONS

1. To Cliff Donaldson, Las Cruces, NM, noted
    Southwestern artist, I owe the most. He held up
    the lantern and showed me the way many times.

    When he paints a horse, he leaves no brush
    marks. Even if it is only a Mexican nag or an
    Apache ridden-down cavalry mount (ready for
    butchering), he goes over it with a curry comb.
    He doesn't paint horses, he just runs them
    across the canvas. We both know you don't
    grease windmills with your spurs on.

2. I picked up a saying over the years when I first
    started my sketching with a paintbrush. It said
    it best of art and book:

    > Them's that can paint, do
    > Them's that cain't
    > Talk about it or teach.
    >   To this I do only talking.
    > To them's that write books, fine
    > To them's that can't, DON'T!
    > You don't know how lucky you are.
    >   *- KJH*

198

Printing Corner owner, Bob Beck (left), standing with author at "book vault" entrance in Las Cruces, NM, August of 1988.

Appendix
Biography of Keith J. Humphries

Daniel D. Aranda

Keith J. Humphries, Artist/Historian

The Dona Ana County Historical Society awarded its 2010 Heritage Award to Mr. Keith J. Humphries for his contributions in painting, writing and recording local history. The author of this article was very pleased to make the posthumous award on January 29, 2011 to his grandson, Keith "Gig" Griffith. I felt that it was unfortunate that many of Keith's friends have crossed over the Great Divide and that many in attendance did not have the good fortune to have known him. I will attempt to fill in that gap.

Keith J. Humphries

Keith James Humphries was born in Retrop, Oklahoma on June 19, 1907 to Eugene A. and Lucy Ann Harris Humphries. Upon his birth, the delivering Doctor Murphy, commented that the newborn baby resembled a fine Irishman. As a result, Keith became known sometimes as "Irishman" and at other times "Irish." Keith was the second of four children

In 1910, the family left Oklahoma and moved to Toyah, Texas. At first they lived at Billingsely Ranch and then at 9-Mile Ranch, where Keith began forming some of his most unforgettable memories. Their mail was often brought to them by passing neighbors, cowboys or by fruit and vegetable peddlers coming up from the Davis Mountains making their rounds. These people, many who were of Mexican descent, were always welcome at the 9-Mile Ranch because they brought in news of the outside and because they shared their stories of old. These passers-by also looked forward to a short stay where they could catch a breather, perhaps a meal and, of course, have a drink of precious water. The water was brackish and smelled of sulfur, but then, water is water and indeed precious in much of West Texas. This is where Keith first met rough grizzled old men such as Evaristo, Calanche, "Burro" Mendoza and an old German simply known as Jo-Bob.

Keith remembered that his father would sometimes leave on long trips to St. Louis and Kansas City to purchase supplies needed on the ranch and in a store that he soon operated in the town of Toyah. Sometime in 1912 the family moved to town and Keith's father operated the largest combination hardware, hay and grain, dry-goods and grocery store in town known as the Reeves County Mercantile Co. Keith's uncle, W. B. Humphries soon joined in as a partner in the business. Toyah was a small railroad town where visitors were welcomed for the news they carried. The store provided young Keith with plenty of old-timers who were glad to recall their past

Keith attended New Mexico A & M (Today's NMSU) earning a degree in engineering in 1931. He was also quite an athlete. He starred in basketball and baseball, which earned him the title of "Greatest Aggie" in 1931 and was offered a chance to play in the minor league farm club for the St. Louis Cardinals. He was also a captain in the ROTC. Keith also took all of the courses available in aeronautics that would later come in handy. During his tenure, A & M registrar, Era Rentfrow, convinced Keith to use his given name, Keith James Humphries, instead of "Irishman" as it would look much better on his diploma.

Soon after graduation in 1931, Keith

married Gertrude Hallick Loomis, who eventually bore their only child, Lois Carol, who he nicknamed "Bunkie" after a friend whom he played basketball with. During this time, Keith made his living by working for the Texas and New Mexico Highway Departments, sometimes with surveying crews, which gave him time to visit with old-timers in remote places. He also found time to submit his first articles for publication in the 1930's and he finished his flying lessons, receiving his flying license as World War II was just beginning.

Keith served honorably during World War II. He joined the army in 1942 and served with the Corps of Engineers in the Pacific. Keith didn't talk much about the war years, but a few tidbits were related to friends and family. He remembered some close calls when Japanese planes bombed the airfield that they were building and where he was nearly struck, several times, by hot shrapnel caused by their phosphorus explosives.

In August of 1945, while on a flight from Okinawa to Saipan and Guam, the pilot, who Keith described as not old enough to shave, asked if anyone there had any flying experience. When he volunteered that he did, he was asked to step into the pilot's seat and take over. To his disgust, the young officer went to the back to start a dice game in which he soon had wounded soldiers dropping their crutches and nurses in baggy overalls down on the floor immersed in their game. Keith guided the plane, listening to Tokyo Rose when all of a sudden excited Japanese voices disrupted the program. "If I had known what was happening," Keith said, "I could have turned the plane forty-five degrees and the gamblers might have looked out to see the world's first mushroom cloud." He also remembered that when on a Jeep ride, several Japanese volunteered to surrender to him.

After receiving a discharge in 1946, Keith worked in Alaska with the Federal Aviation Agency, often in Kodiak, and in 1949 he moved to Las Cruces and began work at the White Sands Proving Grounds. (The facility later became the White Sands Missile Range or WSMR). In the mid 1950's, while employed as a civil engineer at White Sands Missile Range, Keith was awarded a patent for his invention of the tri-axial missile tracking camera mount. The device allowed for cameras to track missiles by rotating on three different axes without shifting positions. This was a tremendous improvement that not only saved the government time and money, but also reduced the chance for errors.

Keith continued writing and had articles published in New Mexico Magazine, Saturday Evening Post, True West, Old West and newspapers in the Southwest that included the Las Cruces Sun News, Las Cruces Bulletin, El Paso Times and El Paso Herald Post, Silver City Southwest and several others in West Texas.

Keith retired in 1972 and took up painting. Like everything he did, he went at it with a passion. He now transferred the incidents from his writings to canvas. He wanted everything to be right so he revisited the sites that he wrote about and even flew over them for a better perspective. He usually took along his trusty companion, a poodle named Bowser. Although not a Charles M. Russell or Frederick Remington, his artwork indeed has merit. This is because Keith painted incidents of local historical significance. Even Keith understood this and stated so in an interview with El Paso Times writer, Ramon Renteria, "It isn't the quality that I'd like to have my name on. My illustrative quality is poor but most of these paintings have a good story behind it. All these characters ought to be remembered." Amen to that. This was around the time that I met Keith.

One day in early 1972, my wife and I were awaiting our hamburgers at the old Burger Time on El Paseo Blvd. when a cheerful older man approached our vehicle.

"That's a pretty good book, isn't it?"

The man was Keith Humphries and the book he was referring to was a brown cloth-covered copy of Dan L. Thrapp's "Conquest of Apacheria. I agreed since at the time it was my favorite book. I also, gladly volunteered that I knew Dan Thrapp. This was the opening of our friendship. Keith also admired Dan, but didn't know him. He did, however know Eve Ball, another well-versed writer on the Apaches. As we continued to converse, much to his surprise, Keith learned that I knew of characters such as Burro Mendoza and Ramon Calanche from the Big Bend country of Texas. My wife's grandparents who resided in Marfa had known these men. Keith also learned that my wife was a descendent of Diedrick Dutchover, also a well-known name in west Texas history. This short visit also was the opening for our introductions to our mutual friends, Keith soon met Dan and I met Eve.

Keith was glad to talk to anyone who knew and understood his passion for history and I spent many hours at his house discussing this and his artwork. On our first visit to his home on Hadley Street, Keith even gave us a newspaper clipping of my wife's mother and father-in-law's wedding picture that had appeared in a West Texas newspaper. He also offered to give us one of his original paintings that hung in his living room. My heart raced, but my wife, undoubtedly matching colors with our décor, didn't feel right about taking it. After all, we didn't have room in our modest home to hang it.

On subsequent visits, Keith showed me the pictures in his "vault" and gladly showed me how he sometimes changed them. He could go on for hours, but anyone who is so immersed as we were, can truly understand.

As mentioned above, Keith met Dan Thrapp and even flew him over some historical sites along the old Butterfield Trail. This is a trip that Keith had offered to take me on many times, but that I never took because my family was afraid that we might crash. Even Keith recognized this and said "I wouldn't want this to be on my conscience anyway. Dan (Thrapp) and me have already lived our lives, but you're still a young man." I really think that he meant it, and to

this day I really feel that he was sincere and not putting me off. My wife summed it nicely when appeasing me with, "I think that it was awfully nice and considerate of him."

Keith Humphries' work did not go unnoticed and in 1979, he received the Hall of Fame Award from the Dona Ana County Historical Society for his contributions in recording the history of the Mesilla Valley.

In the year 1988, Keith finally published the book that he had labored on. It was appropriately titled Apache Land From Those Who Lived It. It consists of the stories that he gathered with the artwork to illustrate them. It is a gem for historians.

Keith passed away on Sunday, July 21, 2002 at La Posada Hospice Facility and was survived by a sister, Anita Oliver of San Angelo, daughter Carol "Bunkie" H. Griffith, three grandchildren and seven great grandchildren.

Keith Humphries collection of paintings, photographs and notes were eventually donated to the Geronimo Springs Museum and I was fortunate to be been given permission by the museum to sort and catalog the collection. The work was tedious because most of it was misfiled and because many of the documents were infected with fungus. Apparently the collection had been exposed to water and much humidity, thus ruining a portion which had to be disposed. With the help of Doug Hamilton of Tucson, Arizona, Berndt Kuhn of Stockholm, Sweden, Frank Brito of Pleasant Hill, California, and fellow Fat Boys Historical Research Group members, Emilio Tapia and Eric Fuller of Las Cruces, we were able to make only a cursory cataloging with the intent to refine it some day.

Authors and Historians such as Dr. Robert N. Watt of the history department at the University of Birmingham in England, Berndt Kuhn of Stockholm, Sweden, Ed Sweeney of St. Charles, Mo., Doug Hamilton of Tucson, Arizona, Karl Laumbach and Herman Weisner of Las Cruces, and the late Eve Ball of Ruidoso,

203

N.M. have benefited from Keith's research. Eminent author, Dan L. Thrapp summed a four page letter praising Keith with "I am most impressed with your research, and your collection and the careful way in which you have accumulated and filed it, and I sincerely hope that you can bring about what you originally intended to do with it."

Well done my old friend.

Daniel Aranda
Las Cruces, New Mexico

Index

by Dawn Santiago

Page numbers in italics represent page number from original edition.

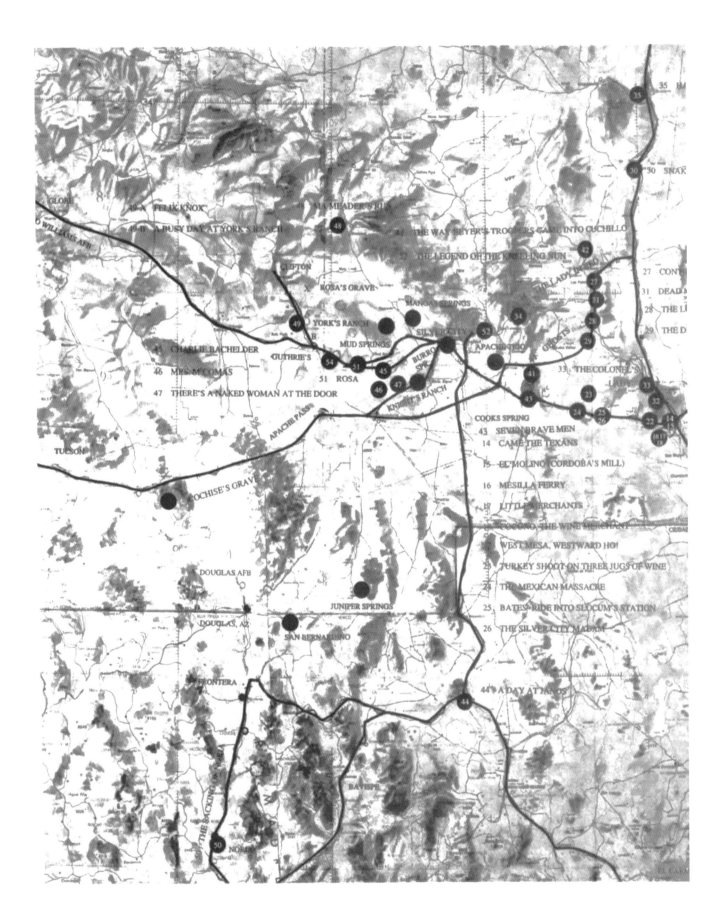

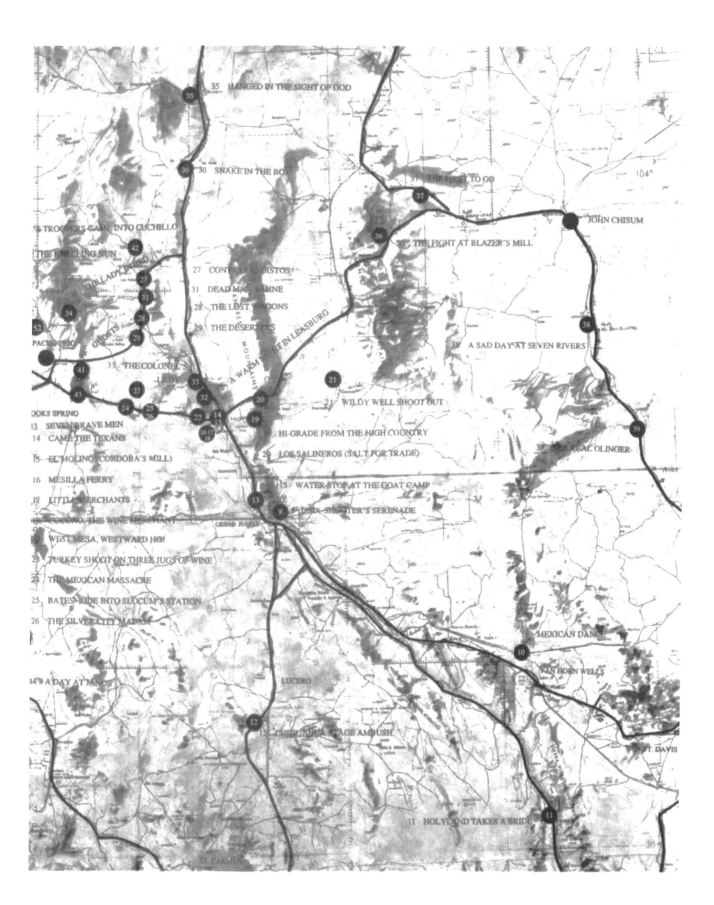

35 HANGED IN THE SIGHT OF GOD

30 SNAKE IN THE BOX

37 THE FIRST TO GO

JOHN CHISUM

'S TROOPERS CAME INTO CUCHILLO

THE KNEELING NUN

36 THE FIGHT AT BLAZER'S MILL

27 CONTRABANDISTOS

31 DEAD MAN'S SHRINE

28 THE LOST WAGONS

29 THE DESERTERS

A SAD DAY AT SEVEN RIVERS

33 THE COLONEL'S LADY

21 WILDY WELL SHOOT OUT

OOKS SPRING

13 SEVEN BRAVE MEN

14 CAME THE TEXANS

HI-GRADE FROM THE HIGH COUNTRY

39 THE REAL OLINGER

15 EL MOLINO (CORDOBA'S MILL)

20 LOS SALINEROS (SALT FOR TRADE)

16 MESILLA FERRY

17 LITTLE MERCHANTS

13 WATER STOP AT THE GOAT CAMP

GUN-SHOOTER'S SERENADE

POCONO, THE WINE MERCHANT

WEST MESA, WESTWARD HO!

TURKEY SHOOT ON THREE JUGS OF WINE

MEXICAN DANCE

THE MEXICAN MASSACRE

VAN HORN WELLS

BATES RIDE INTO SLOCUM'S STATION

26 THE SILVER CITY MADAM

A DAY AT JANOS

LUCERO

FT. DAVIS

12 CHIHUAHUA STAGE AMBUSH

11 HOLYLAND TAKES A BRIDE

Printed in Great Britain
by Amazon